Covenant and Hope

ERIC C. RUST

Covenant and Hope

A Study in the Theology of the Prophets

WORD BOOKS, Publisher
Waco, Texas

Library of Congress catalog card number: 72–84170
Printed in the United States of America

To Duke K. McCall

Contents

Preface

This book is not intended to be an original contribution to Old Testament scholarship. It pointedly sets out to portray for students, ministers, and others who are interested the current understanding of the theology of the prophets. In so doing, I have had to discuss the nature of the prophetic consciousness, the transmission of the prophetic oracles in oral tradition, their basic forms and structure, and the formation and composition of the prophetic books. It has not been my intention to discuss the critical problems in detail, and I hope that footnotes will suffice to help the interested reader to a more detailed critique. I have been much more concerned to draw out the theological content of the oracles of each prophet, relating it always to the historical situation to which it was applied. In so doing, I have sought to show how the prophet's personality and historical experience have played their part in the formulation of his theological outlook, and also to indicate the contribution of each prophetic figure to the ultimate fulfillment in the Christ.

I am very aware that a recent fad in interpreting the prophets is to emphasize their future hope and almost ignore their roots in Israel's covenantal past. Here Von Rad has been a prime mover, and no one would dispute his scholarship. I feel, as does Eichrodt, that Von Rad has strangely gnostic tendencies, but I rejoice that those who have built on his scholarship have sought to reinstitute a concern with eschatology, even though they build their understanding of the Christian faith solely around its future dimension. I refer to Moltmann, Pannenberg, and those who belong to their theological viewpoint. So far as the prophets are concerned, we cannot ignore their backward look while emphasizing their hope. They were declaring their message within the covenant structure of Israel, and elements in that structure were influential in shaping their prophetic insights and their future hope. I have sought to bring out the dual aspect of that covenant structure, showing how the Abrahamic/Davidic covenant tradition with its accompanying royal theology played its part alongside the Exodus/Sinai tradition, both negatively and positively, in the message of the prophets. I have rejected the views of both Martin Noth and Von Rad with regard to the traditions about Moses, the Exodus, and Sinai, but owe much to Von Rad's *Old Testament Theology*, Vol. II.

11

This book is my final contribution to nearly three decades of teaching the theology of the Old Testament. It adds to work already undertaken in *Nature and Man in Biblical Thought; Judges, Ruth, 1 & 2 Samuel* (volume in *Layman's Bible Commentary*); *Salvation History*; and the article on "Old Testament Theology" in the *Broadman Bible Commentary*, Vol. I. I have now handed my Old Testament teaching, at the undergraduate and graduate levels, to my colleague and former student, Dr. Marvin Tate. May he be as happy in teaching it as I have been!

In the preparation of this volume, I have been helped by the advice of my Old Testament colleagues, Dr. Page Kelley and Dr. John Watts. My colleague and former student, Dr. John Polhill, kindly prepared the index and made helpful suggestions about the text. My wife, as always, has been my companion and encourager, and I am indebted to Miss Jean Aiken for her painstaking secretarial work.

I have dedicated this book to Dr. Duke McCall. I have served under his able administration for twenty years, and my friendship with him goes back to the days when we participated in the Baptist World Congress in Copenhagen in 1947. His leadership has contributed, along with a very able faculty, to the prominent position in theological education which Southern Baptist Theological Seminary now enjoys.

ERIC C. RUST

Louisville, Kentucky
1972

Chapter One

Hebrew Prophetism
and the Emergence
of the Classical Prophets

The history of the Hebrew people is unique as a history of di-
vine revelation. The record contained in the Old Testament Scriptures is a testimony to the mighty acts of God within history.
From the beginning of this record God is pictured as a living,
personal reality, in intimate personal relationship with his creatures and acting within the corporate movement of their historical
lives. The testimony carries us back to the days of early civilization when the patriarch Abraham was granted a vision of one
God in the midst of an early culture which was basically poly-
theistic. It contains many traditions, all of which in some way
or other take us back to this central character.

All of these traditions, however, also regard the exodus of a
group of Hebrew slaves from Egypt as a second turning point in
Israel's story. Here too there is a central character. This time it
is Moses who dominates the historical landscape, towering above
it like a gigantic mountain peak. The settlement in Canaan
brought the development of a national consciousness to the tribes
who had entered the promised land. Undoubtedly the covenant
on Sinai's height, made under the shadow of the great deliverance
from Egypt, was the creative center for this sense of nationhood.
It was sealed, however, in the tribal amphictyony at Shechem
in the early days of the conquest. Always Israel is a nation under
God, and its very nationhood has unique religious foundations.
It exists by the creative acts of Yahweh in the Exodus, at Sinai,
and in the conquest, although its faith in God is carried back to
the patriarchs. In the subsequent centuries, Yahweh is the central character in Israel's history. Its monarchy, its national in-
stitutions and social life, its relations with other nations, and
its political organizations are brought under his aegis in judgment and in mercy.

No one reading this story can escape the fact that central in this movement of Israel's history are the great prophetic figures from Moses onward. They were the central media of the divine revelation whereby the history of the Hebrew people became 'salvation history'. They provided the binding link whereby the traditions of the past were made relevant to every generation. They spoke not in the name of some deity whom they had happened upon only in their own experience, but in the name of Yahweh, by whose mighty acts Israel had been delivered from the bondage in Egypt, sustained in the wilderness, and established in Canaan. Their God was a God who had worked in the story of Israel's past and who had a claim upon their hearers because he had graciously made himself their covenant God.

The first prophetical figures have left behind them little record of the actual oracles which they uttered in the name of Yahweh. They are shown to us making and breaking kings from Samuel onward to Elisha. We hear them condemning the oppression of rulers, the presence of social injustice, the corruption of the pure religion of Yahweh by the infiltration of pagan cults, and the tendency to syncretistic forms of worship. Like towering mountain peaks they remind us that Israel's history always revolves around the God who brought it out of Egypt and in whose name they speak. From this prophetic line we cannot separate the great classical or reform prophets with whom we are here particularly concerned. The latter were the heirs of a great prophetic past. Furthermore, neither the prophetic personalities nor the later classical figures can be separated from a more widespread prophetic movement in Israel, even though some differentiation must be made. At the center of all this stands the towering prophetic figure of Moses himself.

In this opening chapter, therefore, we shall consider the traditions of Israel's past as they gather around the prophetic leadership of Moses. We shall survey the prophetic movement of the early years of the settlement and the monarchy in all its wide variety. We shall inquire how the Hebrew prophet envisaged his task and shall examine his authority. Finally, we shall endeavor to place in this setting the great classical prophets, noting any characteristics by which they are differentiated and discussing the forms of the oracular utterances.

The Wilderness Traditions and the Figure of Moses

Behind our Pentateuch lie written sources which, long before they were written down, circulated in oral form. Differentiated by the symbols J, E, P, and D, they represent the accumulated memory of the early years of Israelite history, especially in relation to God's dealing with his people.[1] Although the earliest of them from the written point of view, J, dates from about the tenth century B.C., this does not mean that the authenticity of their records of earlier events is to be discredited. A careful analysis of oral tradition indicates that we are dealing in these written sources with traditions which had a long oral history and which enshrine valid memories of the patriarchal days and of the wilderness journey.

It seems probable that J and E are actually deviant versions of a single original tradition. As we now have them, J, the Yahwist source, possesses greater continuity. It is so styled because it employs the name Yahweh for God from the very beginning of its narrative, in the story of the creation in Genesis 2 and the story of the garden in Genesis 3. It presents a connected history of Israel from the creation through the fall from paradise, the judgment of the flood, the covenant with Noah, the call of Abraham, the stories of the patriarchs, the sojourn in Egypt, the rise and mission of Moses, the deliverance of the Exodus, the wanderings in the wilderness, and the settlement in Canaan. It seems especially concerned with the southern kingdom of Judah and preserves many laws, such as those contained in the Book of the Covenant (Exod. 21–23). It may be regarded as preserving the memories of the southern group of Hebrew peoples and may well have been treasured in a shrine like Hebron in the precarious early days of the settlement.

It is noteworthy that although J includes the covenant on Sinai, it does so mainly by inserting material from the second source, E. This must not be taken to mean that J did not regard the Sinai covenant as significant. Both J and E probably sprang from one origin, but their parallel accounts will reflect the emphasis of the groups in which they were preserved. The Yahwist evidently held to the calling of Abraham and the promises associated with such election. Moreover, he saw the promises to Abraham fulfilled in the exodus from Egypt and the settlement in Canaan. Hence he would seem to make the patriarchal traditions significant and regard the Sinai covenant within this setting. Even though he also acknowledges the greatness of Moses, he significantly holds that God revealed himself as Yahweh to Abraham, whereas the other traditions regard the name Yahweh as a new revelation to the leader of the Exodus.[2]

This divergence can be understood if we recognize that the covenantal structure in the religion of the patriarchs is different from that in the Sinai experience. The covenant with Abraham, preserved in the J tradition (Gen. 15), is made at the divine initiative, but it lays no moral obligations on the patriarch. Rather the emphasis falls on the divine promise. All that was demanded of Abraham was trust (Gen. 15:6).[3] On the other hand, the Sinai covenant, also made at the divine initiative, was cut under the shadow of a gracious deliverance and emphasized moral obligation rather than promise. Some would regard the covenants with the patriarchs as anachronistic, but the very difference in their structure would militate against this. This structural form persisted in the south and became the basis for the Davidic covenant, the covenant between Yahweh and the royal house. It was felt that in David the promise to Abraham had been fulfilled. Israel had now inherited the land and had become a nation great and prosperous (Gen. 12:1–3; 15).

In consequence, a royal theology developed around Jerusalem in the time of David and Solomon. This emphasized two elements in particular. The first was the royal covenant. Not only had God made a covenant with David but also with his descendants. Further, this dynastic covenant was replete with promise and made no stipulations. It was unconditional and thus of the same form as that with Abraham.[4] The second element was the tabernacling presence of Yahweh on Zion's hill. Here David had brought the ark to rest, and Solomon's Temple only served to strengthen the conviction that here Yahweh had chosen to dwell. The Yahwist would appear to share in these convictions, and thus in him we may well see a tension, soon to develop to bigger proportions, between the covenant structure with the patriarchs and its implications for the 'sure blessings of David' and the covenant structure of Sinai with its moral stipulations. The time when he wrote his chronicle was apparently the century of the heyday of the united kingdom, and thus he would stress the election of the patriarchs and the promises to them while not ignoring the work of Moses and the covenant of Sinai.

The Elohist tradition E was probably written down subsequent to J. It seems to have been transmitted in northern Israel.[5] This would certainly account for its distinctive flavor. Allowing for the fact that J includes E only where the latter supplements its own traditions, it would appear that the literary source E was a narrative which also recounted stories of the patriarchs, but which was mainly concerned with Moses, the exodus from Egypt, and the covenant on Sinai's height. To the patriarchs God was known as Elohim, and it is to Moses that the name Yahweh is disclosed for the first time. Hence the Sinaitic covenant is central. This is the wilderness tradition as it is preserved probably in the northern shrines, and it shows little or no trace of the Jerusalem tradition with its royal theology.

In the north, soon after the conquest and as the settlement in Canaan was under way, the tribes formed a tribal amphictyony around Shechem, sealing it by a covenant rite at the Shechem shrine. Many scholars hold that in the Book of Deuteronomy the shape of this covenant and its obligations is preserved.[6] Von Rad has shown conclusively that the 'holy war' theme of the early days of the conquest is preserved in the Deuteronomic framework.[7] In the holy war, Yahweh himself was regarded as a protagonist; the ark, the visible sign of his presence, led the army into battle; and the participating Israelites were required to fulfill certain ritual requirements. The latter were preserved in the Deuteronomic Code and reframed for that later day when it was given written form. This appears to have been sometime in the reigns of Hezekiah or Manasseh, for the Book of Deuteronomy enshrines in its present format the teaching of the great eighth-century prophets with their emphasis on moral retribution. We may imagine that the fall of Samaria and the dissolution of the northern kingdom in 722 B.C. made possible the movement of such traditions, possibly already in written form, to the still secure southern kingdom of Judah.[8] Here they were reshaped and written to form the book of covenant which was discovered in the Temple in Josiah's reign and provided the basis for the far sweeping reformation of 621 B.C.

The traditions enshrined in the Book of Deuteronomy undoubtedly go back to the time of Moses. They stood in conflict with the idea of covenant embodied in the royal theology, for they embodied the demands and stipulations of the covenant relationship initiated at Sinai. Yet their emphasis on a central sanctuary made a point of contact with the Jerusalem theology, for the latter emphasized the Temple as Yahweh's abode and regarded Zion as the center of his earthly rule. We may well assume that the discovery of the law book in Josiah's time was revolutionary, for its covenant basis in the wilderness tradition called in question the covenant ideas expressed in the royal theology. Demand now stood over against promise. The royal theology with its unconditional covenant structure and its tabernacling divine presence was reinforced and revolutionized by the ingression of the Sinai covenant structure with its ethical demands and moral earnestness. Moses stood alongside of Abraham.

From the group who gathered around and preserved this D tradition there sprang the Deuteronomic school of historians which was responsible for the books of Joshua, Judges, Samuel, and Kings. In this school, we find an emphasis on Moses as a prophet (Deut. 18:18), a continuing interest in the prophets of Israel down to the exile, and a moral emphasis which reflects both the spirit of the Mosaic Decalogue and the moral demands of the great prophetic messengers who succeeded Moses. It is noteworthy that Joshua 24 may preserve the account of the Shechem covenant rite, in which the tribes banded themselves together after the conquest.

This D source also shows us the creedal basis of the traditions. We need to remember that Israel's faith was grounded in historical revelation and not in either human rational discovery or the universal affirmations of mystic insight. The God whom Israel believed in was he who acted and disclosed himself in the events of history. He was Yahweh who brought Israel out of Egypt, and the affirmation of faith in him involved a recital of his mighty acts. He was known by what he had done. Undoubtedly this re-

ligious purpose was one factor in the preservation of the traditions at the various shrines. In two D passages this becomes
evident. In connection with the offering of the first fruits, the
Deuteronomic Code requires the worshiper to recite an account
of Yahweh's dealings with the patriarchs, with Israel in Egypt,
with his people in the wilderness, and with the nation in the
settlement (Deut. 26:5–9). The Shechem covenant is also accompanied by a like recital (Josh. 24:16–18). In our study we
shall see how this understanding of God underlies the oracles
of the literary prophets.

The last tradition in Israel which is contained in the Pentateuch
is the Priestly tradition P. Putting its emphasis upon the Temple,
its priesthood, and its sacrifices, this tradition likewise traces
Israel's history back to the patriarchs and gives it the background
of God's creative act (Gen. 1). It tends to think of the covenant
relationship as one made by God with the fathers, so that the
Sinai covenant is of the nature of a reaffirmation. Yet there is a
new revelation of God at the Exodus through Moses, for to the
patriarchs he showed himself as El Shaddai, but to the people
under Moses he was known by his name Yahweh (Exod. 6:5).
The law codes of this tradition, which was finally formulated in
a literary form during the sixth century B.C., constitute the de-
posit of ceremonial rites and moral and civil laws treasured at the
Temple at Jerusalem. We may even see here memories preserved
among the Jebusite priesthood before Jerusalem was taken over
by the Israelites in David's time. We need to remember that the
Jerusalem shrine of those days apparently did worship the high
god El Elyon, a worship akin to the worship of the living God
of the Hebrews, so that it would be easy for elements of this
tradition to be incorporated in Israelite memory.

Closely bound up with this Jerusalem tradition in the preexilic
period were the elements of the royal theology to which we have
already referred. As we have it, the Priestly Code is postexilic.
The cessation of the Davidic monarchy and the ascendancy of the
priesthood means that such elements found little place in the
code. It would seem, however, that the best way of understanding many of the psalms and other references in the Old Testament would be to postulate some new year festival in which the
Davidic monarchy occupied a central place. Scholars vary in their
viewpoint as to the nature of this festival. Some build upon the
concrete evidence provided by similar festivals among the Babylonians and Canaanites. Yet we have too much evidence of the
uniqueness of the Hebrew faith in Yahweh to believe that the
Hebrews could easily absorb cultic elements bound up with naturalistic deities and fertility rites. It may well be that when the
Hebrew monarchy attained an established position under David,
the Hebrews sought to express in some cultic ceremony akin to
those among other peoples their own understanding of the king,

his relation to Yahweh, and his relation to his people. Such a festival would become the focal point of the royal theology.[9] We might postulate an annual ceremony in which God's kingship was celebrated through his earthly representative, the Davidic monarch, and in which Yahweh's and Israel's triumph over all earthly foes was enacted in mime.[10] The victory of the Creator over the chaos in Genesis 1 would be historicized as the triumph of Yahweh over Egypt at the Exodus, and both would be preserved in the tradition partly by cultic deed and memory. H. J. Kraus has suggested that rather than celebrating Yahweh's annual enthronement, the annual festival served to commemorate Yahweh's entrance into Zion as his permanent dwelling place and his everlasting covenant with the Davidic dynasty and with his people.

However such a festival was structured and whatever its distinctive nature, it would serve to perpetuate the Jerusalem tradition and its associated royal theology. Kraus's position might seem the most plausible at this point.[11] In Israel's cult we have the continuing memory of the everlasting covenant of Yahweh with David, wherein the Israelite royal line was assured of its succession. In the center was the Temple itself, the royal chapel, with its ark and with its symbolism that here especially God was pleased to dwell in the midst of his people. The festival, the Davidic kingship, the tabernacling presence in the wilderness tent, in the protecting clouds, in the ark, and in Solomon's temple—all contributed both to the contents of a national and highly uncritical hope and to elements in the developing eschatology of the reform prophets.

At the center of all these traditions stands the massive figure of Moses. As law giver, national leader, and prophet this man dominates the tradition.[12]

Israel as a nation did not begin after the conquest of Canaan around Shechem. It began in the election experience of the Exodus and the covenant rite on Sinai, and the personality of Moses towers above its beginnings. The Deuteronomist records the divine promise that God will raise up another prophet like Moses (Deut. 18:18). Hosea declares that Yahweh brought Israel up out of Egypt by a prophet (Hos. 12:13), and Jeremiah places Moses alongside of Samuel, implying that both are prophetic figures (Jer. 15:1).

We shall see that the divine activity operates in two parallel movements—the revelation through and in certain historical events and the inspiration in the prophetic consciousness which enables the prophet to grasp this meaning of the events. The fact that from Amos onward this is very evident in the ministry of the canonical prophets suggests that it is deeply embedded in Israel's past experience. Th. C. Vriezen argues: "That this certainty [of God's activity in history and in the prophetic consciousness] is found again and again through the course of the centuries can only be attributed to the fact that this connection between prophetic revelation and God's work in the history of his people formed part of Israel's religious conceptions from the very beginning; the figure of Moses must therefore have been prophetic; it is to him that the religious relationship dates back." [13]

It was the faith of Moses that welded into a' religious unity the nucleus of the disparate group of tribes which constituted the later Israel. It was he who by prophetic testimony to the redeeming activity of Yahweh fanned into a flame the loyalty which found expression in Israel's response to divine election, formulated in the Sinai covenant. It was he who laid upon the people the divine claims of the Decalogue [14] (Exod. 20; Deut. 5), and thus established a moral rather than a naturalistic bond between the living God and this people. It is to this religious foundation of the nation that all the traditions bear testimony.

There are two strands very evident in the traditions that we have been considering. One is the wilderness strand, especially evident in J and E but evident also in the Deuteronomic confessions. It emphasizes the Exodus and the deliverance under Moses and places the Sinai covenant in the center with its ethical conditions and rigorous demands. The other is the strand bound up with a royal theology, especially evident in the Jerusalem tradition. This acknowledges the activity of God in Moses, but emphasizes the election of and covenant with Abraham. It pushes the covenant relationship back to this patriarchal figure, interpreting it in an unconditional way. It adds to this a concern for the royal covenant with the house of David and for the abiding presence of God in his Temple. We find elements of this strand very evident in P and increasingly the concern of the Deuteronomists.

These two strands are very evident in the messages of the canonical prophets, with the wilderness tradition and its exodus theology the more dominant. The reason is not hard to see. The royal theology with its unconditional covenant could easily become the basis of a shallow national religion in which the ethical demands were bypassed and on which a false hope could be based. It is against this that the canonical prophets set themselves. They were prophets of reform, concerned to deepen the ethical side of Israel's religion and to awaken the acknowledgment of the divine demands in the Sinai covenant. They had therefore to attack the popular religion and to emphasize the exodus theology over against the royal theology.

Hence we find Amos and Hosea making no mention of Abraham and concentrating on the Exodus as God's redeeming act. Hosea refers to the Sinai covenant (6:1), to the Decalogue (4:2), and to Moses as a prophet (12:13). Isaiah stands more in the Jerusalem temple tradition, and elements of it receive more favorable treatment in his prophetic work. He refers to Abraham, emphasizes the presence of Yahweh in Zion, and promises a Davidic Messiah. Yet although the Sinai covenant does not receive specific mention, his message of divine judgment, his oracles of radical demand for moral conduct, his condemnation of social injustice are all grounded in that covenant. The strong ethical foundations of the wilderness tradition provide the basis for Isaiah's prophetic ministry, and into it is woven a hope in which elements of the royal theology find their place. With the canonical prophets this hope becomes central. The promise assumes an eschatological form.

In Jeremiah we find the revulsion of a man standing in the wilderness tradition who finds himself surrounded by the superficial religion bred in the Jerusalem tradition. So his ethical rigorism again sounds the notes of the exodus theology. Yet into his hope also are woven elements of the royal theology, in part because the Deuteronomic tradition, with its mediating position, exercised some influence on him. In Ezekiel the exodus theology merges into a modified royal theology, as judgment gives place to hope in the latter part of the prophet's ministry. Deutero-Isaiah finally weaves the two strands together. The exodus theme is central, and yet the covenant that comes from it has the form of the 'sure blessings of David'. From these last two prophets, the movement of postexilic prophecy finds its direction.

THE NATURE OF HEBREW PROPHETISM

From Moses onward the prophetic movement is central in Israel's history. It serves as the revelatory medium through which Yahweh and his people enter into dialogue in the midst of the historical vicissitudes of the nation's life. The disclosure of God's nature and purpose takes place through historical crisis-events in which a prophetic figure or figures occupy the central position. As the movements of the current historical scene take place under the divine guidance, they become revelatory because of the inspired prophetic consciousness by which their inner meaning is grasped. Divine revelation through historical happenings and the divine inspiration of the prophet whereby the divine disclosure is made plain are the two prongs of the divine movement into history. Without the inspiration of the prophet, the revelation would not be grasped and communicated. The movements of history would be grasped only in their horizontal and not in their vertical dimension. The activity of Yahweh in them in judgment and in mercy would be of no avail without the inspired insight out of which the prophetic oracles issued. Such oracles addressed to the current historical situation made evident the presence of God as wrath and grace.

In the past decades it has become increasingly evident that Hebrew prophetism parallels other phenomena among other peoples of the ancient Near East. In Babylon there were *mahha*

priests who, in ecstatic frenzy, delivered messages from their
gods, and similar ecstatic utterances are evidenced in Canaan
and Phoenicia.[15] The story of the prophets of Baal on Carmel in
the time of Elijah indicates that a frenzied and ecstatic state
associated with the deliverance of oracles was present outside Israel. The Mari tablets also carry strong parallels to Hebrew
prophecy. Here a message is conveyed from the god Dagan to the
king of Mari with apparently little ecstatic frenzy. The calm style
of the deliverance of the message by the oracular official is much
closer to the central tradition of Hebrew prophetism.[16]

Scholars vary in their estimation of the influence of such phenomena upon Hebrew usage from a total rejection of any influence [17] to a full acceptance of the ecstatic type as formative
in the Hebrew prophetic consciousness.[18] Now there is evidence
of the presence of the ecstatic type during the early days of
the Settlement, but this does not mean that we have to accept
the latter position. Although Samuel does not himself seem to
manifest extreme ecstatic characteristics, yet bands of ecstatics
were associated with him during his ministry. These prophets
were gregarious, forming themselves into prophetic guilds, and
they seem to have been associated with various shrines. They
were given to sacred dances and apparently accompanied their
prophesying by music. Such a group met Saul near Gibeah (1
Sam. 10:5, 10). There was a similar group at Ramah (1 Sam.
19:18 ff.). In their company Saul also manifested their frenzied
behavior and so originated the proverb: "Is Saul also among the
prophets?" (1 Sam. 10:6, 10–12; 19:23, 24). Elijah and Elisha
were later associated with like corporations of prophets (nevi'im)
at Bethel (2 Kings 2:3) and Jericho (2 Kings 2:5), while Elisha
had relations with the group at Gilgal (2 Kings 4:38).

A technical description of such groups was 'sons of the prophets',
and they would appear to be either cultic officials or closely bound
up with the cult. A. R. Johnson has made out a good case for
the existence of such prophets as official members of the Israelite cult, and we shall follow him at this point.[19] The encounter between Ahab and the prophet Micaiah ben Imlah takes
place within the setting of such a cultic group. The four hundred
false prophets of 2 Kings 22 were attached to the court, probably
through the royal sanctuary, and would appear to be of the ecstatic type. Of all the great prophet figures of the early monarchy,
Elijah and Elisha especially manifest abnormal characteristics.
Elisha was apparently induced to prophesy by the aid of music
(2 Kings 3:15), and Elijah showed extraordinary speed and physical endurance as he outraced the chariot of Ahab (1 Kings
18:46).

According to 1 Samuel 9:9, the word prophet (navi') had come
into common usage to describe all types of prophets. Apparently,
in earlier times, one type of prophet had been the seer (ro'eh), and

we may presume that in such days, the word *prophet* (*navi'*) represented another type. It seems probable that the seer was a less ecstatic type whose message came through normal sights presented to the eyes, reflective thought, and that inner sight into the spiritual realm which belongs to the order of intuition. He was thus parallel to the oracular official of the Mari texts. Another name *hozeh* occurs alongside of *ro'eh*. Both are customarily translated "seer," and attempts to differentiate between them are not very successful. It is probable that the *navi'* may originally have been a more ecstatic type, functioning much more at the highly emotional level. It is clear that, by the time of the sources in the books of Samuel, *prophet* (*navi'*) had become an all-embracing term covering many types of prophets. The word *seer* is still used, however, and it is difficult here also precisely to define its boundaries. Later times were less precise in distinguishing one oracular mode from another, and thus Samuel, who was not manifestly ecstatic but more the calm seer type, could be described as a *navi'*.

Ecstatic elements seem actually to be found in the central stream of early Hebrew prophetism. The media of communication were frequently by dream and vision. Samuel's call affords an instance of this (1 Sam. 3:3 ff.), and the place of dream and vision in the divine encounter with the patriarchs is a reminder that such phenomena go back early in the traditions of Israel's life. Balaam describes himself as one who, falling down and having his eyes open, sees the vision of the Almighty (Num. 24:3). The historian of the Books of Samuel tells us that in the last days of Eli prophecy was a rare occurrence and there was no frequent vision (1 Sam. 3:1). In actual fact prophecy at all levels was a charismatic phenomenon. Whether it be at the reflective level of moral and rational judgment or at the extreme position of a heightened ecstaticism, it is attributed to the presence of the divine spirit, the *ruach* of Yahweh. Although in preexilic Israel the latter was thought of in quasi-physical terms as an invasive windlike power which came from beyond man's personal being, the point is that it came from God. It was a divine constraint laid upon a man, a reminder that Hebrew prophetism resulted from the divine initiative.

Let us notice also that the psychic distance between God and man was still maintained in this understanding of the Hebrew prophetic consciousness. There is no pantheistic and mystical suggestion of absorption here. Lindblom [20] points out that we cannot describe any ecstatic phenomena in the Hebrew tradition as if the individual were wholly possessed by the deity, losing his individuality within the all-pervading divine presence. He terms this kind of ecstasy 'absorption ecstasy' and defines that peculiar to Hebrew prophetism as 'concentration ecstasy'. By this he means a concentration upon one aspect of the consciousness to the ex-

clusion of all others. The prophet believed that he participated in
a divine power, but he could not, in the true Hebrew tradition,
identify himself with his God. The spirit took possession of
him, presenting sights to his eyes through which he saw into the
heavenly courts, granting him auditions which had no earthly
source, bringing him into a trance state in which one aspect of
his consciousness dominated his personal being. Sometimes such
a state could verge on apathy as it did later in the case of Ezekiel.
Sometimes it could produce an excess of strength as in the case
of Elijah. Sometimes it made the *navi'* appear like a drunken
man (Jer. 23:9) or a madman (*meshuggah*—Jer. 29:26). Sometimes the Spirit could lift him up and transport him to an isolated
place (2 Kings 2:16; cf. 1 Kings 18:12).

The personality was not lost in the deity, but certain aspects
of it were accentuated. Because the Hebrew saw himself as a
psychosomatic whole, we must not think of this divine activity
as taking possession only of certain aspects of that whole. The
total personality participated in and represented Yahweh, although the particular encounter with God was mediated by ab-
normally excited sense perceptions or unusual responses of feeling. Thus visions were presented to the eyes and auditions came
to the ears. Of such the constituent elements were images and
intelligible sounds drawn from normal sense experience. The
prophet became supersensitive. Out of the stored up memories of
past experience, visions and auditions were lifted into conscious
experience which gave peculiar insight into the ways of Yahweh.
Or the prophet's conscious life was brought to a focus in some
fixed idea in which all his sentiments were sublimated.

We may conclude that however much the religious environment of the ancient Near East may have contributed, the Hebrew
prophetic consciousness carries distinctive characteristics. These
characteristics certainly did not originate in that religious background. Since such phenomena seem to be present wherever there
is intense religious enthusiasm, we might even see them as an
autonomous and spontaneous outgrowth within the specific religious life of Israel. Indeed our emphasis on the towering personality of Moses would suggest that the source of the Israelite
prophetic movement lies in him. The central line of development
stems from him and determines the way in which the ecstatic
elements of the prophetic consciousness are to be understood.
As with Moses, so with his great successors like Samuel, Nathan,
Micaiah, Elijah, Elisha, and Huldah, the focal point was the covenant relation to Yahweh with its understanding of a divine-
human encounter and moral bond, rather than any pantheistic
mysticism.

At this point we might consider the significance of the word
navi' itself. Too much is often made of etymology, but the word
may help us to some understanding of how the prophet regarded

himself, especially when we take into account other features of
the prophetic consciousness. It is now agreed that the word has
at its root the meaning "call." The issue lies between those who
give it an active meaning "one who proclaims"[21] and those
who give it passive meaning "one who has been called."[22] The
first meaning would seem to have the most support, and it is
consonant with a view of the prophetic mission that is rapidly
gaining ground. The prophet as a proclaimer comes as a messenger
of Yahweh. This understanding of a prophet is also found in the
Mari texts.

As such, the prophet does not proclaim his own word but the
Word of Yahweh, for he represents God and must be accepted
as one who stands in God's place. It was commonplace in more
developed Jewish thought that he who represents a man is to be
regarded as if he were the one whom he represents. He who is
sent is as he who sent him. This was held of the later messengers
from the synagogues, the shelamim, and it holds of the early
period. We find the idea quite early in the patriarchal traditions in the figure of the angel of Yahweh. This figure may be a
supernatural being, a visionary, or an actual human figure de-
pending on the situation, but almost with unanimity the records
speak of him as if he were Yahweh himself. So close is the identity
between the sender and the sent! Thus the authority of the messenger is the authority of the one who sends him.

In the early traditions this is borne out in Yahweh's instruc-
tions to Moses about Aaron: ". . . thou shalt speak unto him,
and put the words in his mouth: and I will be with thy mouth,
and with his mouth, and will teach you what ye shall do. And
he shall be thy spokesman unto the people: and it shall come to
pass that he shall be to thee a mouth, and thou shalt be to him
as God" (Exod. 4:15, 16, ASV). Here we have a description of the
function of a messenger and the definition of a prophet at the
same time. The prophet is a divine messenger, and his authority
is that of Yahweh who sends him. God puts his word, his message,
in the mouth of his prophet (Num. 22:38, 23:5, 12, 16; Deut.
18:18).

It is interesting to note that the form of the prophetic oracles
in the canonical prophets, beginning as they do with "Thus saith
Yahweh," bears a striking semblance to the form employed by
royal messengers. Thus when Rabshakeh delivers the message of
the king of Assyria, he commences with the phrases "Hear ye the
word of the great king, the king of Assyria. Thus saith the
king . . ." (2 Kings 18:28, 29, ASV). Nathan is told by Yahweh:
"Go and tell my servant David, Thus saith Yahweh . . ." (2 Sam.
7:5; cf. 2:8).

As messenger of Yahweh, the prophet may best be understood
in the setting of the heavenly council (sôdh Yahweh).[23] "In the
Old Testament sôdh means in the first place consultation, then

a group of men consulting together, and finally a decision, plan, or purpose, which is the result of consultation." [24] The idea of such a council gathered around God appears quite early in Hebrew thought. It is certainly present in the story of the encounter of Ahab with Micaiah ben Imlah. Here Yahweh consults his council of holy ones, and a lying spirit is sent forth to deceive Ahab through his prophets (1 Kings 22:19 ff.). Micaiah's vision of Yahweh surrounded by his heavenly host is only one outstanding description of an image which often occurs (cf. Ps. 89: 5). Psalm 82:1 presents God as standing among the congregation (*'edhah*) of the gods, and the drama of Job portrays God deciding with his council that Job's faithfulness shall be tried by Satan (Job 1:12, 2:7). The frequent occurrence of the plural *us* in connection with the divine activity may well be accounted for as a reference to God and his council of holy ones (Gen. 1:26, 3:22, 11:7). This plural is of peculiar significance when used in connection with the prophets.[25] Isaiah is sent from *us* (6:8). He goes forth to announce the decrees and decisions of the heavenly court gathered around the throne of Yahweh.

Quite often we have the attempt to repair the breach in the covenant relationship. This takes the form of a divine lawsuit (*rîv*) with Israel.[26] There is a controversy between God and his people. The covenant has been breached by a rebellious nation, and now, in a lawsuit, God is seeking to repair the breach. The prophet comes forth as a messenger to declare that the heavenly court is in session and that the nation is arraigned by Yahweh before the tribunal. The terms of the indictment are stated, and the prophet calls on the nations to act as witnesses. Thus in Micah 1:2–9 we have such a controversy or lawsuit in which the prophet calls upon "all peoples" and "the earth and all that is in it" to hear the indictment. In a similar form in Micah 6:1–8, the mountains and the foundations of the earth are called upon to hear the controversy of Yahweh with his people. Sometimes, as in Micah 6:3–5, the prophet recites God's gracious acts in the past. The divine mercy already vouchsafed to Israel is recalled before the witnesses. Again we may have an account of recent calamities which should have recalled the people to God. Isaiah 1:2–31 is on the lawsuit pattern and contains such an account in verses 5–9. The judgment is then pronounced, yet sometimes salvation is also promised. Other examples of such lawsuit patterns are Isaiah 3:13–15; 5:1–7; Jeremiah 2:4–9; Hosea 2:2 ff.; Amos 2:6–16. At times the prophet feels himself so much a part of the heavenly court that he turns from messenger to intercessor, identifies himself with his people, and pleads before the divine throne. This is especially evident in the case of Jeremiah.

The early prophets were politically involved, but appear in the early days to have directed their attention more upon the royal house. In this connection the great figures showed no fear in declaring the divine judgment. From Samuel through Nathan, Gad, and Ahijah, to Elijah and Elisha this remains true. In a sense, the judgment on the king was a judgment upon the nation whose health and righteousness were bound up with the status of the king himself. With the canonical prophets, however, it is the whole nation that is arraigned before the heavenly court, although the kings and other leaders are singled out for specific mention. We note at this point a distinction between Hebrew prophetism and any seeming parallels that may be found elsewhere. At all stages the Hebrew prophet is concerned with moral and not ritual issues. His great plea is for moral righteousness and faithfulness to the covenant with Yahweh. On the other hand, this moral note is absent from the so-called parallels, while the concern with the nation as a whole is not apparent.[27]

As messenger of Yahweh and with the background of Hebrew psychology, the prophet could see himself as an extension of the divine personality. A. R. Johnson [28] has shown how the prophet regarded his total personal being as gathered up in the divine personality and so becoming the divine mouthpiece. He was not merely transmitting a message, but Yahweh so permeated his own personal being that his understanding, feelings, and volition, his body, eyes, and mouth, became God's instruments. This is not mystical absorption, for there was a recognition that the prophet still retained his individual personality. The latter was not suspended, but rather it became the organ employed by God to confront men. The prophet's personality, his emotional characteristics, and his mental capacity were heightened by association with the divine. He shared in the divine *pathos*,[29] knew the divine agony, the tension between grace and wrath, so that from his lips were wrung words which opened a window into the heart of God.

The ecstatic elements may well be due to this heightening of a man's emotional powers, but in the great prophetic figures we do not find a dissolution of personal being. At the center of the great messages there remain moral discernment, reflective judgment, and imaginative sympathy which were possible because God was using all the prophet's gifts and powers as the media whereby he directly confronted men. The prophet remains a personal being with all his idiosyncrasies, but one through whom men immediately encounter Yahweh.

Enough has been said to indicate that Hebrew prophetism covered a variety of types, from extreme ecstatics to more reflective seers, from groups to solitaries like the great prophetic figures, from cult prophets to free prophets. We cannot fit them all into one category. What binds them together is a participation in the great traditions of Israel's faith, especially the wilderness tradition. There seems little doubt that Moses is the focal point of

the movement and that the wilderness tradition was treasured
among the great figures from Deborah and Samuel onward. Here
we have a group of people who sought to preserve the pure religion of the great period of Israel's deliverance.

With the capture of Jerusalem and the establishment of the
monarchy, however, the Jerusalem tradition and its accompanying
royal theology also began to claim a place. The same would be
true when royal shrines were established in the north at Bethel
and Dan. The cultic prophets became influential and often became
sycophants of the monarchy, as witness Ahab's four hundred
court prophets in the Micaiah story. Yet the Elijah tradition shows
that many faithful prophets remained. We hear of Obadiah hid-
ing one hundred faithful prophets of Yahweh in a cave (1 Kings
18:13). Thus all the cultic prophets and groups of prophets must
not be consigned to the category of the false and unfaithful. In
the early days they certainly aided and abetted the great prophetic
figures in their ministry and participated in the overthrow of
evil leadership, for example, the establishment of the dynasty of
Jehu in the place of that of Omri (2 Kings 9).

We have suggested that along with the cultic prophets we
have those not attached to any shrine. Such were men like
Samuel, Nathan, Ahijah, and Elijah. This does not mean a lack
of concern for the ritual and worship of Israel. We find both
Samuel and Elijah officiating at cultic sacrifices. This would be
expected since they were holy persons by virtue of their being
charismatics. Possession of the spirit gave them an entrée into
the shrines and their worship. Yet they entered as free men and
felt free to attack the cult, as did Elijah, when it was prostituted
to pagan and immoral rites. As free men too they declared the
judgment of God on the monarchy in no veiled terms. In the
name of Yahweh, Samuel confronted Saul, Nathan confronted
David, Ahijah advised Jeroboam, and Elijah and Micaiah confronted Ahab. They were consulted officially as the Deuteronomic
history shows, and in every case they exercised an important
function in changing the political situation.

The Degeneration of the Prophets and the Rise of the Classical Prophets

There was always a temptation for the professionals to lose
their charismatic quality and become false prophets. Those attached to a shrine were particularly susceptible to such temptation. First of all, we have the tendency to professionalism. The
prophets had grounded their authority in their charismatic nature. They were possessed by the Spirit of Yahweh and had thus
become his messengers. Yet the outward behavior of religious
ecstaticism, which for the genuine prophet lay in direct encounter
with his God, could also be simulated. The prophets often became
professionals, and either as seers or ecstatics prophesied for hire,

concerned more with the fee than with the divine authority of their message (Mic. 3:11). Dreams and visions were produced by request, and the charismatic basis of the prophetic message, whereby the prophet waited upon Yahweh for his message, tended to recede into the background. The prophet indeed was tempted to control the divine revelation and have the Spirit at his service. The prophetic word, lost in spontaneity, became a set form which met the need of the clientele rather than a Word which came from Yahweh. As we shall see later, Jeremiah was especially concerned with this (Jer. 23). Lies were prophesied in the name of Yahweh. Prophets became preoccupied with the deceits of their own hearts and traded false dreams (Jer. 23:25 ff.).

Secondly, there is evidence in the oracles of the classical prophets that this professionalism bound such prophets in more closely with the shrines. They tended to become increasingly cultic personnel who were classed along with the priests. This does not mean that every cultic prophet was a false prophet. Indeed our Book of Psalms contains a rich treasury of the insight and piety of such men of God. There was, however, a strong temptation to replace reliance on Yahweh by the authority of office. This became more in evidence among those prophets who were associated with the Hebrew monarchy, both in the north and in the south. To prophesy smooth things and to declare peace when there was no peace became an easy way for the sycophants of the royal court, as the story of Micaiah reveals. How easily such a temptation befalls the modern minister!

We may add to such influence the development of a popular misunderstanding of Israel's election and of Yahweh's tabernacling presence on Zion's hill. There seems to have developed a popular eschatology to which Amos testifies. This envisaged a Day when Yahweh [30] would fully establish his people in their heritage and overthrow their enemies. It would be a day of peace and light for Israel, irrespective of its sinful rebellion against Yahweh. Indeed Yahweh himself was reduced often in the popular mind to the level of a fertility deity, and moral responsibility before him was bypassed. His election of Israel placed that nation in a privileged position. It remained for Amos and his successors to declare that privilege meant responsibility.

This particular form of popular eschatology seems to have flourished especially in the northern kingdom of Israel and had its basis in a shallow understanding of the wilderness tradition. In the southern kingdom of Judah this eschatology was un-doubtedly present, but it was also bound up with a false trust in Yahweh's presence in the Temple and his covenant com-mitment to the royal house. In such a setting there was every temptation for the prophet to go along with the crowd. He could easily become a preacher of popular culture rather than the mouthpiece of Yahweh. The modern parallel of ministers who preach to please and who reduce the gospel to the level of current values is apparent!

In the midst of this degeneration of the original prophetic movement there are the classical or reform prophets, whose oracles are preserved in the prophetic writings of the Old Testament. These men are of miscellaneous origin. Some like Amos were not identified with any official group. Amos states categorically that he was not a *navi'* nor a member of a prophetic guild (Amos 7:14). On the other hand, Jeremiah came of a priestly family, the priests of Anathoth, while Ezekiel appears to have been priest as well as prophet. Amos and Micah were countrymen and Isaiah was a city dweller, perhaps even a member of the royal entourage. All are characterized by the conviction that Yahweh has called them to be his prophets. The circumstances of the call vary. Hosea's seems to have been mediated through his marriage experience. Amos received his when following his rural vocation as herdsman. Isaiah's call came to him at temple worship. Jeremiah's was mediated by an inner voice and by two visions presented to his eyes. The occasion of the call of Ezekiel was a thunder cloud above the Babylonian plain. All testify to the pressure of the call, an inner pressure which they cannot resist. When God has spoken, they must prophesy (Amos 3:8; Jer. 20:9).

We find in these men many of the ecstatic elements already found among the professional groups. They too, as we shall see, receive their message through visions presented to the eye and auditions falling upon the ear. They perform symbolic acts in which their message is acted out in miniature and in symbolic form, very much as Zedekiah the son of Chenaanah charged round among Ahab's prophets with horns of iron (1 Kings 22:11). In the case of Ezekiel, these symbolic acts become almost an obsession, while this prophet suffers from periods of aphasia that might suggest his being a cataleptic. Yet, as in the great central line from Moses to Elijah, these men have at the center of their prophetic consciousness a profound moral insight, a capacity for rational judgment, and an imaginative sympathy which lift them above the level of the mere ecstatic. The ecstatic elements undoubtedly served to mediate their message to them and as a means of expressing that message, but the latter is not to be explained by such elements.

The ecstatic element lies at the fringe of the prophetic consciousness, and the great classical prophets were moved by the conviction that they had stood in the council of Yahweh and were his messengers. We shall find recurring in their message this image of the heavenly council, this conviction that they are messengers and mouthpieces of Yahweh. Here their psychology and their religious convictions are of one piece with those of their great predecessors. They enjoyed and claimed the same freedom, standing before kings and nations alike with the courage that is born of profound conviction. They stood free of royal authority and continued the democratic spirit of the wilderness tradition. They were free men under God. And indeed they could validate their utterance by a phrase like "as Yahweh liveth" (Jer. 4:2). The phrase means that they claimed such divine authority for their oracles that they were making God their witness. If their message was false, they had forfeited their life in God's sight, for they had played with the life of Yahweh.

It has been pointed out that the classical prophets usually categorize themselves as having the Word of Yahweh rather than as having his Spirit.[31] Hosea actually says that the man who has the Spirit is mad (Hos. 9:7), while Micah and Jeremiah both suggest that possession of the Spirit may simply mean that the possessor is a windbag (Mic. 2:11; Jer. 5:13). Yet Isaiah declares that the coming messianic king will have the Spirit (Isa. 11), although such possession is here eschatological and future. Generally we may say that the distinction does seem to hold until the Exile, when Ezekiel sets Spirit and Word side by side as differentiating marks of the prophetic consciousness and descriptive of his own experience. It would seem not that the classical prophets did not believe they possessed the Spirit, but rather that they were anxious to disassociate themselves from the false prophets, the degenerate professionals, who claimed such possession. With the Exile this need began to disappear, and thus the old category was used once more.

The emphasis on the Word of Yahweh is, however, important. As Yahweh's mouthpiece, the prophet was convinced that he uttered God's Word. The fact that he rarely described himself as Yahweh's messenger (*mal^e'akh*) may well have been due to the nature of his message.[32] The angelic messengers to the patriarchs had always brought messages of comfort and hope. The preexilic prophets had such a large element of doom in their message that they hesitated to use a word which may have given a wrong impression about them. It is significant that Deutero-Isaiah can use the word to describe the servant (Isa. 42:19) and that Haggai can describe himself as the messenger of Yahweh (Hag. 1:13), although here the cognate word is used (*m^{e}shullam*). Their use of Word, however, served their purpose better, since the uttered word possessed an objective quality, as we shall shortly discuss fully. Once uttered it moved independently in the one who received it to accomplish the intention for which it was uttered. So too with God's Word. Once uttered, it would set in motion the forces that should accomplish God's purpose.

The outstanding differentia of the classical prophets was the content of their message. With them the implicit monotheism in the message of Moses becomes increasingly explicit. God is universal Lord. It is as such that he judges all nations as well as his own people. Every prophet utters oracles against the foreign nations. As universal Lord, God controls history, accomplishing his purpose within it. He manifests his wrath and his grace within historical existence, employing the political and social movements of the time to fulfill his intention. God is increasingly known in what he does, and the concept of a world history centering in the divine purpose for Israel comes to fill the stage. For the first time we are offered a philosophy of history.

This philosophy of history, however, is bound up with eschatology, the doctrine of last things. From the earliest traditions, it is clear that Israel's relation to Yahweh was one of hope. Hence we have the promise to the patriarchs. We have already pointed to the superficial popular eschatology in which this promise was expressed in the time of the classical prophets. The latter, unlike their great precursors, not only spoke to their contemporary situation, but also related their message to an eschatological dimension. For all of them the Day of Yahweh looms ahead and colors their message to the current scene. In the preexilic period, this prophetic eschatology differs from that of the postexilic period. In the former there is some measure of continuity between historical existence and the *eschaton*, the End of history. In the latter a discontinuity becomes evident. The End transcends the historical scene and comes by direct divine intervention rather than through historical forces. Yet we can see within the prophetic messages a developing eschatological pattern which finds its fulfillment and true coherence in Jesus of Nazareth.

Accompanying this emphasis on the lordship of Yahweh over history, we find a deepening sense of sin and guilt and a more profound awareness of the nature of divine grace. As the prophets became aware of the inwardness of sin and the demonic perversion of man's will, they came also to an increasing understanding of God's love and the nature of his redemption.

These emphases of the classical prophets must be understood in relation to the continuing traditions of Israel in which they shared. The historic credos of the people's faith, grounded in God's mighty acts in history, provide the background to the prophets' own encounters with Yahweh. Always God is, for them, the God who brought Israel up out of Egypt and whose tabernacling presence in his Temple guarantees his gracious purpose for his people. All the prophets turned to the wilderness tradition in its differing forms. Some relied also on the Jerusalem tradition with its royal theology and its emphasis on God's presence among his people. All of them found the ground for their own understanding of Yahweh in those historical revelations in which he had disclosed himself redeemingly to his people.

THE UTTERED WORD AND THE SYMBOLIC ACT

One significant feature of the prophetic movement and of the

canonical prophets in particular is the dramatic element in their
behavior. The oracles were not only uttered, but sometimes they
were acted out. In both cases the prophet regarded them as effective acts of the divine power and sovereignty. We need to
remember that the Hebrew word *davar* can mean both "word"
and "thing." Thus, the Word of God may be an act as well as an
utterance. Indeed, in the Hebrew mind, a spoken word was itself an act. As H. W. Robinson puts it: "To the prophet it is of
no account whether his doing be in the realm of speaking or
acting, since speech is itself an act." [33]

We have already indicated that the Hebrew thought of the
uttered word in concrete and objective terms. Once uttered, a
word attained an objectivity of its own and became, as it were,
detached from the speaker though pregnant with the latter's
intention. In some sense a human word gives bodily expression
to the contents of the soul. It is indeed a manifestation of the
soul, and it is strong or weak according as the soul of the speaker
is strong or weak. Thus, what gives power to the word is its
mental content. Once uttered it becomes detached from the
speaker, but behind it lies the utterer's soul. As a medium of
communication it is so objectivized that it conveys the reality
which is in the soul of the speaker to the soul of the hearer,
where it acts in full strength. To quote Johannes Pedersen: "He
who speaks good words to another, creates something good in
his soul, and he who speaks evil words, creates unhappiness in
his soul." [34]

Just here we see how significant a curse and a blessing could
be to the Hebrew mind. Wellhausen cites the case of a father
who, while accompanied by his son, met an enemy. The father
threw the boy upon the ground that the curse might pass harm-
lessly above him.[35] When a man blesses or curses another, he
has created a blessing or a curse in his own soul and transferred
it objectively, by the spoken word, to the soul of the other. The
reality that the word contains expands in the soul of the hearer,
working out the blessing or the curse. To quote Pedersen again:
"It is . . . in full agreement with the general view when the
Israelites, by the verbal form denoting the causative, do not distinguish between *making* a man into something and *saying* that
he is so." [36] He reminds us that a word without a soul behind it
to lend it strength is called 'lip word' and as such is ineffective. "In
all labor there is profit: But the talk of the lips tendeth only to
penury" (Prov. 14:23, ASV).

It is against this background that we must understand the
uttered word of the prophet. Because it comes from Yahweh it is
pregnant with his power and intention. It has objective significance, but the reality it contains is not merely in the soul of
the prophet. It contains a divine content, for it is uttered by one
who is Yahweh's mouthpiece, an extension of the divine per-

sonality. It contains its own inherent power derived from the reality of God himself, and its very utterance means the beginning of its fulfillment.[37] Once the word is winged on its way, it begins its work. It is likened in effectiveness, by Deutero-Isaiah, to the effectiveness of the rain (Isa. 55:10). Again this prophet cries in the name of Yahweh: "By myself have I sworn, the word is gone from my mouth in righteousness, and shall not return, that unto me every knee shall bow, every tongue shall swear" (Isa. 45:23, ASV). Indeed God's word through his prophets is like a hammer that breaks the rock in pieces (Jer. 23:29), and by it men may be slain (Hos. 6:5). Thus we can understand Ezekiel's confidence that the divine word shall be performed (Ezek. 12:25). It will be actualized in history. The Word of God through the prophet not only promises salvation and judgment, but commences the processes by which such promises shall be actualized. It is powerful and effective. So sure is the prophet that the Word will be historically actualized that he uses the Hebrew prophetic perfect, representing the future as if it has already come to pass. He is stating what is actuality.

So objective is this word that it is regarded as something which is placed in the prophet's mouth (Jer. 1) or given on a roll for the prophet to eat (Ezek. 3). The prophet's personality was involved in this, for we need to remember here the background of Hebrew psychology. Yet he only uttered in his human words the Word which had come to him and winged it on its way into actualization in the historical scene.

God's Word through the prophet is thus the instrument of his power. His power brought it forth and his power controls it in its course. It is the 'word of his power'. When uttered by the prophet, it is still not free of God. It is an extension of his personal being into history, a concrete expression of his will and intention. It does not work like a magic spell. As Th. C. Vriezen puts it: "It remains in His [God's] power, He can take it back or carry it into effect. God can relent, He can revoke the word of the prophet and answer a prayer. Not because a prayer or the intercession of someone else could be some kind of counter force that may be opposed to God's power, but because God is and remains God in this respect too, that even His Word is absolutely dependent upon Him and that He remains completely free to dispose of it as He wishes."[38] Neither the prophet himself nor his hearers can stay the course of the divine Word. The Word will initiate what it predicts, unless God intervenes, for he may 'repent', turn back.

This objectivity of the divine Word through the prophets is strongly paralleled by the function of the divine Word in creation. Here we find a parallel idea developing in the 'wisdom circles'. The wise men pictured the divine wisdom in concrete and objective form. In the Book of Proverbs, this portrayal of the divine wisdom is probably poetical personification (8:22-31), but the idea is more concretely and objectively expressed in Ecclesiasticus (chap. 24), while, in the Wisdom of Solomon, Wisdom has become a concrete and objective presence parallel to the thought of the divine Word. Hence Wisdom leaps forth like a mighty warrior from heaven to actualize God's purpose in history (Wisd. of Sol. 18:15). This development is but one indication of the close relationship between the prophetic and the wisdom circles.

Not only did the prophet utter God's Word, but he also acted it. Most of the canonical prophets are associated with dramatic acts in which the divine message is portrayed in deed. Isaiah can walk the streets of Jerusalem in the garb of a slave to indicate the judgment of God on Egypt and Ethiopia (chap. 20); Jeremiah can symbolically purchase the plot of land in Anathoth to signify the sure restoration of God's people (chap. 32); the same prophet can shatter an earthen flask to disclose God's sovereignty over his people (chap. 19); with Ezekiel the symbolic acts are far more frequent, as we shall see later. Now we must understand that such acts were as much divine words or oracles as were verbal utterances. Furthermore, we must understand their significance in the same way.

H. W. Robinson [39] has reminded us that this symbolic behavior has its roots in symbolic magic, in the attempt to put constraint upon the forces of the universe by enacting in miniature what it was desired that those forces should accomplish. He points out that this has been lifted up by the prophetic consciousness, cleansed of its magical associations, and completely inverted. The attempt to control spiritual forces by magic is inverted into an act of God himself. In this act God initiates in miniature what he intends on the large-scale level. The prophet is so identified with God in his dramatic action that his symbolic act is lifted up into the divine Word. The symbolic act thus becomes objective and concrete. It initiates a process in history in which the divine will shall be actualized. This is no longer man seeking to control events by magic. Rather, it is God actively and creatively controlling events by the symbolic acts of his prophets. They perform in miniature what is the divine intention and thereby release the divine power in the world as a creative and victorious force. As Robinson puts it: "Such acts are in miniature the purpose of Yahweh, and they are the natural and instinctive product of the prophet's identification with Him, though it is always the identification of a trusted servant with his Lord's interests . . . . The prophetic act is itself a part of the will of Yahweh, to whose complete fulfilment it points; it brings that will nearer to its completion, not only as declaring it, but in some small degree as effecting it." [40] The symbolic action was, as J. Lindblom says, a "visible word" which "served not only to represent and make evident a particular fact, but also to make this fact a reality." [41]

It is in the light of this that we must understand the prophet's entrance into the social and political arena. His sole weapon was the authentic divine Word that he bore.[42] Yet this was a weapon far more potent than all the expediencies and machinations in which his politically minded contemporaries indulged. For him there was no compromise. To the sovereign and powerful Word that he bore, all political power and military might must be subservient. Once that Word was hurled into the situation the creative and dynamic power of God was released, and the outcome was sure.

The Literary Forms of the Prophetic Message

The literary prophets have left us with complex documents varying from short oracles in poetic form, through longer discourses usually in prose, to autobiographical or biographical sections in which some oracles may be included. The longer discourses are usually the work of an editor, whose prose form often breaks to include prophetic oracles and utterances. Undoubtedly, it is such editors who have preserved for us the prophetic messages. We need not regard these as official figures. Rather, they may be people like Baruch, the scribe, through whom Jeremiah committed many of his oracles to writing (Jer. 36), or like the disciples among whom Isaiah bound up his testimony (Isa. 8:16).

Indeed we may conjecture that every prophetic figure had a group of disciples.[43] Such prophetic circles would collect and treasure the utterances of their leading figures and often would pass them on orally to succeeding generations. Parallel to such oral transmission, we may also see literary compositions. Some of the latter may well have been written down in the prophet's lifetime. Certainly this is so in the cases of Isaiah and Jeremiah. In other cases the loving memory of the circle treasured both the oracles and the experiences of their masters, committing them to writing in after years. To the oracles would be added both biographical and autobiographical material, such as we find in Amos 7:10 ff.; Isaiah 6–8, 36–39; Jeremiah 26–44, 52, and in the autobiographical sections often called Jeremiah's confessions.

Some records are given in the third person, and the setting of an oracle is provided. Sometimes the original poetic form of the oracle is condensed into prose, and an abridged form of the original sermon is offered. This is particularly evident in the cases of Jeremiah and Ezekiel. One outstanding instance is the famous Temple Sermon of Jeremiah, which is furnished in the lengthy and original oracular form in chapter 7, and which in chapter 26 is abridged and set within a biographical setting in the third person. The presence of such doublets is an indication that individual memories were at work preserving parallel traditions until ultimately a collector began to collate the treasured

utterances and experiences. Often both traditions were then preserved, so that in the final collections we see and hear the prophets
through more than one personal remembrance. In Ezekiel we
have evidence of a doublet of the inaugural vision. Chapter 10
may well be a separately preserved tradition parallel to chapters
1–3, placed by the collector in a different position, and yet a
relevant one because of its emphasis on the glory of Yahweh.

The original collections show evidence of subsequent editings.
We can see at work various interests dependent upon later historical conditions and the demands of the religious environment.
As an example, we may look at the Book of Isaiah. Subsequent
editors have added to the original corpus of Isaianic prophecies
oracles uttered against Babylon and thus dating from after the
period when Nineveh was sacked and the Assyrian power had
been replaced by the Babylonian (for example, Isa. 13; 21:1–10).
Such oracles may well have issued from circles which continued
to treasure the memories and traditions of the prophet Isaiah.
The editors may consciously have been concerned to perpetuate
the original tradition, and regarded the authors of the new oracles
as extensions of the initial prophetic figure. To these were later
added the oracles of Second Isaiah (chaps. 40–55), an exilic
prophet with a spirit akin to that of Isaiah himself. The group of
oracles in chapters 56–66 are mainly postexilic, but they also
reflect the spirit of the prophet who prophesied two centuries
before.

We need to remember that the close relation of the prophet to
the cult, made even more close in the postexilic period, would
mean that one important life-setting of the prophetic collections
would be recitation in the public worship of the temple. Thus
cultic needs may have contributed both to the collection and the
editing of prophetic oracles. The presence of the doublet on the
mountain of the Lord's house (Isa. 2:2–4; Mic. 4:1–3) in the collections both of Isaianic oracles and of the utterances of Micah
may indicate that some detached oracle upon the significance
of the postexilic Temple as a center of worship had found a place
because of its relevance to cultic recitation. In this way the
oracles retained their relevance to the contemporary needs and
to the changing situation. As with the gospel traditions of the
New Testament, so with the oracles and collections of oracles in
the Old Testament. They were preserved in a worshiping community, and some of the conditioning and selective factors in
what was preserved were the needs of that community. Nor need
we dismiss from this the divine activity. For the continuing
activity of the Spirit of God who spoke through the original
prophetic figures would also be at work both in the circles which
treasured the traditions and in the cultic leaders who, at the
center, sought to preserve a true worship of the living God.

The finished products of the prophetic circles—the books of

the canonical prophets—do not show chronological or topical unity. Some oracles are prefaced by a note which fixes the time and location of the oracle. Some occur within biographical or autobiographical sections and thus again are placed. Yet others occur without any preface, nor may they be identified by reference to adjacent oracles. Often oracles are grouped together because they have similar themes, but another method of association seems to be a catchword principle. Thus, Amos 7:7–9 is connected with Amos 7:10 ff. probably because *Jeroboam* occurs in both verses 9 and 10. On the other hand, we shall see that in the case of Deutero-Isaiah we seem to have a sustained attempt to develop a theme, so that although oracles and songs seem to break in haphazardly, yet they actually contribute to the general movement of the whole.

Already in this last discussion we have begun to consider not only the mode of collecting and editing the oracles but also their individual form and structure. Evidently, any serious analysis of the literary prophets will have to concern itself with the individual oracles as units. The literary forms of the oracles manifest a general structure.[44] They always begin with "Thus saith Yahweh" and often end with "the oracle of Yahweh." Furthermore, they are poetry and often poetry of a very high order. The latter is especially the case in the oracles of Jeremiah and Deutero-Isaiah, but quite early the oracles of Amos betray a poetic structure which shows him to be far other than an uncultured rustic.

The individual oracles fall into certain groups. Always they are concerned with judgment and salvation. They convey both the divine wrath and the divine grace. Generally the great prophets of the preexilic period emphasized doom, despite their very evident promise of an eschatological redemption and restoration of at least a remnant of God's people. Hence, we find the oracles of reproach, which begin sometimes with "Woe" (Amos 6:1 ff.; Isa. 5:8–23; 29:15 ff.; 30:1–5), and sometimes with "hear this word" (Amos 4:1–3). Often an oracle of doom or threat is attached to the reproach (Isa. 5:11–17), but sometimes only the reproach is uttered (Isa. 5:20, 21). The oracle of doom takes the form of a threat. It begins with "therefore" and details the consequences of the disobedience (Isa. 5:13 ff.; 30:3–5; Amos 6:7 ff.). Sometimes the threat follows a statement of the disobedience introduced by the word *because*. This form appears in the oracles of Amos 1 and 2. A third type of oracle is that which simulates a divine lawsuit, in which God stands over against his people and arraigns them before a tribunal at which the forces of nature are often called in as judges (Isa. 3:12–15; Jer. 2:5b–13; Mic. 6:1–8). Then we have the oracle of admonition in which the wrath is tempered by mercy and salvation begins to sound through the note of doom. Here the characteristic introduction is the use of the phrase "hear this word." There follows an appeal to repent, to turn back to Yahweh, and so to avoid the approaching judgment (Amos 5:1 ff., 5:14, 15; Hos. 14:1 ff.; Jer. 3:12 ff.; Isa. 30:15–18). Finally we have a form which Bentzen describes as the prophetic *torah*. In this the prophet formulates the divine command, and the structure is similar to that of the *toroth*, laws elsewhere (Isa. 56:1–8; Mic. 6:6–8; Isa. 1:10–17). Sometimes such *toroth* are combined with oracles of reproach as in Hosea 6:4–6.

As the prophet opens a window for us into the divine mystery, all the devices of literary structure and poetical expression, of imagination and rhetoric are employed. Yet the power of the prophets did not lie in this. It lay in the fact that in the deeps of their being they were strangely and mysteriously aware of the divine nature and purpose. They were unique figures who knew themselves to be called by Yahweh and who, in their oracles, brought men and nations face to face with God. Their presence is one of the miracles of history, a reminder that spiritual forces are at work behind the materialistic and naturalistic facade which man so easily erects to shut out God.

NOTES

1. J, E, and P are all woven together in Genesis, Exodus, Leviticus, and Numbers. D is contained in and identical with the bulk of the Book of Deuteronomy. The differentiation of the first three written sources has been undertaken by biblical scholars across the last hundred years and is now generally accepted by biblical scholarship. I have not undertaken any discussion of this nor have I sought to identify the passages that belong to each in the first four books of the Old Testament. The reader should consult a good introduction to the Old Testament for detailed information such as Norman K. Gottwald, *A Light to the Nations* (New York: Harper & Bros., 1959) or Artur Weiser, *The Old Testament: Its Formation and Development*, trans. D. M. Barton (New York: Association Press, 1964). Too much has been made of the names given to God as a ground of differentiation, but it still has value. A reader may ascribe to J those passages in Genesis which use Yahweh, whereas E tends to use Elohim and then Yahweh after the Exodus, while P favors El Shaddai and like names prior to revelation of Yahweh at the Exodus.

2. Although too much has often been made of the issue of the divine names in the Pentateuch, I believe that the distinctions must be taken into account and not ignored.

3. Cf. G. E. Mendenhall, *Law and Covenant in Israel and the Ancient Near East* (The Biblical Colloquia, 1955), *passim*.

4. This covenant and its background are formulated in the oracle of Nathan (2 Sam. 7:7–17). They are also reflected in the ancient psalm of 2 Samuel 23:1–7, which may well be Davidic. Cf. Aubrey R. Johnson, *Sacral Kingship in Ancient Israel* (Cardiff: University of Wales Press, 1955), p. 15.

5. The problem of the common origin and milieus of transmission of J and E is discussed in Martin Noth, *Überlieferungsgeschichte des Pentateuch* (Stuttgart: W. Kohlhammer, 1948), pp. 40 ff. My identification of J with the south and E with the north is plausible but difficult to substantiate fully.

6. We may cite Gerhard von Rad, *Studies in Deuteronomy* (Naperville: Allenson, 1953), p. 45: "Deuteronomy renews the cultic tradition of the old Shechem amphictyony." Also Martin North, *Das System der Zwölf Stamme Israels* (Stuttgart: W. Kohlhammer, 1948); A. C. Welch, *The Code of Deuteronomy* (London: James Clarke & Co., 1924); A. C. Welch, *Deuteronomy: The Framework to the Code* (London: Oxford University Press, 1932); William F. Albright, *From the Stone Age to Christianity* (New York: Doubleday & Co., 1957), pp. 315, 319 ff.

7. Von Rad, *Studies in Deuteronomy*, pp. 45 ff.

8. See L. Rost, "Sinaibund und Davidsbund," *Theologische Literaturzeitung* 72 (1947): 132.

9. We omit discussing the extreme views of Scandinavians like Engnell. Ivan Engnell, *Studies in Divine Kingship in the Ancient Near East* (Uppsala: Almgrist and Wicksells, 1943).

10. See Sigmund Mowinckel, *He That Cometh*, trans. G. W. Anderson (Nashville: Abingdon Press, 1956); Johnson, *Sacral Kingship*.

11. See Hans-Joachim Kraus, *Die Königsherrschaft Gottes im Alten Testament* (Tübingen: J.C.B. Mohr, 1951). Also by Kraus, *Worship in Israel*, trans. G. Buswell (Richmond: John Knox Press, 1966).

12. There are those, like Martin Noth, who would divide the traditions into detached units, separating Moses from those units that refer to the Exodus and the Sinai covenant and making him a purely secondary, if not mythical, figure. Undoubtedly later generations did make Moses the focal point of accumulating memories, but I find convincing the arguments of John Bright in which he dismisses Noth's thesis and supports the historicity of the early traditions. Martin Noth, *History of Israel* (New York: Harper & Bros., 1958), pp. 109–137; Noth, *Überlieferungsgeschichte des Pentateuch;* John Bright, *History of Israel* (Philadelphia: Westminster Press, 1959), pp. 110–20; John Bright, *Early Israel in History Writing* (Naperville: Allenson, 1956), pp. 34–55, 79–110.

13. Th. C. Vriezen, *An Outline of Old Testament Theology* (Newton: Charles T. Branford Co., 1960), p. 137.

14. See H. H. Rowley, "Moses and the Decalogue," *Bulletin of the John Rylands Library* 34 (September 1951): 81–118.

15. See Alfred Haldar, *Associations of Cultic Prophets in the Ancient Near East* (Uppsala: Almquist & Wiksells, 1945).

16. See Martin Noth, "History and the Word of God in the Old Testament," *Bulletin of the John Rylands Library* 32 (1949–50): 194–206; Adolphe Lods, "Une Tablette inédite de Mari, interessante pour l'histoire ancienne du prophetisme Sémitique," *Studies in Old Testament Prophecy*, ed. H. H. Rowley (London: Lutterworth Press, 1950), pp. 103–10.

17. Alfred Jepsen, *Nabi: soziologische Studien zur alt. Literatur und Religionsgeschichte* (Munich: Beck, 1934).

18. T. H. Robinson, *Prophecy and the Prophets in Ancient Israel* (London: Duckworth, 1953).

19. Aubrey R. Johnson, *The Cultic Prophet in Ancient Israel* (Cardiff: University of Wales Press, 1944), *passim*.

20. Johannes Lindblom, "Einige Grundfragen der altestamentlichen Wissenchaft," *Festschrift für A. Bertholet* (Tübingen: J.C.B. Mohr, 1951), pp. 325 ff.

21. So the majority of modern scholars. Ed. König, *Hebräisches und aramäisches wörterbuch zum Alten Testament* (Leipzig: Dieterich, 1936), p. 260b.

22. Albright, *From the Stone Age to Christianity*, p. 231.

23. H. Wheeler Robinson, "The Council of Yahweh," *Journal of Theological Studies* 45 (1944): 151–57; Johannes Lindblom, *Prophecy in Ancient Israel* (Oxford: Basil Blackwell, 1962), pp. 112 ff.

24. Ibid., p. 112.

25. See James F. Ross, "The Prophet as Yahweh's Messenger," *Israel's Prophetic Heritage*, ed. W. Harrelson and B. Anderson (New York: Harper & Bros., 1961), pp. 98–107.

26. There is a lengthy discussion of the significance of the *rîv* in Hebrew thought in Berend Gemser, "The *rîv*—or controversy—pattern in Hebrew mentality," *Supplement to Vetus Testamentum* (London: E. J. Brill, 1955), 3: 120–37. This includes a useful treatment of the *rîv* pattern in the prophetic preaching on pages 128 ff.

27. Walther Eichrodt, *Theology of the Old Testament* (Philadelphia: Westminster Press, 1961), 1:322.

28. Aubrey R. Johnson, *The One and the Many in the Israelite Conception of God* (Cardiff: University of Wales Press, 1942), *passim*.

29. Cf. Abraham Heschel, *Die Prophetie* (Kracow: The Polish Academy of Sciences, 1936), pp. 127 ff.; also by Heschel, *The Prophets* (New York: Harper & Bros., 1962), pp. 307 ff.

30. There is a considerable debate as to the origin of this concept. Some would connect it with the hypothetical New Year Festival of Enthronement (Mowinckel). Others would find its origin in a hypothetical widespread eschatology in the ancient Near East (Gressmann). The most feasible seems a hope that sprang out of the traditions of the past. The memories of those days of holy war when Yahweh had intervened to aid his people brought to birth the hope of yet another Day which would be filled full of his saving activity. It would be a Day like the day of Midian, only still more full of Yahweh's glory.

31. Cf. Sigmund Mowinckel, " 'The Spirit' and 'The Word' in the Pre-exilic Reforming Prophets," *Journal of Biblical Literature* 53 (1934):199–277. Mowinckel also argues that, although ecstatic elements are present, the experience of the classical prophet manifests more elevated character (pp. 207 ff.).

32. Cf. Ross, "The Prophet as Yahweh's Messenger," p. 106.

33. H. Wheeler Robinson, *Inspiration and Revelation in the Old Testament* (New York: Oxford University Press, 1946), p. 185.

34. Johannes Pedersen, *Israel I–II* (Copenhagen: Povl Branner, 1926), p. 167.

35. Julius Wellhausen, *Reste Arabishen Heidentums* (Berlin: Walter De Gruyter & Co., 1927), p. 139, n. 4.

36. Pedersen, *Israel*, p. 167.

37. Lindblom, *Prophecy in Ancient Israel*, p. 114, points out that Sumerian and Akkadian texts frequently suggest that the word uttered by a deity is creative and powerful. The same idea is found in Israel.

38. Vriezen, *Outline of Old Testament Theology,* pp. 239 ff.

39. H. Wheeler Robinson, "Prophetic Symbolism," *Old Testament Essays,* ed. D. C. Simpson (London: Charles Griffin & Co., 1927), pp. 1–17.

40. Ibid., pp. 14 ff.

41. Lindblom, *Prophecy in Ancient Israel,* p. 172.

42. Cf. Robinson, *Inspiration and Revelation,* p. 171.

43. See Sigmund Mowinckel, *Prophecy and Tradition* (Oslo: I. Kommisjon Los J. Dybwad, 1946), p. 60; Lindblom, *Prophecy in Ancient Israel,* pp. 239 ff.

44. There is a full and scholarly discussion of these forms in Aage Bentzen, *Introduction to the Old Testament* (Copenhagen: G.E.C. Gads, 1948), pp. 194–202. For the prophetic literature, consult also Johannes Lindblom, *Die literarische Gattung der prophetischen Literatur* (Uppsala: Universitets Arsskrift, 1924), *passim.*

Chapter Two

The Righteousness
of God and the
Day of Yahweh

The earliest canonical prophet, Amos, performed his ministry in the northern kingdom of Israel. His oracles come down to us mixed up with some biographical information, so that as we shall see later, we can form some picture of the prophet himself. These biographical details are offered to us in the opening verse of the first chapter and in chapter 7. It is evident that the prophetic utterances have not come down to us in any chronological order. The first two chapters would seem to form an impressive unity and were probably delivered in one prophetic address.[1] For Amos begins with Damascus in the northeast, and moves successively to Philistria in the southwest, to Phoenicia in the northwest, and to Edom, with its neighbors Moab and Ammon, in the southeast. Only then is he ready to turn his attack upon Israel. In a striking and awesome way the prophet brings the attack on the other nations to a focus in a vigorous condemnation of Israel itself. The whole discourse has what we described in the last chapter as a *rîv* structure.[2] In the next four chapters (3–6) we have a series of detached oracles against the social iniquities and religious corruption of the northern kingdom. In chapters 7 and 8 the book records a series of visions which came to Amos with an accompanying message of judgment. Interlaced in these we have the biographical account of the prophet's visit to the sanctuary at Bethel (7:10–17). The first three visions of 7:1–9 hold out some hope of escape, for Yahweh repents and withholds a final judgment, but the vision of chapter 8 offers no hope of escape—the annihilation of Israel is sure (8:2). In 9:1–10 we have a final oracle of judgment, and then in 9:11–15 the tone changes to one of hope. Some scholars are so convinced that Amos was a prophet of doom that they regard this last oracle as a later addition and not the utterance of Amos himself. We shall see, however, that there are indications that Amos hoped for some kind of restoration.

It would seem that we have here a collection of the prophet's oracles, gathered together and edited by his disciples. They may well have been committed to memory and handed on orally during the troubled days of Israel's fall. Ultimately they found their way to Judah and were there given their final form in the hands of an editor.[3] On this basis, we must proceed to examine the theological insights of the prophetic message.

THE PROPHET AMOS AND THE HISTORICAL SITUATION

No prophet delivered his oracles to a vacuum. The divine stimulation of the prophetic consciousness turned upon the challenge of the national and international scene. History and the prophetic insight were matched, as together they provided the media for a divine revelation.

The historical situation of the two kingdoms of Judah and Israel became increasingly dominated by the imperialistic policies of their two great neighbors, Egypt to the south and Assyria to the north. Naturally Israel's historical fate seemed to be bound up with the history of Assyria. In addition, however, we have to take into account the significant small state of Syria. Centering in Damascus, its power became felt once the united Davidic kingdom had fallen apart. We have traced the earlier association of the future of Israel with the militaristic ambitions of Syria. About the time that Amos came on the scene, however, Syria had been subjugated by Adad-nirari IV (810–782 B.C.), the Assyrian ruler. The realism of the Deuteronomist historians makes the situation in Israel clear. The Syrians oppressed Israel until Yahweh sent them a savior (2 Kings 13:5). Who this savior is is not clear. The Hebrew historians would seem to have identified him with Jeroboam II, whom they specifically define as the one who saved Israel (2 Kings 14:25–27). In actual fact, the unmeasured prosperity and the return of Israel to power under this king was possible only because the Assyrian triumph had removed the menace of Syria and made that state quiescent. Thus the savior may well have been Adad-nirari IV. Even then, Israel's recovery only became possible because Assyria itself soon entered into a period of internal dispute and dynastic changes. It was not until Tiglath-pileser IV appeared on the scene that Assyria reasserted itself. Hence for roughly fifty years Israel had no foreign power menacing its borders and seeking to control its economic and political life.

In consequence, Israel entered upon a period of unexampled prosperity. This begat a materialism and corruption of religious practice which struck at the ethical foundations of society. The foundation of the Hebrew common life had been a covenant brotherhood sealed at Sinai and renewed as the basis of the tribal amphictyony at Schechem. This had brought a spirit of moral responsibility and justice into the society of Israel. Even the Hebrew kings were within this covenant and subject to God. It is true that in the southern kingdom of Judah there was a royal theology, derived partly from Jebusite days but brought to a focus in the Davidic covenant. Yet even in Judah, the prophets (n^evi'im) had delivered their oracles to the monarch. The king was under God, bound to him by covenant obligations and bound to his people likewise. There was a democratic note about the kingship, and whenever the king betrayed the covenant brotherhood, the prophetic voice was heard. As the Hebrew understood it, the king in a deep sense represented the people, and his rightness with God, his righteousness, guaranteed righteousness and justice among the people.

In Israel this democratic or theocratic ideal with its covenanted brotherhood was often challenged by the king. Ahab is one outstanding example. Now, however, it was challenged by the ruling caste. Kings, the aristocracy, the wealthy, and the religious leaders now began to break the fellowship and exploit their fellows. Money began to speak. The judges took bribes in giving judgment at the village gates. Absentee landlords exploited their tenants. Others sought to gain possession of the lands of their poorer neighbors by unjust means, like Ahab and Naboth's vineyard. A love of luxury swept the land, as prosperity filled its borders. The shrines became wealthy, the priesthood shallow, and the religious practice corrupt. Instead of recognizing God as the source of its wealth and newly acquired power, Israel rejoiced in itself, and pride took possession of a people.

Into the midst of this situation stalked Amos. The editorial introduction to the book tells us that he came from Tekoa, to the southeast of Jerusalem and situated in the wilderness of Judah. Thus the man was from the southern kingdom. His presence in and message to the northern kingdom of Israel is understandable in the light of what he tells us of his work. He was a shepherd and a dresser of sycamore trees (1:1; 7:14 ff.). This does not necessarily imply that he was of lowly station. The word *shepherd* is used to describe Mesha, king of Moab (2 Kings 3:4), and may thus describe one who owns sheep. It is probable that Amos owned his own sheep and had extensive property. Tekoa is at 3,000 feet, as has been pointed out, whereas the sycamore line is 1,000 feet. This would suggest that Amos owned land away from Tekoa where he could dress the sycamore trees. He may well have been wealthy, and, in the task of selling the wool from his sheep, he would move from his home on the edge of the wilderness up to the great trading centers of Judah and especially of Israel.

At Samaria and Bethel the social injustice, the moral decadence, the religious corruption, and the love of luxury challenged

his moral earnestness and puritanic spirit. This must not be taken
to imply that he was a proletarian critic of a bourgeois society,
for we have just suggested that he may himself have belonged
to the wealthier group. Thus in Amos we have not a member of
the have-nots attacking the haves, an uncultured rough shepherd
of the desert vastnesses criticizing wealth and material splendor
as such. The poetical style and classical language of the prophet,
as well as his insights, indicate some degree of culture. He was
familiar with the vocabulary and style of the wisdom circles
and may well have received some of his ideas from them.[4] He
was not some uncultured rustic and rebel reformer from below,
but one whose own standard of living was implicated in that
which he attacked. He was in the north quite possibly to trade
the results of his own sheepfarming, and he attacked the north
on moral and religious grounds.

One can imagine that after his visits north he returned to his
southern wilderness to brood upon the civilization he had en-
countered. His powers of observation had been sharpened by his
life so close to nature, and his moral insight was that of an austere
man of the southland close to the wilderness traditions of Israel's
faith (J and E). He was no man of the city. Jerusalem, its culture
and its tradition, its Temple and its royal theology, seem to have
exercised little effect upon this Judahite. He was able to speak
to the north because, to a large extent, he shared in their traditions. The memory of the Exodus and the wilderness traditions
with their moral obligations and divine demands still remained
real, and his keen insight saw that this portended inevitable
judgment upon a corrupt and luxury-loving Israel.

We may add to this the fact that Amos, coming from outside
the northern kingdom, was able to take a more objective look at
Israel's prosperity and new access of power. He must have been
aware already of the lengthening shadow of a resurgent Assyria.
To his conviction of judgment such an awareness would be linked,
although he, unlike his contemporary Hosea, did not clearly
identify Assyria as the agent of divine judgment.

He began his ministry two years before the earthquake. This
is mentioned also in Zechariah 14:4 and apparently was a cata-
clysmic event, but it provides us with little help for dating the
prophet. The editorial note also identifies his ministry with the
reigns of Uzziah in Judah and Jeroboam II in Israel. It has been
suggested that the solar eclipse of 763 B.C. is reflected in 8:9.
We must, at any rate, date him a little earlier than Hosea, for
the identification of Assyria with the coming judgment has not
yet become so evident to him as it was to his northern contemporary. It is customary to place his ministry in the period
760–745 B.C.

He gives us little information about his call, although he
clearly states that he received one. He calls himself a prophet

and yet sharply differentiates himself from the professional group. He tells us that he was not a *navi'* and did not belong to a prophetic guild (this is the meaning of the phrase "one of the sons of the prophets" in 7:14).

Amos manifests the experience of his successors in the canonical prophets. The features of the prophetic consciousness are present. There is the conviction of standing in the divine council, sharing in Yahweh's decrees, and being sent as a messenger (3:6, 7). There is the sense of an inner pressure which sends him out to proclaim his message, very much like that later experienced by Jeremiah (3:8).

Although Amos differentiates himself from the professional group, he clearly identifies himself as a prophet and commends the orthodox type of prophet. It is God who has raised up the prophets and who reveals his will to them (2:11; 3:7, 8). His trouble with the professional group would seem to be the mercenary motive that activated them. This weakness is attacked again and again by Amos's successors. It meant that such prophets would prophesy smooth things. Such an issue is evident in the autobiographical section, which records the visit of Amos to Bethel. His clash with the priest Amaziah evidently arises out of the form of his message. He is told to go and eat bread, earn his living from such a message, in Judah. His threats against Israel may well bring him financial return in the rival southern kingdom, but they will not do so up north. Amos's response to this challenge is to affirm that he is not a professional and has no mercenary motive (7:10–17).

It has been suggested that the visions of chapters 7 and 8 were associated with the prophet's call. Yet they seem to be spread across his ministry and to manifest a change in his experience of God and his inner convictions. In the first two visions of judgment, the locusts and the drought, the message of an imminent doom is lifted through the intercession of Amos. In the second two visions, the plumbline and the basket of summer fruit, the message of judgment is upheld. It would appear that the conviction is now brought home to the prophetic consciousness that ultimate judgment is inevitable and cannot be revoked by Yahweh. The visions are of value in showing how some aspects of his message came to the prophet. Elements in the common life and natural order around him became revelatory media through which his oracles were formulated. This is, of course, a typical aspect of the prophetic consciousness.

Yahweh, the God of All the Earth

With Amos the monotheism, the belief in *one* God of the whole earth implicit in the Mosaic understanding of God, comes to expression in the prophetic consciousness for the first time. Although an explicit monotheism waited upon the revelatory insight granted to Deutero-Isaiah, Amos sees already that Yahweh of Israel is also Lord and Judge of the nations.

The opening chapters of the book contain what we have already defined as a long prophetic utterance. It consists of a series of oracles specifically addressed to Israel's neighbors: Damascus, Philistia, Tyre, Moab, Edom, and Judah. The whole is brought to a climax in a denunciation of Israel. Two things are striking in this series of oracles. The first is the fact that Israel's neighbors are brought directly under the aegis of Israel's God. Yahweh is no tribal deity but one who claims jurisdiction over all peoples. By implication the deities of the other nations are put out of court. The second fact is that the nations are arraigned not on the grounds of their relation to Israel, but on the grounds of their unrighteousness toward God and toward one another. They do not meet the divine standard for righteous conduct.

Hence Ammon and Damascus are condemned for barbarity in warfare; Edom for its open hostility to Israel, its brother; Philistia and Tyre for slave raiding and trading; Moab for its desecration of the remains of the dead king of Edom; and Judah for rejecting the divine Torah. When he turns to Israel, the prophet stands it alongside the rest and arraigns it also on moral grounds. He assumes a universal morality because he believes in one universal God. We note that only in the case of Edom is a specific crime against Israel cited. Moab's crime is against Edom. And all the cases before the divine tribunal are instances of a breach of man's moral responsibility to his brother man under God.

The universal rule of Yahweh naturally goes with such a moral emphasis. We find the prophet putting Israel on the same footing as the other nations, not only in this opening arraignment before the divine court but also in one of his final oracles (9:7). Here the foreign peoples are brought into a positive relationship to God. Not only are they related negatively as under the divine judgment, but they are also under his overruling. Their history is subject to his sovereign purpose. From the Ethiopians who stood at the fringe of the ancient world, to Israel's nearest neighbors in Syria and Philistia, Amos sees Yahweh at work. All the inhabitants of the world, including Israel's closest enemies, stand in a positive relation to God. The prophet even thinks of brotherhood between Edom and Tyre and between Edom and Israel (1:9, 11). If Israel is specially chosen out of the group, then its moral responsibility is all the greater, and its privilege gives it no reason for a false sense of security and for moral depravity (3:1, 2). Even Sheol comes under Yahweh's surveillance, and the realm of the dead is not beyond the reach of his power (9:2). God is indeed universal Lord. He is God of hosts.

It is noteworthy that although Amos speaks of Israel's election by God, he does not speak of Yahweh as the God of Israel. He is Yahweh, the 'God of hosts'. This description occurs many times in the book of Amos (3:13; 4:13; 5:15, 16, 27; 6:8, 14; 9:5). In its roots, the title was originally associated with the holy war period of Israel's history, when Yahweh fought for his people and led their armies, as the ark went before them into battle. Clearly, however, it is not so related in the oracles of Amos, with their universalism. It is much more likely that the term has been given a celestial rather than a terrestrial reference and that the hosts refer to the heavenly bodies. The pagan deities were associated with the stars, and thus, the title infers that Yahweh is lord over the nations because he controls the heavenly hosts. As E. Jacob reminds us, ". . . the best way of neutralizing these powers was to integrate them into the being of Yahweh, the only Lord." [5] In Amos there are three doxologies which are probably authentic.[6] In one of these (5:8), Yahweh is declared to be the creator of the constellations of the stars. Elsewhere he is declared to be lord over the sun and to control its eclipse (8:9). Stars and sun are no deities but powers subservient to the God of hosts.[7] The title thus refers to God's lordship over his universe, the totality of whose powers is under his control. Yahweh could not be inferior to foreign deities for his true worshiper. He must be universal ruler over all peoples.

THE SINS OF ISRAEL

As Lord of the nations, Yahweh is characterized by his righteousness. Amos does not describe Yahweh himself as righteousness, but righteousness and judgment characterize his actions and his demands of his people. Those who turn judgment (*mishpat*) to wormwood and cast down righteousness (*tsedheq*) to the earth are urged to seek the Lord that they may live (5:7). Because they have turned righteousness to wormwood and judgment into gall, Yahweh has decreed their destruction (6:14). Thus God is the living source of righteousness and judgment.

The two words have a law court flavor and are legal terms. *Righteousness* means basically conformity to the norm or standard, and *judgment* means the right sentence of a judge. The implication is that the personal God, the living Lord, is righteous because he abides true to himself, for he sets his own standard in his dealings with Israel and for Israel's behavior. Righteousness is to be measured by the covenant demands of Yahweh on his people and by the obligations which he has himself freely accepted in that relationship. God's standard or norm is his "personal being in his totality; this personal being is the sovereign Lord and all he does conforms to that fundamental attitude." [8] Hosea later can remind Israel that Yahweh has betrothed them to him in the covenant relation in righteousness and in judgment (Hos. 2:19). God's righteousness is also judgment. God is the judge who passes his sentence upon Israel in accord with his righteousness. Israel's righteousness and judgment as a social whole are grounded in this divine source. They are not based on social or moral principles merely, but on God's activity.

The righteousness of Yahweh flows down from heaven into Israel and to the ends of the earth. But Israel refuses the divine demands and by its sin dams back the flood of righteousness, until the dam bursts, and like a mighty flood of waters, judgment comes on Israel (5:24).[9] Israel has turned the fruit of righteousness into wormwood and judgment into gall (6:12). Amos can describe Israel as in rebellion (*pesha'*) against God, but he is not concerned with the inner spirit of rebellion, its internal motivation. Rather he is concerned with outward expression and behavior. He is concerned with rebellions or transgressions rather than with rebellion, with sins rather than sin (3:14). Furthermore, he is concerned with Israel as a corporate whole, rather than with the individual Israelite. Sin and guilt are primarily national, and the sins that he attacks are generally social and corporate.

Amos attacks the social injustice of his time. Covenant brotherhood has been undermined with the occasion of prosperity, and the haves have become the oppressors rather than the succorers of the have-nots. The rich have waxed wealthy at the expense of the increasing poverty of the poor, and the old social order is disintegrating. So we find the prophet indicting those who sell the poor for silver and the needy for a pair of shoes (2:6; 4:1; 5:11; 8:6). Religious observance of the sabbath and the festivals is objected to by those whose major concern is trading and who falsify their measures in order to make more profit (8:5 ff.). Rapacious landowners are swallowing up the land of their poor neighbors (8:4). The leaders are storing up robbery and violence in their palaces (3:10). On every hand there is a debilitating love of luxury and increasing drunkenness (6:4–6; 3:12, 15). The wives of the wealthy are as depraved as their lords (4:1). Justice has become so debased that judgment is turned to wormwood and gall, and the judges take bribes as they administer justice at the village gate (5:10, 12).

Conjoined to the social ills is the corruption of religion. The terrible fact is that Israel is very religious. Its citizens throng the shrines and make costly sacrifices, but their social deeds belie their religious acts. Man's inhumanity to man denies the very covenant which is brought to a focus in the worship of the shrines. The ideals of the covenant have been replaced by material values, and the new situation of prosperity has not been matched by an increased depth in religious faith. Rather religion has become superficial, and the cult has become the servant of a materialistically minded social order. Religious practice has become a cover for social injustice, and the cult ritual has been harnessed to the support of the wealthy and the unjust. The common belief is that because Israel is God's covenanted people, therefore they are bound to be secure. There is a failure to realize that the privilege of the divine election brings moral obligation in its train. God is bound to look after Israel, runs the popular argument, and the religious practice is harnessed to the support of an unjust order.

Hence Amos attacks the sacrificial system. He does not attack the bull worship and the baalism as did his later contemporary, Hosea. We have just a hint of this in the indictment of religious prostitution (2:7). The sledge hammer blows fall on the sacrifices and the motive that underlies them. The abundance of sacrifices could not make up for the absence of the right spirit. Rich shrines could not cover up social iniquity. However much men might advertise the number and richness of their offerings on the altar, proclaiming them to the crowd on some religious festival, this would not avert the divine judgment. Indeed, it had not done so already (4:4–10). It was no use seeking the shrine, if they were not seeking Yahweh (5:4–6). Punctilious observance of public worship does not atone for evil living.

So Amos inveighs against the sacrifices in the name of Yahweh. He even implies that God had not intended them (5:25).[10] Certainly he will not accept them as they are now offered (5:21, 22). The prophet could hardly mean that the sacrificial aspect of the approach to God was not required and should be replaced solely by ethical behavior. Righteousness in the nation should be the outward expression of worship, but worship there must be, and it is difficult to see how worship could be offered to God without some form of sacrifice in its center. It would seem that Amos is not denying sacrifice a legitimate place in the cult. Rather he is pointing out that there was little or no opportunity for it in the wilderness, and yet God was Israel's God even then. The sacrifices were no magic spell by which God's favor was released irrespective of the inner attitude of Israel's spirit. They were only effective when conjoined to moral behavior and when they expressed the commitment of Israel to the covenant bond. Israel was closer to Yahweh in the wilderness days, when sacrifices could rarely be offered, if at all, than in these days of prosperity with their abundant offerings. Sacrifices were irrelevant if the divine demands were not met. How relevant to our own contemporary situation!

THE DAY OF YAHWEH—THE JUDGMENT OF ISRAEL

The popular religion of the day held an optimistic view of the future. The moral rigor of the Sinai covenant had long since been slackened by a perverted interpretation of the covenant with the patriarchs and with the Davidic dynasty. Even though the latter no longer counted for the northern kingdom, yet the royal theology was undoubtedly influential even if reinterpreted. In consequence there had grown up a popular optimism reinforced by the apparent prosperity of the times. Since Yahweh had chosen Israel and bound himself to it by covenant, he was bound to protect and further its destiny. In the common thought of the time there developed, as we have seen, a popular eschatology which envisaged a glorious future Day of Yahweh, when in prosperity and splendor Israel would enjoy to the full the privilege of being God's people.

Undoubtedly, one root of this concept lies back in the holy war when Yahweh had come to do battle for his people. The Day of Yahweh was a day filled with Yahweh's triumph. It is highly probable too that the eschatological concept contained other contributing elements. It may well be that the hope was also fostered by new year festivals which celebrated annually the kingship of Yahweh and by the infiltration into such festivals of naturalistic fertility rites with their emphasis on material prosperity and natural fecundity! [11]

Be that as it may, Amos would have nothing to do with it. He boldly declares that the Day of Yahweh, the day of his kingship, would be darkness and not light (5:18-20). The popular conception of the day as the time when Israel would be exalted was challenged. Rather, Israel would be humiliated and judged. Yahweh was coming, but he was coming as judgment, and the flood of his righteousness would overwhelm unrighteous Israel (5:24). Privilege meant responsibility. Because Yahweh had chosen Israel out of all the peoples, he would visit upon it all its iniquities (3:2). Indeed, 9:7 would suggest that Yahweh's election of Israel involved no favoritism, for he had also controlled the destinies of the other historical peoples. In a moving lament, Amos declares the fall of the virgin of Israel (5:1 ff.). Already the judgment has come in part. Drought and famine, pestilence and disease in the crops have afflicted Israel. Yet Israel has not returned to God, repented, turned back its will to Yahweh (4:6-12). Its very failure to turn meant that the ultimate doom was inevitable.

We find the same theme repeated in the visions of judgment. In the visions of the locusts and the drought (7:1-3, 4-6), Amos interceded and Yahweh held back his judgment. But the visions of the plumb line and the basket of summer fruit declare an inevitable doom that cannot be averted (7:7-9; 8:1 ff.).

The prophet is vague about the agent of the final catastrophe. Clearly it will be a military disaster and will result in the captivity of Israel (5:27; 6:7, 14; 7:11, 17). It is evident that Amos believed that the final disaster would move in from the north, and he may have identified it with the policies of Assyria rising once more to power. He does not specifically make this identification, however, and he was actually more concerned with the fact that it was Yahweh who was acting. This inevitability of final judgment occurs also in the repeated refrain of the long address of chapters 1 and 2. Yahweh declares that he will not cause the judgment to return, he will not lift his decree.

Amos has often been cited as a prophet of doom, and this is especially true if we reject 9:11–15 as unauthentic. In 5:4, 6 we have an evangelical appeal to seek Yahweh which, in 5:14 ff., becomes an evangelical promise that Yahweh may yet be gracious to the remnant of Israel. It would seem that even here the hope lies beyond the judgment. If we regard 9:8b–10 as in the original corpus of Amos's oracles, we find the same hope repeated. Israel will be sifted among the nations, and the solid remnant will be preserved.

Probably this is as far as Amos himself was prepared to go. The closing oracle apparently belongs to the period of the exile of 587 B.C., when the 'booth of David' had fallen and would be restored by Yahweh. Chapter 9, verses 14 and 15 specifically mention the captivity, but Amos does this elsewhere. Actually the reference to David would be the chief reason for dating the oracle late, apart from the belief that Amos was solely a prophet of doom. We have just discredited the latter view in part, and thus the detached oracle of 9:11–15 may have a core derivable from Amos, although in its present form it is exilic.

Amos began a new day in Israel. Under God, he became a conscience to the covenant people and a revealer of the greatness of Yahweh. In his message monotheism becomes very evident, and the universal moral claim of God is clearly expressed. That he should be a prophet of judgment and a messenger of darkness ought not to blind us to glimpses of light and hope that come breaking through. Amos was not a northern Israelite and thus was detached emotionally from his hearers. It was left for Hosea to plumb the depths of the divine pathos and to declare a grace that went beyond judgment in redeeming mercy.

NOTES

1. Johannes Lindblom is convinced that the oracles form a coherent composition in "Wisdom in the Old Testament Prophets," *Supplement to Vetus Testamentum* (London: E. J. Brill, 1955), 3:202. He sees Wisdom influence in the rhetorical trick at the commencement of each of the oracles. The use of numbers is characteristic of wisdom literature (for example, Job 30:14; 33:2; Prov. 30:15–16; 18–19). Cf. Samuel Terrien, "Amos and Wisdom," *Israel's Prophetic Heritage*, ed. W. Harrelson and B. Anderson (New York: Harper & Bros., 1962), pp. 109 ff.

2. Berend Gemser believes that this section of Amos follows such a *rîv* pattern and likens it "to the monotonous summoning by the officers of the court of a panel of accused and sentenced persons"

in "The *rîv*—or controversy—pattern in Hebrew mentality," *Supplement to Vetus Testamentum*, 3:129.

3. See J. D. W. Watts, "The Origin of the Book of Amos," *Expository Times* 66 (1954–55): 109 ff., and Johannes Lindblom, *Prophecy in Ancient Israel* (Oxford: Basil Blackwell, 1962), pp. 241 ff.

4. See Terrien, "Amos and Wisdom," pp. 108–115. Terrien points out that "Like the wise, Amos was uncommonly well versed in Oriental learning, especially in astronomy. He was acquainted with the geography, the history, and the social customs of nations outside of Israel." He holds that in matters of terminology and style, peculiar affinities existed between Amos and the wise men. He makes the conjecture that the prophet received some of his ideas from wisdom circles, although Amos set them within his own prophetic framework rather than that of moral humanism (pp. 114 ff.). Living near the borders of Edom with its ancient wisdom tradition (1 Kings 4:30–31; Jer. 49:7), Amos may well have been subjected to such cultural influences in this location.

5. Edmond Jacob, *Theology of the Old Testament* (New York: Harper & Bros., 1958), p. 55.

6. It has been suggested that these doxologies may have been added in the process of editing to fit the writing for cultic usage. This does not mean that they do not reflect the thought of Amos. See J. D. W. Watts, *Vision and Prophecy in Amos* (Leiden: E.J. Brill, 1958), pp. 57 ff.

7. Cf. Ludwig Köhler, *Old Testament Theology* (Philadelphia: Westminster Press, 1957), pp. 50 ff.

8. Jacob, *Theology of the Old Testament*, p. 96.

9. Cf. Martin Buber, *The Prophetic Faith* (New York: Macmillan, 1949), p. 102.

10. For a discussion of this consult H. H. Rowley, *The Unity of the Bible* (London: The Carey Kingsgate Press, 1953), pp. 30–43. A differing and more radical interpretation is offered by Lindblom, *Prophecy in Ancient Israel*, pp. 353 ff.

11. See Gerhard von Rad, "The Origin of the Concept of the Day of Yahweh," *Journal of Semitic Studies* 4 (1959): 97–108. Cf. Lindblom, *Prophecy in Ancient Israel*, p. 352.

Chapter Three

The Covenant Love
of Yahweh

The prophets Hosea and Amos were contemporary messengers to Israel, the northern kingdom. Hosea began his ministry before the close of the reign of Jeroboam II. How long it extended, we cannot say. Unlike Amos he seems to belong to the people he is addressing. He is the only prophet of the northern kingdom who has left a written record of his oracles. He and Amos are the first two great literary prophets, and many of the notes that he sounded recur in the messages of those who follow him.

Like the other books, Hosea is a collection of oracles compiled by disciples who treasured the utterances of the master. Evidently chapters 1 and 3 are separate transmissions, one in the third person and the other in the first, of Hosea's marriage experiences. We must defer until later a discussion of how far they are duplicates or descriptions of different stages of that marital relationship. The use of biographical and autobiographical forms, however, would indicate separate transmissions. It may well be that the collector who assembled the detached oracles of chapters 4–13 was also responsible for the introductory section of chapters 1–3, since the theme of adultery knits the whole together.[1] The catchword principle is evident in the work of the collector. Chapter 8, verses 8–10 and 1–7 are connected by the word *devour* (8:7 and 8:8). Chapters 8:11–14 and 9:1–9 have the reiterated sentence, "He will remember their guilt, and punish their sins" (8:13 and 9:9). Chapters 4:1–11 and 4:12–19 seem connected by the image of harlotry (4:10 and 4:12). The latter case also indicates how similarity of content brings individual units together in the collector's mind. Chapter 5:1–7 and 8–14 have in common the theme of forgiveness. We find the same in other oracles.

The result is that we have no indication of any chronological order in the oracles. We have a collection of detached oracles against priests, rulers, and people, analyzing the depths of their faithlessness, attacking their immorality, pointing out the inner nature of sin, and affirming the unfailing covenant-love and faithfulness of Yahweh. The collector was a disciple sufficiently near the prophet to be heir to some recollection of the prophet's family problems, and to collect remembrances of them in the introductory section in such a way that he showed their relation to the prophet's message to Israel (chap. 2). Yet he was sufficiently remote to have no recollection of the chronological order of the utterances. He was probably a second generation disciple. One principle is evident in his collection. He alternates oracles of judgment with oracles of hope.

HOSEA'S MARITAL EXPERIENCE

The key to the prophetic message lies in the first three chapters. In chapter 1 we have an account, in the third person, of Hosea's marriage to Gomer and of his naming of his children in accord with certain dominant themes in his message: Jezreel, Lo-ruhamah, and Lo-ammi. We are told that the prophet was commanded by God to take a wife of harlotry and children of harlotry. In chapter 3 we have an autobiographical account, in the first person, of how Hosea was commanded to love a woman who was an adulteress, loved by a paramour. He obeyed the command by purchasing her and compelling her to live in isolation for a period. The name Gomer is not used in this chapter. In chapter 2 the relation of Hosea to his wife is made the basis for an allegory on the relation of Yahweh to Israel. The two relationships are often bound together in such a way that it is not clear which the prophet is referring to. This has led some scholars to infer that all of Hosea is allegory and that we are not here dealing with real events in the prophet's life. There are, however, details which are difficult to reconcile with pure allegorization. The name Gomer seems to possess no allegorical significance. The weaning of Lo-ruhamah and the purchase price are details which have no bearing in the allegorical interpretation. They are evidently descriptive of concrete happenings. Hence we shall assume that the basis of these chapters is an actual marriage of Hosea to Gomer.

Our troubles are, however, still not over. Are we to identify Gomer in chapter 1 with the redeemed harlot of chapter 3? There are those who argue that such identification does not hold. The redeemed harlot was a second wife and Gomer was innocent.[2] Yet the whole movement of thought is against this. It is difficult to explain the phrase "wife of harlotry" as a reading of the apostate state of Israel into Hosea's marriage (1:2). It is the like conditions of Gomer and Israel that make the figure significant. Further, Yahweh in chapter 3 says to the prophet:

"Go *again* love a woman" (3:1), an evident indication that Hosea
has been previously related to her. Again, we have to ask why
Hosea should attach the thought of whoredom to his wife and
children when the term did not apply. It is hardly consonant with
the lofty moral principles so evident in his teaching. The truth,
yes. But to apply to his own family symbolism that has a false
foundation in reality raises real questions when we remember
the prophet's character. Furthermore, the prophet uses the marriage as the symbol of God's relation to Israel, and there is no
thought of God having another wife than Israel. We must assume
that in chapter 3 Gomer is the harlot who is redeemed, and that
she becomes symbolic of Israel. Finally, we find it difficult to
understand how the enduring covenant bond between Yahweh and
Israel could be symbolized by the chance purchase of a whore,
rather than with the purchase of one to whom the prophet was
already bound in the covenant of marriage.

When we have identified the woman of chapter 3 with Gomer
of chapter 1, we still have to ask whether chapter 3 is subsequent to or parallel to chapter 1. Many argue that the two chapters are parallel,[3] chapter 3 being a biographical description by
another hand of what the prophet describes himself in chapter
1. Yet the details are different, and the two hardly fit as parallels.
The most satisfactory solution is that which regards chapter 3
as the sequel to chapter 1. We might even suggest a dislocation
of text such that 3:1–5 should belong between 1:9 and 1:10.
Then chapter 2 would be a fitting climax to the whole experience which, in a real sense, constitutes the prophet's call.

There are two possible interpretations open to us in this se-
quence. Both turn on our understanding of the phrase "wife of
harlotry." The first takes the phrase literally and assumes that
Hosea, under divine constraint, knowingly married a woman who
was a harlot. We need to remember that religious prostitution
was rampant at the Israelite shrines, where Yahweh had been
baalized and his worship associated with the practices of the
fertility cults. Hosea might knowingly have developed a love for
one who was such a prostitute at a sanctuary.[4] It is true that
he attacked the baalistic forms of worship and their attendant
immorality in his oracles. But in marrying one associated with
these, he may well, in his own understanding, have been joining
issue with them at the redemptive level. Now it was customary
for such religious prostitutes to continue their duties when married,
and Gomer may have done this. Hosea, however, did not tolerate
this, tried to win her complete loyalty and fidelity within the
marriage bond, and at last succeeded. He freed her from her
service at the shrine by paying the purchase price, or gaining
legal possession, and thus set her free to be his wife within an
uncontaminated bond. In this time when she still carried on
her practice of ritual prostitution, he showed his attitude to her

behavior and the whole fertility practice by the names he gave their children. Our difficulty with this interpretation lies in the fact that it belies the original relation of Yahweh to Israel, expressed in chapter 2 and presumably having as its background Hosea's initial relationship to Gomer.

The second alternative is to interpret the phrase "wife of harlotry" as a later reading of Gomer's subsequent behavior back into the beginning.[5] The prophet had been commanded to marry her and was convinced that his marriage and all its later developments were within the divine purpose. As she fell into wayward practices, he became increasingly aware of her infidelity and named his children accordingly. The last child was given a name Lo-ammi ("not my people"), which may indicate that he had doubts of this child's parentage. He now found that Yahweh's command had involved his marrying a harlot. God evidently intended this, for it was in his foreknowledge, and so the prophet threw back his subsequent experience into the initial command. The consequences were in the original purpose. This view is fully consonant with prophetic realism. Seen *post eventum*, Hosea can spell out the purpose of God in his marriage. As H. W. Robinson puts it: ". . . when the prophet did interpret his own life prophetically in the light of after events as being under the providential guidance of God, he saw that he had, in fact, though unconsciously at the time, taken to himself a woman *destined* to be a wife of harlotry and to bear children of harlotry." [6] The full nature of his call and message became clear when Hosea's love triumphed and he redeemed Gomer from those who were exploiting her, reestablishing her in his home. This view can still be bound up with the thought of ritual prostitution, for Gomer may well have been a religious devotee who, despite her marriage to Hosea, gave herself to the practice of the shrine.

Both views show a depth of spiritual revelation, but the second would seem to be more appealing. The first view appears to suggest that even the prophet's marriage was a symbolic act, and would be quite in keeping with the view of marriage in his own time. The second view may savor of romanticism and is often attacked on this ground.[7] It is held to be too modern, whereas the first view would involve no difficulty for a man of that time, especially if he were a charismatic person convinced of God's purpose. One point already made needs, however, to be stressed again. The initial relation of God to Israel, described in chapter 2 and allegorically grounded in Hosea's marriage experience, seems better fitted to the second alternative.

Whichever view we take, Hosea's marriage and its consequences became the window through which he saw into the heart of God and came to share in the divine travail over a faithless Israel. The call of the prophet and his understanding of God's nature and purpose came to him through his own marital experience. We have here no ecstatic or visionary experience. Through the crisis of his life situation the prophet comes into encounter with the living God and enters into that *pathos* with the divine which characterizes the prophetic consciousness.

THE COVENANT IN HISTORY AND EXPERIENCE— THE UNVEILING OF GOD'S LOVE

This insight into the mind and will of God must be seen within the context of that wider faith which Hosea shared with the people of God and which was grounded in the great historic act of deliverance. Hosea stands in a succession which looks back to the deliverance from Egypt. The God who came to him was Yahweh, the God of Israel, and within the matrix of Hosea's own experience was born a vision of the travail of Yahweh with his covenant people. This God was the covenant-God, and Israel was the covenant-people. The vicissitudes of Israel's history and its contemporary situation must be understood in terms of that covenant by which it was related to the living God. The judgment and mercy of God, the sin and rebellion of Israel, were alike within the aegis of such a relation. But now new light was thrown on the significance of that covenant relation by Hosea's own marriage experience.

Two matters need to be elaborated at this point. The first is the Hebrew understanding of marriage. In Hebrew thought generally, as J. Pedersen has made very evident,[8] a guiding concept is that of wholeness. The image of God in Genesis 1:27 is specifically indicated as male and female, and the marriage bond was regarded as the making of the two into one whole. This psychic whole created by marriage belonged to the same order as the psychic whole which resulted from the covenant bond, such as that between Jonathan and David. Hence it was a natural movement in the Hebrew mind to transfer the marriage image to the covenant relationship, to see in married love and loyalty an indication of the covenant love (*ḥesedh*) and faithfulness (*'emunah*) which must characterize the covenant bond.

The second matter to bear in mind is the background of Hosea's own time. The naturalistic religion of Canaan into which the Hebrews came at the settlement had, as had the religions of the ancient Near East generally, a fertility background and was accompanied by rites which, based on sympathetic magic, sought to stimulate the fertility of the land and its people by sexual orgies. These were realized in the functions of the king who acted at the new year festival ceremony as representative of the people and also as the adopted son of the gods. Hence the idea of a marriage between the god, the land, and the people was not alien to the thought of the Canaanite world, and, in the time of Hosea, the attempt to baalize or naturalize Yahwism and to reduce Yahweh to the level of a fertility god had reached so far that ideas and practices of this type were associated with the Yahwistic cultus. If Hosea's wife had become a sacred prostitute in this kind of movement, it was all the more remarkable that Hosea should apply the marriage image to the living God and display the spiritual truth contained in the naturalistic perversions to which the marriage image had been subjected by pagan practice.

Out of this experience Hosea came with a deep understanding of God's love in the election of and covenant with Israel. These concepts were deeply wrought into the texture of Israel's life. Israel, as a people, was characterized by a unique religious faith, and in this faith the initiative was declared to be Yahweh's. Amos had emphasized God's election of Israel. God had known Israel in the sense that it became the special object of his gracious act and the peculiar instrument of his redemptive purpose. This election was expressed in the call of the patriarchs, but the seal was set by the covenant relationship established on Sinai through the prophet Moses.

Hosea is told to love Gomer (3:1). Such a command is impossible of fulfillment unless love is already in the heart. The commandment is understandable if Hosea already loved his wife. The command is now to go the extra mile, to put his love in action, and to redeem her. He is to continue in his loving. The Hebrew words used for love in this sense occur sparingly in Hosea. They are employed of Hosea's attitude to his wife and of God's attitude to Israel, but never of Israel's response to God. N. H. Snaith has investigated the general usage of such words in the Old Testament and notes that they carry a connotation of choice. Thus a man may love one wife and hate another, but here the meaning is that the loved one is preferred. The hate is not necessarily active animosity but simply implies that the wife is not preferred. The loved one is the chosen one. In this sense the word *love* (*ahᵃvah*) can be used of God's love for Israel. It is electing love. The covenant with Israel originates in such love. Yahweh preferred Israel above all other peoples. Such love cannot be ordered and cannot be merited, it is utterly free.

The Deuteronomic Code probably represents originally the code at Shechem. If it was preserved in the northern kingdom, finding its way south to become the foundation of Josiah's reformation, it is significant that it too is dominated by this thought of Yahweh's election love. Hosea's thought shows many points of contact with the Deuteronomic tradition, and this may be one of them. The Code declares that Yahweh's love is unconditional. He did not love Israel because they were more righteous than their neighbors nor because they were great in number (Deut. 9:4 ff.; 7:7 ff.). The mystery of Israel's election was an act of sheer grace. "Only Yahweh had a delight in thy fathers to love them, and he chose their seed after them, even you above all peoples, as at this day" (Deut. 10:15).

Hosea can likewise describe God's love for Israel in this way, employing the father-son image to portray it. "When Israel was a child, I loved him, and out of Egypt I called my son" (11:1, RSV). Here is a love which is utterly free and unconditioned, a love that is spontaneous and free to express itself as God wills. He draws Israel with the bands of love, a love akin to the emotional response of man (11:4). Indeed he will love Israel freely (14:4). Here is a love that is merciful, but that can also be wrathful. Because of Israel's sin, Yahweh can say that he will love it no more (9:15), and yet such love in the end triumphs over wrath, for God will heal their backsliding (14:4).

It is within this divine electing love, this free and spontaneous kind of love which Hosea has known in his own emotional attachment to his wife, that Yahweh's covenant with Israel is set. Hosea moves from the covenant bond of marriage to the covenant of Sinai's height. It is significant that he says little about the election, although he implies it by his use of the phrase "my people" for Israel (1:9; 2:23). Israel is God's people, chosen by him. The covenant is, however, pivotal in his message.

The covenant idea in Israel was a characteristic one in the Semitic thought world of the time.[9] It served to describe a relationship of mutual loyalty and obligation between two parties not related by blood ties. We have already discussed at some length the distinction between the divine covenant with the patriarchs and that with Israel at Sinai. The former was unconditional in the sense that it was constituted on the basis of a promise by Yahweh, while all that was demanded of the fathers was trust. On the other hand, the Sinai covenant involved moral demands from Yahweh which Israel was obligated to obey. It is this second type of covenant structure with which Hosea is concerned.

To understand this, we shall first examine it in the situation where the two parties are both at the human level. In this case, it serves to bind together two persons not related by blood ties, under obligations akin to those of natural kinship. A typical example is the covenant between David and Jonathan (1 Sam. 20:12 ff.). It describes a community of souls of such intensity that the souls of the two parties, their personalities, cleave together and become one whole. At the human level, the two parties to a covenant lay mutual obligations upon one another. In the case of the covenant of God with Israel, however, the two parties were never regarded as standing on the same footing. It is God who takes the initiative in choosing Israel, in knowing them. And so the covenant relationship stands within the aegis of God's free and unconditioned elective love, a love which Israel does not deserve and which follows it in its waywardness. Such had been Hosea's love for his wife.

Yahweh had found Israel in the wilderness and bound them to himself (9:10; 13:4–5). Hosea saw the gracious calling of God behind the deliverance from Egypt (11:1). In the days of its youth, when it came out from Egypt, Israel had been responsive within the covenant relationship, and Hosea pictures this in the marriage image (2:15). Taking it from the experience of his own marriage and daringly employing it despite its pagan usage in the fertility cultus, the prophet uses this image to describe the covenant relationship of God with Israel. There is a fundamental difference, however, from the pagan usage. In the fertility cultus the Baal was regarded as wedded to the land, and the rites of the cult were directed upon sustaining the fertility of the soil. Hosea overcame the Israelite baalization of Yahweh not by dismissing the marriage image, but by replacing the land by the people. As Buber puts it: "The baalization of YHWH appears to be overcome where Israel is thought of as His wife, and so His husbandship is pictured as something not of nature but of history." [10] God is no longer *baali*, "my baal," but *'ishi*, "my husband" (2:16).

Within the divine election, Israel's part in the covenant relationship is to accept and to obey. It cannot bargain with God, for the covenant is the result of his gracious initiative and choice. Israel can lay no obligations on Yahweh. The only obligations are those which God freely takes upon himself toward Israel and which he lays upon Israel toward himself. Such a covenant makes Israel into God's people, a whole that is his special concern and to which he has freely bound himself in gracious activity.

Thus, the idea of the covenant between God and Israel is filled with the conception of grace. Covenant appears as an external and legalized framework, a mutual contract. Its inner content, however, is a word translated as *steadfast love* or *covenant love* (*ḥesedh*), a word which is central in the message of Hosea. It characterizes the relationship of the parties to a covenant at any level. It is marked by the quality of steadfastness or faithfulness. This is indicated by the way in which the word is associated in many Old Testament passages with the words for *faithfulness* and *righteousness* (for example, Isa. 16:5; Hos. 4:1; Ps. 26:3; 89:2; Isa. 57:1; Ps. 36:10). The Authorized Version rendering of the word as *lovingkindness* is thus somewhat weak. The word conveys the sense of enduring and unchanging faithfulness, of unwavering responsibility to obligations undertaken, of loyalty to the covenant.

Of such steadfast love on the part of Yahweh, Hosea is quite sure. Steadfast or covenant love has characterized God's treatment of Israel in the treasured memories of past history (2), and, in his own marital experience, he has discovered a replica of it, however imperfect. The real issue for the prophet was the response of Israel, its humble covenant love, its loyalty to the covenant and obedience to the obligations which Yahweh had graciously imposed. The nation had so responded in the wilderness in the days of its youth (2:15), but now, despite its outward formality of worship, its heart was distant (6:1-6). The prophet's challenge to Israel was covenant love, not sacrifice. So Yahweh had a controversy with his people, for covenant love was not to be found in the land (4:1). Israel must turn to God and keep covenant love, steadfast love.

There is a contractual flavor about covenant love, a kind of externality. But Hosea made it a very inward thing. There was certainly nothing contractual about the covenant love of Yahweh, for his steadfast covenant love and faithfulness were grounded in a free and unconditioned elective love. The emotional warmth that had driven Hosea to redeem his wife, keeping him faithful to her in her unfaithfulness, making him show her covenant love when such a response was lacking on her part, was a window through which the prophet saw the love of God. Hence he uses another familiar word. God is a God of mercy. The Hebrew word *ramah*, "to have mercy," is related to the word for *womb*. It is a maternity word, and is again full of the warmth of spontaneous love. When his people go astray, God refuses to show mercy (1:6), and yet, in the end, the prophet believes that in spite of it all, God will say "I will have mercy" (2:19, 23; 14:3).

Hosea marks a tremendous move forward in the understanding of God. To him there came, through his own experience, a deeper vision of the divine nature. No longer could God be pictured merely in symbols borrowed from man's physical experience. It is true that words like *hands, feet,* and *mouth* are still figuratively employed of Yahweh and his activity. But now the revelation takes us deeper and employs images taken from the realm of personal relations. Father-son and husband-wife become for Hosea ways of understanding God's relation to his people. Amos sees God as judge. God is in controversy with his people but is not involved with them. He demands righteousness, and his final day will be darkness and not light. Hosea sees God as redeemer. For him the center is not righteousness but covenant love. Yahweh is involved with his people, and in the end he will have mercy.

For all subsequent prophetic voices, Hosea's insight was central. His emphasis on the covenant and on Yahweh's love remained abiding themes. The covenant concept of Israel was an all-embracing one. At Shechem the Sinai covenant associated with the prophet Moses (12:13) was extended to all the tribes and made the basis of the tribal amphictyony. In the days of Hezekiah and Josiah it appears to have been renewed and made the basis of religious reformation. In such reformations the prophetic voices of Isaiah and Jeremiah were heard. Beside the covenant with Israel was set the differently conceived covenant with the house of David and the establishment of the Davidic monarchy. Here was one of the strands out of which the prophets wove their Messianic expectations. Further, Israel and Hosea himself saw this covenant of God with his people as implying a covenant with the natural order, and, as we shall see, the restoration of this covenant was also a part of the prophet's hope.

THE REBELLION OF THE COVENANT PEOPLE

Just as Gomer had proved faithless to her marriage covenant with Hosea, so Israel, the bride of Yahweh, had proved faithless too. It had rebelled against the living God. Amos had attacked the sins of Israel and had been concerned with outward behavior. For him sin was an act not conforming to the norm of God's righteousness. Hosea likewise deals with the external aspect of sin, but he also probes sin to its roots. With a deep sympathy and understanding born of his own experience, he penetrates more deeply into the human heart. He sees, as our Lord later declared, that what is inside a man is the final determinant of his relation to God. Man's external acts spring from an inner heart, and it is to this inner attitude that we must finally turn if we would understand the nature of sin. Hence Hosea has a characteristic word to describe sin. It is the *spirit of whoredom* (4:12; 5:4). Just as Gomer went wrong because of a spirit of lust and sensual desire which expressed itself in the outward acts of adultery, so Israel had rebelled against the living God because its heart was wrong. It had gone awhoring after strange gods. The fertility deities of Canaan, the baalim, had awakened wrong desires, and the spirit of whoredom had entered into the heart of Israel.

Hosea sees this inner malady manifested at two levels, the religious and the political. At both there was shown unfaithfulness to Yahweh, a rebellion against the covenant bond. At the religious level the spirit of whoredom resulted in practices that were marked by gross immorality in the cult and on the part of the priests. Hosea indicts the priests with multiplying sacrifices and making profit out of them, with making the sanctuaries centers of robbery and murder (6:9; 4:7-9). The bull, the Canaanite image of fertility first set up at Dan and Bethel by Jeroboam I, had been retained, and idolatry had become rampant (8:4-6; 10:5; 11:2; 13:2). The Israelites worshiped the Canaanite baalim in the sacred groves (11:2). They kissed and worshiped the calves (13:2).

This would seem to imply both idolatry and the baalization of the worship of Yahweh. That is to say, we have both the worship of pagan deities and the transfer to Yahweh of pagan practices and ideas. The latter meant that the God of Israel was represented as the source of the fertility of the soil, not in the lofty sense of the holy, creative, righteous God who had spoken to Moses, but in the language, imagery, and practice of the surrounding paganism. In its worship, therefore, Israel was no longer worshiping the living God, even though its sanctuaries and priests still used his name. They simply transferred to Yahweh the practices of baal worship, with all their accompanying immorality.

Hence we find Hosea attacking such immorality. Ritual prostitution, perhaps a real factor in the prophet's own marital relationships, comes in for violent attack (4:13–14). The people take counsel, that is to say, consult divination, at the pagan symbol of deity and fertility, the stock (4:12). Drunkenness is rife, probably in association with ritual orgies (4:11, 18). The sacrifices of the cult are empty things for they manifest no covenant love and loyalty to Yahweh on the part of Israel (6:6; 8:13; 9:4). Israel has multiplied its altars and shrines, but all to no avail. Its heart is far removed from Yahweh (10:1). And so Hosea returns to the inwardness of Israel's sin.

At the political level, Israel's sin was manifested in a desire for foreign alliances rather than a trust in Yahweh as the Lord of history. The prophet describes Israel as a "half-baked cake" (7:8) and a "silly dove" (7:11), because of this propensity to seek for external aid rather than to abide secure in the covenant with Yahweh. Situated between the two great imperial powers of Egypt and Assyria, a veritable cockpit of the nations, Israel and Judah too were liable to set off one power against the other and to flee from one to the other for aid (5:13; 12:1). Against the aggressive activity of Assyria, it was natural to seek help from Egypt and vice versa. Hosea likens Israel to a "wild ass," alone by itself going up to Assyria (8:9). But Yahweh will rend it like a lion (5:14), and they who now sow a wind will reap a whirlwind (8:7). Political factions appear to have arisen within Israel which favored one imperial power or the other, but the true solution did not lie in such political alliances and advocated policies. That way lay judgment and destruction. The true solution lay in a penitent return to Israel's God and to the covenant bond.

In the center of this political turmoil we have a failure on the part of the monarchy. Rebellions and intrigues centered in the royal court, and the "burden of king and princes" was a very real one (8:10). The best rendering of this passage would appear to be "they shall cease for a little while from the burden of king and princes." Hosea's attitude toward the monarchy is reflected in the declarations that Israel had set up kings but not of Yahweh (8:4), and that Yahweh had given them kings in his anger and would take them away in his wrath (13:11).

There is an antimonarchical spirit in this prophet which is very close to that of the Deuteronomic Code (Deut. 28:36) and of the later source in the Book of Samuel. The latter attributes the kingship of Saul, not to God's intention, but to the people's desire at Gibeah. God goes along with their will but warns them of the dread consequences (1 Sam. 8:4–22). If the Deuteronomic tradition originates, as many now believe, in the shrine at Shechem, it would reflect one stream of tradition in the northern kingdom, and thus we should not be surprised if it and Hosea manifest a similar attitude toward the monarchy. Hosea's reference to the days of Gibeah may actually reflect the ideas of the late source in Samuel (9:9; 10:9), although it may equally refer to the Benjamite outrage referred to in Judges 19 and 20.

In any case, Hosea's attack upon monarchical tyranny and usurpation of power reflects the experience of the monarchy in the northern kingdom, where dynasty had followed dynasty with alarming regularity and with a monotonous repetition of oppression and injustice. Although Judah had continued to abide by the Davidic monarchy, Israel had not. As far as the northern kingdom was concerned, the covenant of Yahweh with the House of David, so cherished by the south, had no meaning. Hosea could declare the judgment of God upon the royal house, both because of their own iniquity (7:5-7; 9:15), and because of the situation in which they were involved (10:7). The successive acts of desecration at Gibeah and at Jezreel, in the Benjamite incident and under Jehu respectively (10:9; 7:3 ff.), had meant that Yahweh had a lawsuit with the disloyal monarchy. They had dethroned God and put themselves in his place. Now Hosea, as messenger from the heavenly court, was declaring the divine sentence on them.

The explanation turns upon the representative capacity of the king as a holy person. In Hebrew thought, he is the divine representative as well as the representative of the people. If he cleaves to God he becomes righteous, and the people are righteous in him. If the king was associated with fertility rites and bull worship, he became like that which he worshiped, and his corruption spread to the people. So in 8:4 the prophet associates the wrongful appointment of kings without God's direction with the setting up of idols in the sanctuary. A pretender in the sanctuary would mean a pretender on the throne.[11] Hosea's putting away of his wife for a season may symbolize Yahweh's putting away of the kings from Israel. The people would abide many days without a king and thus without Yahweh, for there would be no true representative of God upon the throne in whom their own righteousness could be secured.[12] Like king, like people. No anointed one, and the covenant bond is broken!

Hosea's deep inner analysis of sin means, however, that these outward manifestations point to the spirit of whoredom that produces them. Priests and kings, people and rulers do what they do because they are wrong within. The external activity covers an inner deficiency. God requires covenant love and not sacrifice (6:6). Knowledge of God is more significant than an accumulation of burnt offerings. There is no steadfast and loyal love of God in the land (4:1), and here Hosea means a love that issues in obedience. Instead of faithfulness, Israel manifests faithlessness, rebellion, and idolatry.

There is an absence of knowledge of God (4:6). Hosea does not mean lack of information about God. This is not rational, propositional knowledge. It means personal awareness of and response to the presence of God, which are shown in loyalty to the covenant, in unfailing love and obedience, and thus in right relationship to fellow Israelites. It is existential knowing. It implies commitment and involvement and is a synonym for covenant love. Sin is a matter of the will and not of the intellect, and it carries with it a corruption of the inner being, a misdirection and perversion of the will. The will is directed on idols, it goes awhoring, it is sensual. It means that Israel has cast off that which is good (8:3). Without true knowledge and covenant love, Israel may offer whole flocks and herds as sacrifices, and yet they will not avail (5:6). Indeed God has withdrawn himself and judgment is sure. Israel declares that it has goodness, but it is knowledge without commitment, it is false covenant love, and like the morning dew it passes quickly away (6:4).

The prophet is convinced that Israel's sickness is beyond its own cure, an infirmity of will which it cannot put right. One of the most terrible effects of sin is the bondage of will that it produces in the sinner. The more a man sins, the more infirm does his will become. John Greenleaf Whittier saw this when he wrote:

> Forever round the Mercy-Seat
> The guiding lights of love shall burn;
> But what if, habit-bound, thy feet
> Shall lack the will to turn?
> What if thine eye refuse to see,
> Thine ear to Heaven's free welcome fail,
> And thou a willing captive be
> Thyself thy own dark jail.[13]

So the prophet sees the impossibility of return. Long disloyalty to the covenant has resulted in the loss of any desire to return, of any sense of need. Israel's doings will not suffer them to return to God, for the spirit of whoredom is in them (5:4), and the spirit of whoredom means infirmity of will. Even when Israel goes with its flocks and herds to sacrifice to Yahweh, it will not find him (5:6). God has withdrawn himself. Indeed he has returned to his place, to the inner recesses of his being, until they repent and long for him (5:15).

Whoredom and wine have deprived Israel of volition, however. They have taken away its heart, which is the center of volitional activity (4:11). The nation has become as abominable as that which it loves (9:10). Hence even when it repents, its repentance is a shallow thing like the dew which goes early away (6:4–6). Its response to God is as transient as the morning cloud. It is not genuine, but a superficial formality, a movement that has its ground in purely selfish concern. In 9:12–13 the prophet proclaims the inevitable nemesis that attends all sin, the fact that

sin begets its own harvest and brings its own doom. There is a
moral deterioration, a spiritual dry rot, which sin produces and
from which the sinner cannot escape. Israel is beset about by its
rebellion and cannot escape (6:11; 7:12). It is unable to repent
and thus undeserving of the divine mercy.

Hosea hints here at the true nature of judgment, for the very
bondage is the working out of the judgment. Israel has sown a
wind, and it will reap a whirlwind (8:7; cf. 9:13). Like Amos,
Hosea sounds the note of wrath and darkness. By ignoring
Yahweh and running from political alliance to political alliance,
Israel is creating a situation which will be its own undoing. The
spirit of whoredom within brings on a bondage which spells
destruction for the nation.

Is there, then, any hope? As we have noted, Hosea does call for
and promises repentance. Here is the mysterious paradox which
he could not resolve. Israel's sin is its responsibility, its choice,
and yet there is an infirmity of will, a spirit of whoredom within.
The prophet is a moral analyst of depth who sees the mystery
of sinfulness, the strange paradox of responsibility and necessity. But because this mystery is open to God, he dares to hope,
to hope that responsibility may yet turn to repentance even though
the necessity born of infirmity of will denies it. Hosea's successors grasped the content of this hope more clearly than he did.

Before we turn to this hope, two things should be noted. The
first is that Hosea, like Amos and Isaiah, is concerned with the
northern kingdom as a corporate whole, rather than with individual
Israelites within or even apart from that whole. It is Israel as a
whole that must repent, and the judgment and salvation are alike
corporate. Hence in the second place, Hosea is as drastic in his
declaration of judgment as his contemporary, Amos. The note
of retribution is struck throughout his prophecy. God has forsaken
Israel. He will be like a lion to it and carry it off to destruction.
None will be able to save it. The wind has wrapped Israel up in
its wings and will carry it clean away (4:19). The destruction of
the nation will be so complete that even the life of nature will
be wiped out (4:3). There would seem to be no future but the end
of Israel. Yet the note of hope is still there. Judgment would be
corporate, but somehow redemption would be in it. It would be a
purging judgment, and out of it a remnant would be saved. The
corporate whole would be refined, and a penitent people would
emerge. Israel as a corporate whole would remain, but saved as
by fire.

THE TRIUMPH OF COVENANT LOVE

Hesedh has an element of steadfastness and loyalty about it.
As H. W. Robinson has written, it expresses "the moral bondage
of love, the loving discharge of an admitted obligation, the volun-
tary acceptance of a responsibility." [14] It is this quality of stead-

fastness in the divine love which gives the prophet cause for hope. Whereas Amos seems to have almost no hope at all, Hosea, equally sure of judgment and destruction, yet hopes. And he hopes because God is a covenant God. The difference lies in the emphasis on covenant love, to which Amos never refers.

The prophet begins by naming his children symbolically— Jezreel, Lo-ammi, Lo-ruhamah—all names which are pregnant with the coming judgment and which speak of Yahweh forsaking Israel. Yet out of the deeps of his own marital experience and his redemptive search for Gomer, Hosea stretches up to heaven and grasps the reality of the divine grace. Hence he calls on Israel to repent, to turn its infirm will back to Yahweh, and does so despite his conviction of the bondage of that will and the evil compulsion under which the nation labors.

The evangelical appeal goes far, even despite Israel's demonic refusal to repent (7:10; 11:5; 14:1). We have the gracious call to repentance in 6:1-3 and 14:1-3. In chapter 2 Hosea sees God pleading with his bride, Israel, and declares that he who had definitely declared that he would not have mercy (*Lo-ruhamah*), would yet say to Israel, "I will have mercy" (*ruhamah*). Just as long years ago God had taken the initiative and called Israel up out of Egypt, so he would do it again. He would betroth Israel to him in covenant love and faithfulness (2:19 ff.). He would once more say, "Thou art my people," and Israel would repent and say, "Thou art our God" (2:23). Here is the promise. After the judgment, Israel would return and seek Yahweh (3:5). In the latter days love would find a way. The compulsive power of evil in the heart of Israel would be overcome by the compulsive power of new affection awakened in that heart.

How could Yahweh forsake Israel, whom he has graciously chosen and bound to himself in covenant relationship (11:8)? He could no more do so than Hosea could give up Gomer. So the prophet could cry in the name of God, "I will not execute the fierceness of my anger, I will not return to destroy Ephraim" (11: 9, ASV). Yet the promise does not mean that judgment and destruction are not accepted. It is assumed that Israel will be scattered among the nations, yet its children will cease trembling at the lionlike roar of Yahweh, and he will make them again to dwell in their house (11:10, 11).

Here we come on the image of resurrection for the first time, yet not resurrection of the individual, resurrection of the nation (6:2). The people would not escape death. They would be put away for a time, but they would also be raised up. God would heal their backsliding and love them freely, turning away his anger (14:4). Grace would triumph in the end. Israel would confess the failure of political alliances and return unto Yahweh (14:1-3). God had known Israel in the wilderness, and now at long last they would know him. The circle of knowledge and covenant love would be completed in Israel's response (13:5; 14:8).

In this restoration the land would also be involved. Hosea had a deep sense of the presence of God in the natural order and of the intimate relation between the people and the land. The judgment on Israel was also a judgment on its natural environment. Because the nation was God's people, he had given it fertility and natural prosperity, even though the people turned to the fertility cults and the baalim both in thanksgiving and in hope of perpetuating this happy state of affairs (2:8). God's judgment on them would involve his bringing barrenness to the land (2:9), even barrenness to the women of Israel (9:14).

So too the restoration of the nation would involve the land. God would make a covenant for them with the whole order of nature, with all living things. In this setting the covenant would also be with the nations that they might live in peace. There would indeed be a new marriage covenant in which Yahweh would betroth Israel to him in covenant love forever (2:18 ff.). The chain of responses would be complete once more as God, through the natural order, answered Israel with gifts of corn and wine and oil. All nature is a psychic whole whose parts—heavens, earth, the food crops, Jezreel—function in harmony and answer successively the divine call (2:21 ff.).

How would grace accomplish this resurrection? How would genuine repentance be evoked from such a stubborn people? Hosea's southern contemporary, Isaiah, was preaching the doctrine of a remnant that should escape the purging fires of judgment and be saved when the Day of Yahweh supervened. But, as we shall see, he too had no answer as to how such purging should be possible when the peoples were so corrupt. It waited for Ezekiel to grasp the reality of the activity of God's Spirit creating a new heart and a new spirit within men (Ezek. 11:19; 36:26), and for Jeremiah to see God making a new covenant within the individual Israelite which shall be so inwardly transforming that Yahweh's law shall be written on his heart (Jer. 31:31 ff.). God's redemptive activity in the end would not wait for the impossible repentance of a rebellious people. God, as Hosea saw, would take the initiative, would woo Israel, and would create the conditions that would make possible a true repentance, a turning back to God. Jeremiah, Ezekiel, and Deutero-Isaiah spelled out in detail what those conditions must be and saw them as the work of redemptive grace. Our Lord made the vision an actuality on Calvary, and continually actualizes it in our lives by the activity of his Spirit.

One closing thought is appropriate. The mark of the true prophet is a pathos with the divine, an inner sympathy which gives insight into the divine mind and will. This bond of sympathy was forged in the heart of Hosea by his own experience with Gomer. Out of the redemptive initiative and activity of his own love for his wayward wife, he looked into the heart of God.

That window into the inner life of the divine was flung wide
open when God became man and issued forth from his heavenly
splendor in the garb of a servant. In seeing Jesus we are seeing
God, and the heart of our Lord's work was a cross on which he
paid the price for our redemption. Yet the price that was there
paid in the actuality of history was already borne in the heart
of the eternal God, and it was given to Hosea, along with his
prophetic successors, to grasp from afar the truth that love
cannot redeem without suffering, that there is no atonement
with God unless God himself pays the price, and that grace is
God meeting his own demands himself and doing so in a covenant-love that will not give up his people.

Already, extended downward into history through the personality of his prophet, the living God was bearing redemptively
the sin of man. He was pointing to that decisive and ultimate
act in which, by the suffering of the divine, our sins are forgiven and our lives remade.

NOTES

1. This is the view of Johannes Lindblom, *Prophecy in Ancient
Israel* (Oxford: Basil Blackwell, 1962), pp. 242 ff.

2. Cf. Robert H. Pfeiffer, *Introduction to the Old Testament*
(New York: Harper & Bros., 1948), pp. 567 ff.

3. Lindblom, *Prophecy in Ancient Israel*, p. 225, adopts such a
position, arguing that chapter 1 is biographical and chapter 3 is
autobiographical. He would regard the two chapters as doublets re-
sulting from the parallel transmission of tradition.

4. This is the view of Norman Gottwald, *A Light to the Nations*
(New York: Harper & Bros., 1959), pp. 297 ff.

5. Cf. G. A. Smith, *The Book of the Twelve Prophets*, 2 vols. (London: Hodder & Stoughton, 1928), 2:241 ff.

6. H. Wheeler Robinson, *Two Hebrew Prophets* (London: Lutterworth Press, 1948), p. 13.

7. Cf. Gottwald, *Light to the Nations,* p. 297.

8. Johannes Pedersen, *Israel* (London: Oxford University Press,
1926, 1940) 1–2, 3–4: *passim*.

9. Cf. G. E. Mendenhall, *Law and Covenant in Israel and the
Ancient Near East* (The Biblical Colloquium, 1955).

10. Martin Buber, *The Prophetic Faith* (New York: Macmillan,
1949), p. 120.

11. Cf. ibid, p. 123.

12. Ibid.

13. "The Answer" in *Selected Poems of John Greenleaf Whittier*
(London: Oxford University Press, 1945), pp. 415 ff.

14. Robinson, *Two Hebrew Prophets,* p. 49.

Chapter Four

The Lord of History
and the Holy One
of Israel

*Isaiah of Jerusalem is the towering figure among the eighth-cen-*tury prophets. Any student of the book of Isaiah is early made familiar with the fact that only the first thirty-nine chapters bear any direct relation to this prophetic messenger, and that, even of these, some sections belong to a later date. Actually these thirty-nine chapters are quite diverse in structure, for they include oracles, some of which are dated, and biographical sections in which oracles are included, often in a condensed form. In addition, the chapters 36–39 are historical material taken directly from the Second Book of Kings. Thus, as we have them, the first thirty-nine chapters have an editorial history all their own, quite apart from the later editing which included with them chapters 40–55 and chapters 56–66.

In chapters 1–35, the only major non-Isaianic section is what is often termed "the little apocalypse" (chaps. 24–27). The eschatological emphasis of this passage appears to indicate a much later, postexilic origin. Chapters 13:1–14:23 and 21:1–10 refer to Babylon, and since Babylon replaced Assyria as the dominant imperial power in 612 B.C., these groups of oracles are also referred to a later period. For the rest, we have collections of Isaianic oracles of various types. They include 'reproach' oracles usually introduced by the characteristic word *Woe* and calling for witnesses to hear Yahweh's complaint against his people (1:2–9; 5:8–10, 18–23). Sometimes reproach oracles are conjoined to 'threat' oracles, beginning with some declaration of consequences, and introduced by the word *therefore* (5:24; 30:3–5). But along with messages of doom we also have oracles of 'promise' (30:15–18). In addition, the *rîv* type of oracle occurs with its echo of judicial procedure (3:13–15; 5:1–7). This rich selection of oracular types also contains the *torah* type (1:10–17). In the midst of these collections we have the significant autobiographical section from 6:1–9:6 which offers the historical setting and oracles of the period of the Syro-Ephraimitic War and which carries the theme of Immanuel through to the promise of 9:1–6. Some of the oracles are evidently condensed and offered in prose form, as, for example, the address to Ahaz in 7:4–9.

Undoubtedly these oracles include many that were treasured in the memory and orally communicated until written down. Actually we are told that early in his ministry the prophet did himself commit some to writing and bind up the roll of them among his disciples. Thus in his own lifetime he began to gather around himself a group of disciples who would treasure his utterances. In this way collections began to grow, and, in the course of the years, they were written down, for example, 2:1–5:30 and 6:1–9:6.

Later editors gathered these many collections together, adding other oracles, until finally with the addition of Deutero-Isaiah and chapters 56–66 the roll was completed. The acknowledged fact that the Second Isaiah of chapters 40–55 does echo some of the insights of the earlier prophet, even though living two centuries later, would indicate the presence of a circle which treasured the oracles of the original Isaiah and had bound up his *torah* in their hearts long after his death. Indeed, the unity which pervades the roll of Isaiah, despite the differing styles and historical settings of the various sections, would indicate the greatness of the first prophet who, for nearly four decades, was a strong voice for God in the life of Israel.

ISAIAH OF JERUSALEM AND HIS HISTORICAL BACKGROUND

Isaiah commenced his ministry under the menacing shadow of Assyrian imperialism. We have already seen the effect of this world power on the ministry and message of Amos and Hosea. It is against the same background that we must set the work of the prophet Isaiah. His ministry was mainly to Judah, but some of his oracles were addressed to Israel, while the early part of his work was concerned with the relationships of the northern and southern kingdoms.

The unparalleled prosperity of the northern kingdom of Israel under Jeroboam II had been aided by the decline of Assyrian power. Under Tiglath-pileser III this power revived, however, and by 743 B.C. Assyrian ascendancy was again becoming evident. It would appear that the small western states formed a coalition against it, probably led by Azariah of Judah.[1] Azariah (or Uzziah) died soon after. The other states, including Israel, were subdued and had to pay tribute. Judah so far escaped, but the

menace of Assyria loomed ever larger. Such may well have
been the external occasion for Isaiah's inaugural vision recorded
in chapter 6.

At the time of his call, the prophet must have been a young
man, for he was still an active power in the state of Judah some
forty years later. If the background of the call was the growing
Assyrian power and the triumph of Tiglath-pileser over the Pales-
tinian and Syrian coalition, its immediate foreground was the influence of the Temple at Jerusalem and its worship. The prophet
had long been a worshiper of Yahweh, but now he fell into an
ecstasy and beheld a vision of the divine glory. In the vision,
Yahweh was the heavenly king sitting on a lofty throne, far
above the prophet, around whom swirled the skirts of his long
robes. With the half-serpentine seraphim attending him, God prepared his prophet for his task. Isaiah heard Yahweh's call and
responded, despite his initial hesitancy. As we shall see, all his
later experience served but to confirm the initial assurance of
Yahweh that the people would not listen to his message but
would be destroyed. Thus at the very beginning of his ministry a strange and terrible task was laid on the prophet. He was
to declare the Word which God gave him, and yet this Word would
but serve to harden the hearts of his hearers. A word of judgment
which was also a promise of salvation would gain no true lodging
place in the heart of the listeners. As we analyze Isaiah's message we must ask ourselves what is implied in this mysterious
contradiction in the initial experience of Isaiah's ministry.

Within a few years of his call, 734 B.C., Isaiah found himself involved with his king against the background of the Syro-
Ephraimitic War. This was the attempt of Pekah of Israel and
Remaliah of Syria to force the young King Ahaz of Judah into a
coalition with them against Assyria. Isaiah comes upon Ahaz as
the latter is inspecting the water supply of the beleaguered capital
city. The prophet counsels a quiet confidence in Yahweh and fore-
tells the coming overthrow of the enemy (chaps. 7, 8). The prophecy
to the king does not state how the actual deliverance will come.
Isaiah was opposed to any external entanglement. He seems to
have seen Assyria as the agent of deliverance, but not because
Judah had sought an alliance with this imperial power. He was
sure that God would find a way.

Closely bound up with this encounter with Ahaz are the symbolic naming of Isaiah's own children and the giving of a sign.
Ahaz refused to ask a sign of Yahweh, but the prophet gave him
one nevertheless. The refusal was couched in pious language,
but undoubtedly had its grounds in a tacit rejection of confidence
in Yahweh and the acceptance of political involvement with
Assyria. A child would be born, presumably in the royal house,
and he would be named Immanuel, "God with us," because by
the time he was able to manifest intelligent discernment, both

Israel and Syria would have been disposed of by Assyria. God would not fail.

The prophet expressed his hope of deliverance in the names he gave his two sons. Shear-jashub carried the message of both judgment and hope that a remnant would turn to God and be saved. The prophet was instructed to name a second child Maher-shalal-hash-baz ("speed-spoil-haste-prey") as a sign that Assyria was destined to carry off the spoil of the two allies and to save Judah. Ahaz had only to have confidence in God.

Ahaz refused to abide by the prophetic word. He played politics and sought the help of Assyria instead of relying on God. He was delivered, but only at the price of becoming an Assyrian vassal. In the decades that followed, the results of foreign entanglement became more evident. Always to the south lay the other power of Egypt, and what could be more tempting than to seek its help as the Assyrian shadow loomed larger. Isaiah had continually to preach his political quietism and to attack foreign entanglement as the years came and went. His immediate reaction to Ahaz's obdurate rejection of the divine word was to write down his prophetic testimony on a roll and bind it up among his disciples (8:16–18). So his little circle would keep alive the saving content of the prophet's hope until a better day when the incorrigibility of Israel would be righted.

In 722 B.C. Samaria fell and Israel disappeared as an independent state. Until then, some of Isaiah's oracles had been directed to the northern kingdom. They may even have been delivered at Bethel. He attacks the pride, the luxury, the false leaders, and the unjust judges of Israel, and prophesies a series of disasters culminating in the ultimate destruction of this northern group.

After 722 B.C., Judah remained untouched since it was a vassal of Assyria. In 711 B.C., however, there was a further revolt against the Mesopotamian power. The revolt centered in Ashdod, and Judah's participation was sought. Egypt and Ethiopia were now in the background, aiding and abetting the rebellion. In chapter 20 we find Isaiah warning against both participation in the revolt and listening to the blandishments of Egypt. Just as he had earlier employed prophetic symbolism in the naming of his children, so he now acted out his message. He walked naked and barefoot in the streets of Jerusalem for a period of time, acting out the role of a slave. He thereby affirmed in act his conviction that Egypt and Ethiopia were but weak reeds to lean on. They too would be led captive by Assyria. The situation is not clear. The revolt was quashed, and, since Judah escaped trouble, we may presume that Isaiah was listened to.

In 705 B.C. Sargon of Assyria died, and once more the states on the Mediterranean seaboard sought freedom. Egypt fomented the opposition, and Judah was active, negotiating with this imperial power for help. Isaiah again denounced such foreign alliances and foretold disaster (28:7–13, 14–22; 29:15–16; 30:1–7; 31:1–3). Judah should trust in Yahweh and leave all such political maneuvering on one side. Hezekiah made such overtures to Egypt, and Isaiah declared all such attempts to be a covenant with death (28:15). Hezekiah was, however, too involved to withdraw. His leaders apparently mocked Isaiah and told him to quit his prophesying (28:9–13, 14; 30:9–11). Sennacherib of Assyria acted swiftly. He crushed all the states involved except Judah, and then turned his attention on Hezekiah. Jerusalem became a beleaguered city.

Now Isaiah rose to new heights. He still recognized that Assyria was an instrument of the divine judgment, but he also recognized the arrogance of this despotic power. God's patience would ultimately be exhausted by the pride of his instrument, and he would humble Assyria to the dust once it had accomplished his purpose (10:5–16). Jerusalem would survive, and the invading power would depart, crushed apparently on the eve of triumph (14:24–27; 17:12–14; 29:7–8; 30:30–31; 31:4–5).[2]

The prophetic word was actualized in history, and the nation was delivered. Yet the last oracle we have of Isaiah is that which he uttered after the siege was lifted and the Assyrian host had fled. In his oracle on the burden of the valley of vision (22:1–14), he denounces the Jews for their lack of concern with the God who had delivered them. They had escaped destruction by the skin of their teeth, and this deliverance owed nothing to them, for their conduct had been worthy of judgment. God had delivered them, and yet they had no thought for him who had shaped their history. So the prophet ends his recorded ministry as it begins, with the incorrigible nature of Israel's sinful rebellion, its deafness to God's redeeming word, and its blindness to his grace.

The Prophetic Call and Its
Implications for Isaiah's Ministry

It has frequently been noted that Isaiah makes no explicit mention of the exodus theology and the wilderness tradition. Indeed, he seems to rely much less on the historical traditions of Israel's faith than did either Amos or Hosea. For him the revelation of the living God appears to center not in the Exodus experience, but in the Temple. It is, of course, significant that the latter was the center of his call, yet the strong element of moral demand and judgment in his message indicates that the Sinai covenant with its moral conditions formed the basis of his theology. What he says is rooted in the wilderness tradition, and he continually describes Israel as the people of God (1:3; 3:12, 15; 5:13; 10:2; 22:4; 32:13, 18). In the Song of the Vineyard the Sinai covenant between God and his people is pictured as the relation of an owner to his vineyard (5:1–13), while 10:24–26 may refer to the Exodus—Yahweh will yet deliver his people as once he brought them up out of the land of Egypt.

Certain strands of thought from the royal theology are ingredients of the prophetic message. Isaiah's call came through the meditation of the temple worship, and Engnell has even associated it with an annual enthronement ceremony.[3] This may account for the concern with Zion and the Temple, while the messianic element becomes, for the first time, a significant part of the prophetic hope. We have seen already that the unconditional form of the covenant with Abraham and David could give rise to a popular hope which carried no moral rigor. Isaiah could not accept this. He was a reform prophet of judgment, and this theme is dominant even in his inaugural vision. He was to declare the judgment and even the destruction of Judah. Yet he saw truth in the royal theology and thus dared to hope when all seemed to spell doom. He believed that judgment was inevitable, and yet he was sure that Yahweh had come to dwell on Zion's hill in the midst of his people and that the Davidic covenant would remain sure. Hence he saw the judgment as one which would not mean that God's tabernacling presence would be taken from his people or that the Davidic line would cease. The judgment would be a purging, but Yahweh's presence in Zion would provide the redemptive center for the people. On Zion's hill the faithful would find refuge from the flood of judgment, and ultimately a true Davidic king would reestablish Yahweh's rule of justice and equity. It is significant that, early in his ministry, Isaiah makes his Immanuel prophecy to Ahaz.

Hence Isaiah was warned at the very commencement of his ministry that the prophetic word would actually produce a hardening of heart in Israel and increase its stubborn rebellion. He was to prophesy, despite the lack of positive response, until the land was utterly wasted and the inhabitants were decimated (6:9–12). The people were incapable of correction. The text of 6:13 is so difficult to exegete that we must not take it as any true remnant hope. It might even suggest that any remnant would meet fresh catastrophe.[4] It is probable, however, that a remnant conception was in Isaiah's mind at the call. His vision of God as King, lifted above all earthly kings, combined with his acceptance of the Davidic covenant and the theology of salvation implied in it, led him to an understanding of the divine truth in which hope was blended with the conviction of the severity of the judgment impending because of disobedience to the Exodus covenant.

Why then the reference to the hardening of heart? It was just this Davidic theology, with its promise of salvation, that might tend to harden the heart. We have seen in the case of Amos (5:18 ff.) that popular ideas in the northern kingdom had led to a trust in the covenant without the acceptance of the obligations,

an expectation of privilege without responsibility. In the same
way the south with its Davidic tradition tended to an assurance
about the continuation of its Davidic line of kings and thus of
their kingdom, without accepting the moral obligations and the
responsible trust in God which were also necessary, and which the
Exodus covenant prescribed.

It was Isaiah's tragedy that he felt called to emphasize both
aspects—salvation because of God's word to David, and judgment because of failure to respond to the demands of the Exodus
covenant. The first element of his message fell upon welcoming
ears, which were immediately closed to the second and significant
aspect of his preaching. Judah heard as much as it wanted to
hear and continued to believe that God was on its side irrespective of its attitude. Rather than 6:9 ff. being a later reading
back into his call of his later experience, we may see the statement as an indication that his message would be misunderstood. The divine claims must first issue in a judgment before
the promise of salvation could become effective in a remnant.[5]

The Holy One of Israel—Holiness and Guilt

The vision of God in the call is the key to Isaiah's theology.
The prophet sees Yahweh high and lifted up, so that his angelic
attendants chant of his exalted holiness, and yet God's glory
fills the temple and the skirts of his garments envelop Isaiah.
Here we have a vision of God as both transcendent and immanent,
as the Holy One of Israel whose glory fills the whole earth. In
Hebrew thought, *glory* was used to describe the manifest appearance, a kind of radiation from the divine presence which suffused
into the created order. Thus we have two central conceptions of
God in the prophet's thought, holiness and glory.

God's holiness (*qadhosh*) is his otherness, his transcendence.
Among the Semites the description *holy* was used to distinguish
the gods from man, and carried a numinous quality. Twelve times
in the oracles of Isaiah of Jerusalem, God is described as the
Holy One of Israel, and the title might at first sight be understood as synonymous with describing him as divine. Yet a deeper
significance is attached to the title in the case of Isaiah. In the
inaugural vision, the angelic attendants hail Yahweh as thrice
holy (6:3). God is the most unique and separate Being who stands
apart from men. He is transcendent in his splendor and majesty,
towering in his enthroned glory above the Temple, the prophet,
and the people. He is not like other holy ones and his holiness
takes its unique quality from his own exalted character. Indeed,
the other gods are *idols* or *nonentities* (*ᵉlilîm*), the "work of men's
hands" (2:8, 18, 20 ff.; 31:7; 37:19). Such deities shall pass away,
but men will flee in fear before the terror of Yahweh (2:18, 20 ff.).
Thus although Isaiah is not explicit in his monotheism like
his successor, Deutero-Isaiah, yet implicit in his teaching is the

affirmation that beside Yahweh there is none other. The whole earth is filled with God's manifest presence, his glory.

Yahweh's holiness or otherness betokens his mystery. The numinous quality is present, and Yahweh is unapproachable in his awesome presence. Even his angelic attendants cannot approach him. Yet he is no terrifying irrational power. His otherness is not irrational but essentially moral. He is personal being whose moral purity makes him unapproachable by sinful man. Thus the transcendence of Yahweh is not mere spatial remoteness. Rather it is ethical distance. The Holy One of Israel is exalted and transcendent, but the final measure of his exalted splendor is his moral perfection.[6] His holiness has a moral content.

Hence Isaiah binds in closely God's righteousness with his holiness. The divine holiness is not ethically neutral. The measure of God's transcendence is seen in his righteous will. Amos had declared the righteousness of Yahweh, but Isaiah bound up this righteousness with God's innermost character. The Holy One of Israel is essentially righteous. Justice is the very foundation of his throne. Here the great wilderness and exodus tradition surges into the center of Isaiah's message. The Sinai covenant with its moral demands points to the innermost character of God. What God is in himself is expressed in his demands of men. He is a righteous God and he demands righteousness of men. Only in his own character can righteousness be clearly defined.

In his inaugural vision Isaiah is overwhelmed not only by his own moral guilt, but also by the moral guilt of his people. He is a man of unclean lips, and he dwells among a people of unclean lips (6:5). Israel, like himself, is guilty before God. Here the Sinai covenant tradition is very evident. God is the Holy One *of Israel,* but by its sin Israel has set a distance between itself and God. In his words to his prophet, God can describe it as "this people." By the divine forgiveness, actualized in the imagery of the cleansing coals from the altar, the prophet is set apart for his task and made to stand on the divine side in the controversy of Yahweh with his people. In his own sense of guilt before God, Isaiah experiences the corporate guilt of his people. Now, in his prophetic consciousness, he becomes the divine representative to a rebellious Israel. For him, too, they are "this people."

God is in controversy with his people. Israel has not met his righteous demands. The prophet sets the plumb line of the divine righteousness against the life of the nation, and attacks Israel's sin. The sacrifices of the Temple were unavailing and its ritual was without effect. The elaborate offerings and repeated festivals were of little significance when there was no moral counterpart in social behavior (1:10–17). It was no use honoring Yahweh with the lips when the heart was far from him (29:13). Indeed, the combination of insincere worship and social wrongs would only be an offense to the Holy One of Israel (1:14 ff.).

The prophet commences his attack at the level of social injustice and the manifest evils of the communal life. Then he cites the grinding tyranny of the upper classes (3:13–15), the corrupt administration of justice (1:23; 5:23; 10:14), the luxurious fashions of the women of Jerusalem (3:16 ff.), the rapacious landholders (5:8 ff.), and the intemperance of dissolute living (5:11 ff.; 28:7 ff.). Again and again Isaiah utters his woes, some addressed to the northern kingdom of Israel but more to the southern kingdom of Judah. This people is corrupt socially, and for this corruption religion is no antidote. The worship of the Temple only serves to make matters worse.

Here Isaiah, like Hosea, penetrates more deeply. He sees all of this as symptomatic of a deep-seated ungodliness and apostasy. Israel is a sinful nation in revolt against the Holy One of Israel (1:2, 4), contemptuous of Yahweh (5:18 ff.; 29:16), a nation in rebellion (1:5, 23; 30:1), wise in its own eyes (5:21; 28:14 ff.). The core of its trouble is its pride and arrogance (29:16). Two characteristic descriptions of Israel's sin are thus rebellion and pride. Yahweh has adopted Israel as his sons and they have rebelled against him (1:2–4). The prophet sees the gracious relationship of the Sinai covenant torn asunder by the rebellious spirit of Israel. This spirit has at its center an arrogance which would invert the relation of Yahweh to his people, of the potter to his clay (29:16). Here we see the complacence of the Jerusalem tradition and the royal theology breaking through. Yahweh is bound to preserve his people. Israel is secure in itself, its material possessions, and its religious idols.

The prophet arraigns Judah for its arrogant self-sufficiency. It glories in its wealth and luxury (2:7; 22:9–14). It trusts in its own political schemes and foreign coalitions (30:1). It relies on armed strength and military leagues (20; 30:16; 31:1). Thus, Isaiah sees arrogance in Judah's trust in foreign alliances, both that of Ahaz with Assyria (7) and that of Hezekiah with Egypt (30:2). In a symbolic act, walking naked and barefoot in the garb of a slave, he attacks the trust in Egypt which provided the background for the Ashdod revolt of 711 B.C. (20). All is misplaced trust, for the cause of Judah's sin is its arrogant self-sufficiency, its refusal to trust in God (22:11; 31:1). Instead of putting its trust in Yahweh, Judah was placing its confidence in supports which God himself would shake. In pungent words the prophet contrasts the wisdom of Yahweh with the sagacity of politicians who counseled foreign aid against Assyria and the power of Yahweh against the weakness of fleshly military strength.

Isaiah's profound analysis of sin takes us down to the depths of the human heart and reflects the same understanding as in the story of the garden (Gen. 3), where man is tempted by the

thought of being like God. Sin is seen in terms of the imagery of
height and exaltation. It is man endeavoring to place himself
on the heavenly throne and to cast God from his seat (cf. the
Tower of Babel story in Gen. 11:1–9). Furthermore, it is not
Judah alone which suffers from this malady. All men are sinners.
The attitudes of Judah and Israel are matched by the pride of
Yahweh's instrument of judgment, Assyria (10:5 ff.). While exe-
cuting the divine sentence on Judah and the other nations, that
imperial power did not recognize its condition. Arrogantly it had
set out on world domination, unaware that it was but an instrument in God's hand, boasting rather that its achievements were
by its own strength and wisdom. But the day would come when
the haughty pride of Assyria too would be brought low (10:12–
19). Indeed, in the final day of judgment, all men would stand
condemned because of their pride. Then the haughtiness of men
would be humbled and the pride of men would be brought
low (2:17).

Judah's malady is so deep-seated that it is not willing to be
obedient. It *will* not hear (28:12; 30:9, 15). It suffers from a
willful rebellion, a defiant rejection of God. It is contemptuous
of the divine word and rejects the divine law (5:24). Hence the
prophet writes down and binds up his word, the divine *torah,*
among his disciples (8:16 ff.). This arrogant rebellion has brought
the nation to such a condition that it cannot discern the difference
between good and evil (5:19 ff.). They are blind to the truth and
spiritually dead (29:9–12). Thus the prophet sees in Judah, as his
prophetic mission progresses, a hardness of heart and a demonic
bondage which seems to make it incapable of responding to the
note of judgment which he sounds.

The Lord of History—Glory and Judgment

Because Israel was sinful, the Holy One of Israel manifested
himself in judgment. His glory filled the earth, but this radiation of the divine presence was evident in judgment. Isaiah is
unrelenting in his affirmation of the divine justice. The divine
righteousness will be manifested in a historical process of destruction. The judgment of God will destroy like a fire burning up the
stubble (5:24; 9:19). In it, social disintegration will be manifested by every man's hand being turned against his brother
(9:19). Rebellion against God leads to internal social strife. Furthermore, the rebellion against Yahweh will lay Judah open to
foreign invasion, just as confidence in him would have meant deliverance from alien aggression. The rejection of God means to
perish by the sword (1:20).

The Day of Yahweh is indeed at hand, the day when judgment
will be consummated (2:9–22; 28:22). Then men will flee from
the cataclysm in which the forces of nature and of history will
be unloosed on a rebellious people. In such a consummation the

whole land will be involved. All the historical instances of divine judgment in the past will be small compared with the strange work that God will then perform (28:18–22). In the center of this controversy of Yahweh with his people are the national leaders, and most of all upon them his judgment will fall (3:13–15).

In this process of judgment, Isaiah manifests a profound sense of God's lordship over history. For him Yahweh is King, not only in the initial vision, but also throughout his prophetic mission (6:5; 30:33). He is the Lord, a title used almost exclusively by Isaiah (1:24; 3:1; 10:33; 19:4). Indeed God is Lord of hosts, Yahweh *tseva'oth,* uniting in himself the whole fullness of the powers on earth and in heaven. The Holy One is glorious in his majesty. So much is he the Lord of history that he needs only to whistle, and nations will move at his behest (5:26). It is his activity which determines the movement of history, even though men may not discern its presence (5:19 ff.). He is the maker of Israel (17:7), and, despite its sin, he will yet do marvelous things with his people, restoring its relationship to him as it was in earlier days (29:13–14). The other nations are under his control, for his glory fills the earth. In the foreign oracles (chaps. 13–23), omitting some non-Isaianic material, we have a series of doom-oracles proclaiming the judgment of God on foreign nations. Philistia (14:28–32), Damascus (17:1–6), Arabia (21:13–15), Egypt (18), and Tyre (23:1–12) are arraigned in turn. Yahweh is no national deity. He is the God of the whole earth. His hand is stretched out over all nations and his purpose concerns the whole earth (14:26).

This lordship over history is especially evident in the prophet's attitude toward Assyria. In one oracle (14:24–27), Isaiah declares that Yahweh will overthrow Assyria. In the oracles already cited (10:5–11, 12–19), we have a much more incisive understanding of the relation of Assyria to the divine plan. Assyria in its pride is bent on imperialistic aggression, but actually it is a rod in God's hand. It is powerless once Yahweh lets it fall. When it has accomplished its divinely appointed task of judgment on Judah, God will punish the stout heart of its despotic ruler and bring its pride to the dust. Assyria too will come under judgment and learn that God is sovereign.

Yet the judgment has a redemptive goal. Its cumulative force is to bring Judah to repentance, if only Israel *will* repent. Repentance here means an active turning back to God, a conversion of will. If sin is grounded in willful disobedience, salvation must lie in a willing return to Yahweh. Although one almost feels in some passages that the judgment is absolute (6:10; 9:12), the prophet still offers hope on the ground of repentance. The corrupt judges and false rulers will be destroyed, but the judgment will also be a cleansing and a purging (1:21–26). God will ultimately restore his people. And so the prophet holds out the hope that, in returning, the rest of Israel may yet be saved (30:15). Here is the paradox. He sees that obduracy will inevitably bring judgment (28:22), and his initial call, reinforced by his experience as prophet, confirms the conviction that the heart of Israel is hardening against God's message. Yet he still dares to hope. God will find a way. There is a note of hope in the midst of denunciation and of a sense of doom.

THE CENTRALITY OF ZION AND THE SALVATION OF THE REMNANT

We have suggested that the hardening of Israel's heart was paradoxically due to this element of hope and salvation in Isaiah's message. He was a prophet of judgment who yet, by the very setting of his call, was heir of the royal theology of Jerusalem and the traditions associated with her temple. But so also were the people who received his oracles, and there was an element in his message which they could receive, while closing their ears to the note of doom and judgment. It is to this element that we must turn our attention. What made Isaiah hopeful?

The answer lies in the presence of the Jerusalem tradition and its royal theology alongside of the wilderness tradition and its exodus theology in the consciousness of the prophet. Although he was fearless in declaring the divine judgment and ruthless in·his expression of the divine demands, Isaiah was yet bound in closely with the Temple cult and the royal house. His relations to Ahaz and Hezekiah would suggest that for him the Davidic covenant and its accompanying royal cult had a real significance. His inaugural vision in the Temple gave to his message, from the beginning of his mission, a sense of the divine presence tabernacling on Zion's hill. If Engnell is right, some royal festival may well have provided the occasion for that vision. Thus, by his very conditioning, Isaiah had a profound sense of the centrality of Zion in God's purpose.

Zion was God's. In her Yahweh was pleased to dwell. In the Temple on Zion's hill the prophet had seen the Lord high and lifted up. Here God had made his power known, and from here his glory radiated over all the earth. The Temple could not be destroyed. The implicit logic is evident. Yahweh had established Zion for his dwelling place, and therefore it could not be destroyed.

Here we face a question. Did Isaiah differentiate Zion from Jerusalem? Was Zion the Temple on its hill? This may well be so, for he can declare that Jerusalem is a harlot (1:21), that it is like Sodom and Gomorrah (1:10), and that its walls have not been built on God's foundations (30:9–14). Yet he also affirms that God has established Zion and that the afflicted of God's people will find refuge there (14:32). Indeed, when the invading judgment takes place, every stronghold of a rebellious people will be over-

thrown, and only in Zion will be left a tried and precious cornerstone of sure foundation (28:16 ff.). Surely, however, the rebellious leaders as well as the faithful would flee within the strong
walls of Jerusalem, and it may well be that Isaiah did envisage
even the fall of the city.[7] But the Temple would stand, and there
God would reconstitute his people.

In the prophet's thought, Zion is the center from which God
would reconstitute a faithful people. There can be no such re-
creation until the catastrophic judgment has descended (30:15),
but its purging fires will cleanse away the dross, and wise leadership will be reinstituted (1:24–27). Thus Zion shall be redeemed
with judgment and called the faithful city. The judgment will
leave Judah ravaged and Zion a besieged city, but total destruction
will not overtake it because a faithful remnant will remain
(1:7–9).

So we come to yet another of the contributions of Isaiah to
Israel's religious heritage. Isaiah begins to differentiate a true
Israel out of the corporate whole. Amos may have seen some
hope along this line (Amos 5:15), but Isaiah makes it clear.
Israel 'after the flesh' is not to be identified with Israel 'after the
Spirit.' The purging fires of judgment will cleanse away the dross
and a true and faithful Israel will remain. So Isaiah symbolically
calls his son Shear-jashub, "a remnant shall return" (7:3). *Return*
must not here be taken to mean a return from captivity. Rather
it means a turning back to God, a conversion to holiness, and thus
the phrase could be taken to mean "a remnant shall be saved."
Even then we need to note the finer nuance of meaning that he
enshrined in the name. Isaiah is speaking to Ahaz, encouraging
him to trust in Yahweh and not to put his confidence in foreign
alliances. The name of his son is both a promise and a threat.
The emphatic position of the subject in the Hebrew suggests that
the title should be understood enigmatically as "*only* a remnant
shall return." At least a remnant, but only a remnant, will survive
the judgment if Ahaz pursues his disastrous policies. Thus originally the name of Isaiah's son is more a sign of threat than one
of promise. Closely bound up with this experience, we may see
Isaiah actually forming such a remnant proleptically in the circle
of disciples which he gathered around him, and among whom
he binds up his *torah* (8:16–18).

We have seen that 6:13 in the inaugural vision may be a gloss
or, at least, is difficult to exegete. Yet it would appear that the
remnant idea was early a constituent element in his message.
This faithful remnant will be gathered in Zion and can thus be
symbolized in the cornerstone which Yahweh has established in
Zion (28:16). Here Isaiah is evidently concerned that all nations
shall see the glory of Yahweh of which the Temple vision has
made him so aware. The persistence of Zion and the remnant
in it would demonstrate God's sovereignty to the world. A group

of oracles (10:20–27), in prose and thus condensed at best, would, if authentic, support the prophet's hope.[8] Those who dwell in Zion are not to be fearful, for Yahweh will lift the yoke off their shoulder (10:24–27). Yet judgment is sure, and only a remnant shall escape (10:22–23). Here we have a doom oracle which is tempered in our text by a preceding oracle of promise (10:20–21). Having trusted in war with disastrous consequences, the remnant will learn not to trust in war but to lean on God (cf. 31:1).[9] What in the naming of his son was mere threat became increasingly promise. Isaiah became more and more aware of the obdurate evil of Judah and its inevitable destruction. Yet now he saw that Yahweh was still with his people if even a remnant could be saved out of the coming judgment and gathered around God's glorious presence (1:4–9).

This hope stayed the prophet even though he was burdened by Judah's hardness of heart. Israel seemed so obdurate (9:13). Indeed it had made a "covenant with death" (28:15, 18). Yet a remnant would stay on God and find refuge under God's tabernacling presence in Zion (28:16). Righteousness would overflow and only a remnant would return, but it would return. Indeed, judgment had this end in view. It was a refining process. It provided the extremity which made redemption possible.

THE CHALLENGE TO FAITH

In the light of this, the prophet calls for faith. This alone is the ground for a reconstituted remnant. Of all the prophets, Isaiah is preeminently a prophet of faith. God is Israel's defender, not that of Egypt or any other foreign power. The deliverance of Israel will not result from any human activity. It will be by the act of Yahweh (31:1–3; 29:14). Such an act is bound up in Isaiah's thought with Yahweh's presence in the Temple. Hence we have the enigmatic sign to Ahaz of the birth of a child whose name shall be symbolically Immanuel, "God with us" (7:14 ff.). Isaiah can call on Ahaz for a trust in Yahweh and not in Assyrian aid. If Ahaz does not believe on Yahweh, he will not be established (7:9). God is in the midst of his people and his purpose shall be accomplished (14:24–27).

Isaiah is the first to use the root *'mn* in the form *he'ᵉmin*, "to believe."[10] It means fundamentally to acknowledge God as steadfast, to put oneself into a relationship with God which is divinely initiated. So fundamental is the attitude it describes that such belief springs out of an act of will. It is a decision. It has existential import and covers the whole of a man's being. It carries with it the connotation of steadfastness and is associated with the idea of righteousness. A faithful city is one full of righteousness (1:21, 26). Thus, to believe in God means to commit oneself to God as steadfast and to manifest that commitment as obedience in one's own existence. Such belief issues in righteousness. He who thus believes in God will not make haste (28:16). By so believing a man will be established, that is to say, will have a real, a meaningful existence (7:9).

For Isaiah this was all that Judah had to do. He condemned all trust in imperial powers and political alliances (7:1 ff.), in human strength (30:15 ff.), in protection against danger (28:14 ff.). He demanded absolute belief in and commitment to Yahweh. This is the attitude of the whole man, and it means the rejection of all other sources of security. The word *to believe* can thus be used by Isaiah only of God, for such faith can brook no rival object.

The word which Isaiah uses of faith in other methods and powers is *batah*, "to trust." He also employs the word *sha'an* ("to stay"—30:12; 31:1; 32:9–11). Both words can also be used of trusting or confiding in Yahweh (30:15; 10:20). These words do not convey the absolute sense or objective import that we have found in the word translated "to believe." "To trust" has not the developed sense that our English word conveys. It later came to have this connotation in the Book of Psalms. But, in Isaiah, the Hebrew word hardly gets beyond the level of a feeling of security. It thus does not convey the sense of existential commitment, a steadfast act of will, that the Hebrew word translated "to believe" does. It may be applied equally to feeling secure in God or in false objects. Yet in the former connection, its association with the word *shuv*, "to turn," "to repent," might add the appropriate sense of commitment, of an act of will. A man may feel safe in God, but this is not the kind of experience that Isaiah desires to convey when he speaks of believing. Artur Weiser suggests that Isaiah "has played a decisive part in giving the ultimate depth of meaning to the content of this word" [11] (*he'emin*, "to believe"), and in his vocabulary *to trust* does not reach this depth. [12]

Yet if the remnant which escapes the purging judgment is to be characterized by faith of this existential quality, how can such faith be awakened in the human heart? Israel, as the prophet saw, had not the will to obey or to believe. It was obdurate and hard of heart. Here Isaiah has no counsel except to imply that God will find a way. It was left for his successors to see more deeply into the divine counsels at this point.

The prophet was certain, however, that Yahweh was a wonder-working God. He was wonderful in counsel and excellent in wisdom (28:29). He would perform a marvelous work and wonder, in which the wisdom of the wise and the understanding of the prudent would be confounded (29:14). Although Isaiah is here referring to the coming judgment, we need to bear in mind that for him judgment had a purging and saving aspect. The next verses of chapter 29 indicate such a hope. Yahweh would perform a wonder that would be beyond all human devising, and his counsel, his design for Israel, would be accomplished.

The Day of Yahweh—The Messiah and His Kingdom

We must not be surprised, in the light of this, at the eschatological element in the prophet's thought. The kind of faith which he demanded carried a sense of destiny because it was existential. Yet such a faith could only result from God's act.

There are many scholars who differentiate the preexilic prophets from the postexilic by holding that only the latter are eschatological. The former were concerned with the continuity of history, and their hope for a better future lay solely within the historical plane, its fulfillment being achieved by Yahweh through historical forces. None would dispute that there is much more of a sense of continuity in the preexilic prophets. It is true that developed eschatology is concerned with an end that arises out of a transcendent act of God. Yet Isaiah is concerned with the last things, and it is by no means clear that this element of transcendence is absent. When he describes the end, it is true that he seems to associate it with historical forces, and yet he also employs language that implies a transcendent and suprahistorical act. There will be a miraculous divine intervention. There has to be total destruction and purging before the new day dawns. The remnant will be reconstituted out of ruin.

There will be more than historical reconstruction here, for the result of the Day of Yahweh will be a totally new state of affairs. It will be on the historical plane, but the old order of things can never return. War will cease (2:4), justice will prevail (1:26), and the ground will become supernaturally fertile (30:23 ff.; 32:15). God will pour out his Spirit from on high (32:15), and Yahweh will transform nature as he binds up the heart of his people (30:25). Spiritually, morally, and even physically the whole order will be transformed by the act of God, and in the oracle of chapter 4 this is evidently to be God's act. The mingling of the historical and the suprahistorical should not surprise us here, for how else are we to describe the consummation of the divine purpose, which is the actual meaning of history and yet points beyond history? We can understand why Vriezen can describe Isaiah as "the creator of eschatology." [13]

As Isaiah describes the life of the reconstituted people of God, the restored remnant, he brings in the thought of the Davidic monarchy. His own close association with the royal house and the place occupied in his thought by the royal theology made him sure that the covenant with David had to be fulfilled. The Immanuel sign and the messianic oracles of 9:2–7 and 11:1–9 are central in our understanding of the prophet's message at this point.

Let us first consider the Immanuel sign (7:14). In his advice to Ahaz, Isaiah counsels him not to seek foreign aid against the Syro-Ephraimitic alliance but to have faith in Yahweh. In confirmation he offers a sign, even though Ahaz refuses it. A child shall shortly be born or has been born,[14] and, by the time that he reaches the stage of moral discernment, Israel and Syria will both be overthrown. Since the word *'almah* (often translated "virgin") denotes a young woman of marriageable age until the birth of her first child,[15] the early Christian attempts to find support here for the virgin birth must be left on one side. This does not mean, however, that the passage has no messianic significance. Further, the addition of the definite article to *'almah* would seem to suggest that a specific situation is in the prophet's mind. In other words, we are concerned with some actual historical event, a fact consonant with Isaiah's offering of his oracle as a sign.

Yet there is with this viewpoint a possible resuscitation of interest in some messianic significance for 7:14. In part this springs from the fact that similar language is applied in the Ras Shamra tablets to the begetting of a divine or royal offspring. Engnell and other Scandinavian scholars [16] hence associate Isaiah's sign with the royal cult at Jerusalem, arguing that the prophet is echoing a cultic cry. Ahaz, faced with the fall of his dynasty, is assured of its continuation and the perpetuity of the Davidic covenant. Here we see the royal theology and Isaiah's concern with the Temple and its royal cultus finding a place in the prophetic message. Hence there may be truth in the suggestion that Hezekiah was the sign-child, and *ha'almah* is the wife of Ahaz.[17]

The best answer would seem to be the suggestion that the Immanuel-utterance has both a proximate and a futurist reference.[18] The immediate Immanuel may well have been Hezekiah, and yet there may also have been a deeper messianic significance to the sign in the mind of Isaiah. Certainly, if Micah was under Isaianic influence, Micah 5:3 applied the same idea to a Davidic Messiah. In some sense the prophetic word is always detached from its immediate historical environment and has a wider application. As the prophet saw it, its fulfillment in Hezekiah might be but the beginning of a movement which would culminate in the full Messianic King.

If the coming age was to result from a divine act it would be through God's giving of a Messiah. The fact that he is born indicates the historical continuity in the prophet's mind. This brings us to two oracles, 9:1–6 and 11:1–9, which are increasingly regarded as Isaianic. The first oracle would seem to belong to the biographical section, chapter 7, and the autobiographical section, chapter 8. It thus may well continue the promise of Isaiah 7:14, and yet it is more specifically messianic. It is a question whether the perfect tenses of the verbs in this oracle are to be taken in their normal sense or to be understood as 'prophetic perfects.' The latter would probably be the original intention of the prophet, yet, as we now have it, there may be some truth that the oracle has been used liturgically in the royal cult. Isaiah appears to have been closely associated, as we have seen, with the royal house and may well have uttered this oracle also with a double sense in view.[19] In emphasizing the double sense, we are once more suggesting that the oracle may have been addressed to a specific historical situation and yet also possess a futuristic reference. The latter would explain more adequately the ascriptions "Wonderful Counsellor, Mighty God, Everlasting Father, Prince of Peace" (9:6), which are attached to the anointed one. We seem here to be moving into the realm of a transcendent eschatology which yet has historical continuity with what precedes it. Here is the child of miracle, the act of God that breaks into the continuity of history and works the extraordinary. Here is Immanuel, God with us.

The oracle in 11:1–9 would seem to be yet more directly messianic. It has often been regarded as non-Isaianic and post-exilic, the reference to "the stump of Jesse" in 11:1 suggesting that the Davidic dynasty has fallen. Again, the reference to peace among the animals savors of postexilic eschatology. Yet modern scholars tend more to regard this also as an oracle of Isaiah, and many would interpret it as originally a cultic utterance composed by the prophet for some ceremony of royal accession.[20] If so, it also would have a double reference. Our own judgment would be that it is bound up with the prophet's remnant hope and that it envisages a Messiah who shall fulfill the hope of the Davidic covenant and be truly Yahweh's vicegerent. The failure of both Ahaz and Hezekiah may well have driven Isaiah to prophesy a divine act in which God would set his chosen king upon the throne of his re-created kingdom. Is it an accident that the Spirit who broods over the deep at the first creation becomes the indwelling moral and spiritual presence in the Messiah (11:2)? A new creation is to be a reality. "The zeal of *Yahweh* of hosts will perform this." Here is a true eschatology, even though the original reference may have been to an actual king. There shall be a king who shall rule in righteousness. Maybe this eschatological hope was expressed by Isaiah before the accession of a new monarch, always with the hope that this might yet usher in God's day. It is fitting that such oracles should thus be regarded as fulfilled in Jesus Christ when the fullness of time dawned.

This is Isaiah's hope expressed in varying ways. It was left for later prophets to fill in the fragmentary pattern, and to see how, in the counsels of God, the coming anointed one would accomplish the redemption. Israel's stubbornness of heart and obduracy of spirit required a new creative and redemptive act. What would God do that Israel might believe and thus be established as the people of God? Isaiah believed that God would do something through his anointed one, who would be like rivers of water in a dry land. Eyes would no longer be dimmed, nor ears darkened, nor hearts hardened (32:2, 3). Here was the prophet's hope. The faith he called for had this strong element of expectation in it. Those who believed must wait for God's day and God's act (8:17; 30:18). Indeed, included in the roll which Isaiah bound up among his disciples may well have been his messianic prophecies. For these were so open to misinterpretation and false hopes, so liable to harden the hearts of those who did not want to hear the truth and who believed in a political kingship and its foreign alliances, that Isaiah and his followers could only bind them up and wait for the Day of Yahweh when this redemptive and transcendent meaning would be made plain.

A PROPHETIC CONTEMPORARY FORESEES THE FALL OF ZION

The prophecy of Micah is, like all the other prophetic books, a collection of oracles, and some of these evidently belong to a later date than that of the eighth century prophet. Thus we find references to the Exile (4:6 ff.; 7:12) and an allusion to Babylon (4:10), which suggest that later elements are included. Yet we need to beware of attempts to break up the book and scatter its message across the centuries. Most of the oracles could well have come from Micah himself. We shall attribute to Micah, at least, chapters 1–3 and 5:10–7:7. Chapter 4:1–5 is repeated in Isaiah 2:1–4, and it is difficult to determine which was original, but the oracle probably belongs to Isaiah's and Micah's period. Chapter 7:8–20 is probably a postexilic oracle, yet it may refer to the desolation of the northern kingdom and not to the exile of Judah. We see no reason to assume that 5:1–9 is not by Micah, unless we do not believe that the prophet had a message of hope.

The latter is the crucial point. A century later Micah is remembered in Jeremiah's time as a prophet of judgment (Jer. 26: 18). On this basis, it is assumed that the real Micah was solely a prophet of doom and that all oracles of promise and hope must be rejected as unauthentic. Such critics will thus accept generally chapters 1–3 and yet dismiss the passage in this section which gives a glimmer of hope (2:12–13). We have no right, however, to make such sweeping generalizations from the position in the time of Jeremiah. Micah's contemporaries, like Isaiah, have a mingling of promise with their condemnation, and we have no right to deny the same attitude in Micah himself. If an oracle has nothing in it which intrinsically refers to a later date and another situation, we have no right to regard it as not from Micah. In any case, we may assume that the oracles result from the devoted remembrance of a group of Micah's disciples, as in the case of Isaiah. They represent, therefore, in spirit, the man and his message, even where doubts as to origin may be raised.

Coming from Moresheth-Gath in the Philistine plain, Micah

was a country man in contrast to his contemporary Isaiah, who was a man of the city. He shows the same lively sense of social evil and has a profound sympathy with the poor and the farmers. He condemns the oppressive rulers of Judah for their tyranny and partiality in dealing with the poor (3:11). The agrarian problem, in the specific form of the covetous absorption of land and the eviction of the owners of small holdings, comes under his attack (2:1 ff.). He scathingly indicts the men who should have protested against this but have not, namely, the prophets who are not willing to become unpopular (3:5 ff.). Princes, priests, and prophets—the political and religious leaders—are all alike responsible for the running sores of Hebrew society (3:9–12). Upon them the judgment of God will come.

More clearly than Isaiah he saw that the judgment entailed the fall of Jerusalem. It is probable that his rustic background contributed to this. Isaiah bound up the Temple with the worship of Yahweh, but Micah made no such identification. The perpetuation of Jerusalem was not necessary for the continuance of the nation. His rural outlook convinced him that the national backbone was to be found in the farming population of the countryside. Around these he built his hope. Jerusalem might be destroyed and Zion become like a plowed field, but that was not the end of God's people (3:12; 2:12, 13). With the indignation of a countryman against the city rulers, he declares that the chastisement of God will fall on both Samaria and Jerusalem (1:5 ff., 12).

We have to remember that the situation of Israel after the fall of Samaria in 722 B.C. may well have encouraged his thinking. Few northern Israelites had been deported. The majority remained in the land and retained their religious faith and practices. The Samaritan Pentateuch of later years is a testimony to this. The shrines outside Samaria would and did make up for the loss of the royal sanctuary. The faith of the north persisted among the rural population, and Micah may well have believed that this would happen in the south.

If this be so, we can understand the admixture of hope and promise in his message as in that of Isaiah. We know that the popular eschatology was totally hope, a belief in privilege without responsibility. We have suggested that the presence of such an element in Isaiah's message may have helped to harden the heart of the Jewish people against his correlative emphasis on sin and judgment. We certainly cannot exclude the same element from the work of Micah, and we find it in the later oracles of his prophecy. In 5:2–4 we have an echo of the Immanuel hope of Isaiah. The phrase "she who travailed" may refer like Isaiah 7:14 to some royal person. A second David will come, and the remnant of Judah will be restored under his rule. Judah will be purged of false worship (5:10–15), but beyond this threat there is also promise. Even if 7:8–20 were not from Micah, we have the hope that God will gather the dispersed of his people and forgive their iniquity.

In the midst of the last group of oracles, the quintessence of the Hebrew prophetic message is gathered up. The demands of Yahweh are to do justly, to love mercy, and to walk humbly with him (6:8). Here the prophecy touches the highlights. Micah and the oracles gathered in with his own have little to contribute to the major movement of the prophetic message. But he shared in the deep pathos in the heart of God, and because of this he dared to hope. We see some of this divine sympathy as he breaks through his message of doom in 2:6, 7. There results a mixture of judgment and hope, threat and promise. This finds its focus in a classic statement of God's demands and in an assurance that the Messiah will come, a second David.

NOTES

1. We identify the Azriau of Yaudi of the records (see J. B. Pritchard, *Ancient Near Eastern Texts* [Princeton: Princeton University Press, 1950], pp. 282 ff.) with Azariah of Judah, despite some difficulties such as the locale of the reported conflict in northern Syria. Cf. John Bright, *A History of Israel* (Philadelphia: Westminster Press, [1959]), pp. 252 ff.

2. Bright, *History of Israel*, pp. 269–71 and Excursus I, associates the passages in chapters 10, 14, and 17 with a later Assyrian invasion about 688 B.C., and thus endeavors to deal with the critical problems in the narrative of 2 Kings 18:17–19:37 ff., and Isaiah 36–39. I have preferred to retain the usual dating of the material.

3. See Ivan Engnell, *The Call of Isaiah* (Uppsala: Lundequistska Bokhandeln, 1949), *passim*.

4. Cf. William F. Albright, *Supplement to Vetus Testamentum*, (Leiden: E. J. Brill, 1957), 4:254 ff.

5. This view is supported by Martin Buber, *The Prophetic Faith* (New York: Macmillan, 1949), pp. 131 ff.

6. Cf. G. W. Wade, *The Book of the Prophet Isaiah*, Westminster Commentaries (London: Methuen & Co., 1929), p. xxxiv. "It [holiness] implied that the Lord was separated from mankind not merely by perfection of power but by perfection of moral purity."

7. Th. C. Vriezen, in an essay on "The Theology of Isaiah," *Israel's Prophetic Heritage*, ed. W. Harrelson and B. Anderson (New York: Harper & Bros., 1962), pp. 128–46, has argued that the prophet did envisage the fall of Jerusalem. Yahweh transcended the Temple even in the inaugural vision (6:1), and the absence of an explicit reference to the destruction of the city is no justification for arguing that Jerusalem would be spared because Yahweh dwelt in it. Zion was holy only because of Yahweh himself. On this view both Temple and city might be destroyed. It is true that this is the thought of Jeremiah, but it is by no means so evident that we should read this

thinking back into Isaiah. I do not believe that Vriezen has established his case. My own differentiation between Zion and Jerusalem might better meet the situation.

8. We shall assume that 11:11 and 16 are postexilic material. Here the reference is evidently to the dispersed exiles and the dominant motif is a geographical return to the homeland rather than a spiritual return to God.

9. So R. B. Y. Scott in "Commentary on Isaiah chapters 1–39," *The Interpreter's Bible*, 12 vols. (Nashville: Abingdon Press, 1956), 5:244 ff.

10. There is an excellent discussion of this issue in Kittel's *Bible Key Words*, Vol. 10: Faith (New York: Harper & Bros., 1961), pp. 10–23. This English translation of the contribution of Arthur Weiser to KTW repays careful reading.

11. Ibid., p. 17.

12. There is an interesting analysis of Isaiah's understanding of faith in Sheldon Blank, *Prophetic Faith in Isaiah* (New York: Harper & Bros., 1958), pp. 34 ff., although it is marred by Blank's unusual and not well-founded views about the structure of the book and its portrait of the prophet.

13. Th. C. Vriezen, *An Outline of Old Testament Theology* (Newton: Charles T. Branford Co., 1960), p. 360.

14. The Hebrew verb system makes the tense indefinite.

15. So Ludwig Köhler and Walter Baumgartner, eds., *Lexicon in veteris testamenti libros* (Leiden: E. J. Brill, 1953).

16. See Ivan Engnell, *Studies in Divine Kingship in the Ancient Near East* (Uppsala: Almquist and Wiksells, 1943), p. 133; Helmer Ringgren, *The Messiah in the Old Testament* (London: SCMP, 1956), pp. 25 ff.

17. See Johannes Lindblom, *Prophecy in Ancient Israel* (Oxford: Basil Blackwell, 1962), pp. 246 ff., 368 ff. If it be argued that Hezekiah was already born and nine years old at this time, it may be noted that the chronology of 2 Kings 16:2 and 18:2 is exceedingly difficult. According to this Ahaz would be only eleven years old when Hezekiah was born.

18. Cf. H. Wheeler Robinson, *Inspiration and Revelation in the Old Testament* (Oxford: Clarendon Press, 1956), pp. 171 ff.

19. Scott, "Commentary on Isaiah," p. 232, suggests that the oracle was composed to celebrate the accession of an actual Judean king, and that the exalted language and transcendent elements in the description would be normal for such an occasion. He holds that Isaiah composed the oracle for the cult at a coronation ceremony. Lindblom, *Prophecy in Ancient Israel*, pp. 368 ff., writes: "the oracle of Immanuel refers to the birth of a royal child, a successor to the throne of Ahaz. With the birth of this child Isaiah associated the most exalted hopes. . . . I hold also that the poem in ix:1–6 refers to the same Immanuel–child. . . . In exalted language based on oriental court and cult style Isaiah describes the coming reign of the newborn prince."

20. For example, Scott, "Commentary on Isaiah," pp. 247 ff.

Chapter Five

The Hope of an
Individual Covenant

As with the other prophets, the Book of Jeremiah does not present the oracles of the prophet to us in chronological order. Perhaps of all the major prophets, this book confronts us with the least number of critical problems. It is not generally disputed that the oracles are genuinely Jeremianic and that the biographical sections give us an authentic picture of the prophet. The Septuagint version presents us with a rearrangement of some of the material and is considerably shorter than the present Hebrew text, but this need not lead to doubt about the historical authenticity of the latter. As a whole the book presents us with the oracles of Jeremiah of Jerusalem, some highly revealing autobiographical sections or confessions, and some biographical narratives in which oracles are interspersed. We can penetrate through these to the inner life of the prophet much more easily than is the case with Isaiah of Jerusalem or Ezekiel in Babylon. In consequence, the book of Jeremiah is significant for understanding the prophetic consciousness and its significance as a medium of revelation.

In its present form, the roll of Jeremiah is divided into four major sections. Chapters 1–25 consist of individual oracles of the prophet in poetry and in prose, interspersed with his intercessory prayers for Israel and his confessions. The confessions consist of a mingling of laments and personal petitions with the answers of Yahweh to his tortured soul and thus take dialogue form (15: 10–21; 20:7–18; 11:18–23; 12:1–5; 17:14–18; 18:18–23). Chapters 26–45 are a collection of biographical narratives written about Jeremiah in the third person, but containing in their text some of the prophet's oracles. Doublets like the Temple sermon recorded in chapters 7 and 26 indicate the presence of parallel traditions. Chapter 23, verses 7 ff. may be a separate memory of

the oracle in 16:14 ff. The biographical section indicates that
the Jeremianic circles had variant ways of remembering and re-
cording their traditions. Often the poetic form which is retained
in the autobiographical section is transformed into prose and
the content is condensed in the biographical sections. The Temple
sermon illustrates this. Even in the autobiographical section oracles
are often condensed too, and lose the vivid color and imagery of
the original utterance, as for instance, Jeremiah 11. Chapters
46–51 present us with a series of oracles against foreign nations.
Finally, in chapter 52, we have a historical appendix which re-
produces the text of 2 Kings 24:18–25:30.

How the book achieved its present form is a question that has
been variously answered. Mowinckel, among other scholars, has
suggested that the nucleus of the roll must be found in the
scroll compiled by Baruch, under Jeremiah's direction, during the
reign of Jehoiakim. This would have contained many of the
oracles contained in chapters 1–25, those oracles relating to
events after 605 B.C. being excluded. This was later enlarged
after the commencement of the exile by the addition of the other
oracles and Jeremiah's confessions. At the same time, there was
added to it the biographical section chapters 26–45. Here scholars
are not in agreement. I am inclined to believe that Baruch was
responsible for these biographical memoirs and brought the first
two sections of the roll together.

In taking Baruch's scroll as the nucleus of the prophet's book,
we may actually trace the way in which the written records of
a prophet's testimony were compiled. We need to remember
that the prophetic oracles of Jeremiah are especially good examples of lyrical poetry, that their preservation in the memory of
disciples like Baruch would thus be easier, and that they were
preserved in the tradition as detached units. As with the other
prophets, we have no reason to ascribe all the oracles in a collection to the same date as that appended to the first oracle of
the group. Often they were remembered together because of a
common theme or objective. We shall see that Jeremiah's confessions, his lamentations and petitions, and his dialogues with
Yahweh also follow a fairly fixed pattern which would make
preservation in memory and tradition easy. Thus, though the
final completion of the roll may be long after Jeremiah's death,
we may assume that his words were preserved and treasured by
the circle to which Baruch belonged. The scribe himself, out of
love and regard for his leader, would strive to remember the
oracles and confessions that fell from Jeremiah's lips, and we
would imagine that much of our present roll was, directly or
indirectly, his handiwork.

THE HISTORICAL SCENE IN RELATION
TO JEREMIAH AND HIS MINISTRY

For three quarters of a century after the last appearance of

Isaiah of Jerusalem, no prophetic voice was heard on the hills of Judah. Then four prophets came: Zephaniah, Nahum, Habakkuk, and Jeremiah. Jeremiah was the dominating figure, and his ministry covered roughly half a century.

The prophet's call came in the thirtieth year of Josiah's reign, 626 B.C. There has been some dispute as to this date, since both biographical memoirs and oracles for the years 626–609 B.C. are noticeable by their absence. Hence some contend that the call came in 608 B.C. One ingenious suggestion has been made that since the call assured Jeremiah that he was predestined from his mother's womb, he would identify the inception of his ministry with his birth and that this occurred in 626 B.C.[1] We are here in an area of speculation and there seems no reason for not accepting the actual dating. Actually there is no reason why the bulk of chapters 1–6 should not be attributed to the period 626–621 B.C., prior to the Josianic reform and just after the call. Jeremiah's premonition of an invasion in chapters 4–6 may well have dated back so early, since the barbarian Scythians were then moving down from the north.

The prophet came of the priestly family of Anathoth (1:1), and thus had cultic connections. His family would have been dispossessed by the Josianic Reformation in 621 B.C., which centralized the worship in Jerusalem and dismantled all the surrounding shrines. This may well have caused a breach with the prophet who seems, at one stage, to have supported the Deuteronomic reforms.

The call came to the prophet in the year that the last great imperial leader of Assyria, Ashurbanipal, died. His death delivered Judah from the Assyrian domination which had covered the preceding half-century. It also made it possible for invading hordes like the Scythians to make inroads upon the outskirts of the great empire. Herodotus [2] records a Scythian raid on Palestine somewhere around the period 626 B.C., and the advent of this barbarian horde with its predatory excursions may well have portrayed judgment to Jeremiah. He discerned this as the "movement among the nations" which would issue in the divine chastisement of Judah. Thus, to the threatening collapse of Assyrian power, we must add the formidable danger of invading barbarian hordes. We may see these as constituting the historical situation in which the divine call came to Jeremiah. The Scythian hordes were threatening the north, but in his imagination he saw them moving down on Judah as the advance guard of the Day of Yahweh (4:23–29). The descriptive passages of chapter 4 would fit such a barbarian group.

God confronted Jeremiah in a complex of experiences consisting of one audition (1:4–10) and two visions (1:11–14). In his audition, Jeremiah's sense of election was carried back beyond his conception. He was predestined to his prophetic mission and was a thought in the divine mind before he was conceived in his mother's womb. Thus, in some sense, he was the incarnation of a divine thought. The manner of his calling involved for him not a discovery of his own inner powers and gifts, but his surrender to one who had planned and devised his life before he was born. It is always God who takes the initiative in an encounter with him, and this is demonstrated in the case of every prophet. For instance: "The Lord God has spoken; who can but prophesy?" (Amos 3:8, RSV). Supremely of the prophets it may be said that they chose God and surrendered themselves to his purpose because first of all he had chosen them. In Jeremiah's case, this sense of inner compulsion of the divine grace takes the form of a conviction that his whole inner life has been planned beforehand by God. As Skinner has finely put it:

> The sense of predestination in Jeremiah's consciousness means the conviction that the endowments of his whole nature, his physical and social environment, all the influences of heredity and education that had shaped his life and made him what he was, had worked together under the hand of God to prepare him for the task to which he is now summoned.[3]

The prophet complains of his sinfulness and youth, but he is rebuked by God. Yahweh will be with him, and he is to be God's mouthpiece. So like Isaiah but with different symbolism, his mouth is touched, and God prepares him for his task. He is promised God's presence and power.

The two visions provide the center of the prophet's message. He sees the branch of an almond tree (*shaqedh*), and the consonants of the name conjure up in his mind, by a change of vowels, the thought of watcher (*shoqedh*). God is waking and watching over his people. The sight of the boiling cauldron, with its face directed away from the north, reveals the unhappy lot of Judah. So at his call, Jeremiah becomes a prophet of judgment.

Within five years of his call, the Josianic Reformation took place, and it would appear that, in the beginning, the prophet hailed it with approval. This reformation (2 Kings 22:1–23:30) is generally believed to have been undertaken by Josiah upon the basis of the core of law and injunction contained in our Book of Deuteronomy. Josiah's centralization of worship in Jerusalem and destruction of pagan and even Yahwistic shrines apart from the Temple reflects the injunction of Deuteronomy 12:1–7. This document discovered in the Temple may well have been given written form in the time between Isaiah and Josiah's reign. In the evil reign of Manasseh, prophets and priests sought to formulate a codal basis for the elimination of the evils that then became rampant. The influence of prophets like Isaiah shines through the concern with moral righteousness and judgment. Chapter 11:1–14 explicitly connects Jeremiah with an itinerant mission in support of the reformation. He goes around Judah preaching the words of "this covenant," a phrase which can only be interpreted as a reference to the Book of Deuteronomy. The reformation was needed. The period of Assyrian overlordship, under the evil and pliable Manasseh, had led to a syncretization of religion and the introduction of pagan cults into the life of Judah. The real problem about Jeremiah and the reformation is the opposition toward the cult which is most certainly expressed by him in the rest of his ministry, and that despite his connection with a priestly family.

It has been pointed out by many scholars that there are sayings throughout the roll of Jeremiah which have a distinctively Deuteronomic flavor. The suggestion is often made that Jeremiah never supported the reformation and that these oracles have been edited from a Deuteronomic point of view.[4] It is certainly true, in support of this thesis, that Jeremiah was not consulted when the law book was discovered in the Temple (2 Kings 22:14); at least, no mention is made of him. But the central figure in the discovery was Shaphan the scribe, and throughout his ministry Jeremiah was protected and supported by a court party which had intimate contact with this man and which included his sons Ahikam, Elasah, and Gemariah. Baruch read the roll in Gemariah's chamber in the Temple (36:10); Elasah helped to deliver the prophet's letter to the first deportees in Babylon (29:3); Ahikam, also mentioned with Shaphan in the original discovery of the law book, saved Jeremiah from the angry mob (26:24). In addition, Gedaliah, the governor set by Babylon over those who remained in Judah after the deportation of 586 B.C., was the grandson of Shaphan, was strongly supported by the prophet, and afforded him protection. It may be true that, down in Egypt, a remnant of Deuteronomists of this type treasured Jeremiah's oracles and gave them a Deuteronomic flavor actually absent from them. But this is no grounds for eliminating all Deuteronomic support from the prophet's ministry, least of all the period covered by chapter 11. It is noteworthy that Jeremiah supported Josiah and mourned his death. In attacking Johoiakim, he praised his father (22:15 ff.).

One incident which seems to belong to this period confirms our estimate of the situation. Jeremiah's kinfolk at Anathoth turned against him and threatened him with death if he continued prophesying (11:18-23). The cause may well have been the dismantling of the shrine at Anathoth and the unemployment of its priests because of Josiah's reforms. The incident is certainly recorded in the same chapter that represents the prophet as a preacher of the reforming movement. In one passage of his confessions (12:1-6), we learn of the prophet's agony of heart as his own family deal treacherously with him. The inner torture of his soul, his loneliness because of his prophetic task, his agonized colloquies with Yahweh, thus began quite early in his ministry.

What is evident is that Jeremiah increasingly realized that the

Deuteronomic reformation would not be achieved. He clearly stood in the wilderness tradition with its Mosaic covenant and moral vigor. Yet the people to whom he came were dominated by the Jerusalem tradition with its royal theology and its unconditional covenant. The popular attitude was still a shallow optimism. Yahweh had promised perpetuity to David's line, and the tabernacling presence of God on Zion's hill assured Judah's safety and future. The unconditional nature of the covenant with the Davidic dynasty had bred a moral indifference. Jeremiah set himself against this with all the moral rigorism of his character. He had welcomed the Deuteronomic reform because of its return to the Mosaic covenant and its moral claims. It seemed as if the wilderness tradition was about to take its rightful place in Judah's life. But the Deuteronomic Code also emphasized the central sanctuary and tended to reinforce the royal theology at this point. As Jeremiah saw it, the latter emphasis was what the people really heard. Judah did not manifest any signs of becoming truly God's people, and the time-honored measures of political expediency and foreign alliances still remained. There was not any great fidelity to or trust in Yahweh. Hence Jeremiah was turned against the very measures that he had originally supported, because of their external nature. The Deuteronomic reform did not penetrate to the heart of Judah's problem. Jeremiah 8:8 shows Jeremiah's later attitude: ". . . the false pen of the scribes hath wrought falsely."

In consequence, we find Jeremiah turning against the Temple in which the Deuteronomists had centered their reform. The royal theology was still prevailing over the wilderness tradition, and Jeremiah had no alternative but to become a prophet of doom and judgment. The next period of Jeremiah's life from 621 to 608 B.C. shows him in increasing opposition to the reform movement and its practical consequences in the life of Judah. He attacked the law of a central and single sanctuary as mere externalism. Toward the end of Josiah's reign Jeremiah grew out of touch with contemporary religion.[5]

On the political horizon, however, great events were stirring once more. The neo-Babylonian dynasty overthrew the Assyrian power with the help of the Medes, and Nineveh fell in 612 B.C. The internal trouble in Assyria meant increasing relaxation of pressure on Judah, but now Egypt became prominent. Pharaoh Necho went unsuccessfully to the assistance of the Assyrians against the Babylonians. On his return in 609 B.C., he met the forces of Judah under Josiah. This may have been an attempt to win Judaean independence from the one imperial power that still threatened, now that Babylonia was removed as an active threat. In any case, Josiah was killed at Megiddo and his young son, Jehoahaz, enthroned in his place. Necho took Jehoahaz from the throne and replaced him with his older brother, Jehoiakim. Jere-

miah's lament over Jehoahaz is contained in 22:10–12, while
22:13–17 gives a picture and condemnation of Jehoiakim.
Jehoiakim was a vassal of Egypt and had been established on the
throne with no royal covenant with the people. Jeremiah's oracle
shows him to have been a tyrant, an oppressive ruler, bent on
satisfying his own luxurious tastes and using forced labor to accomplish them.

In 605 B.C. Nebuchadrezzar of Babylon defeated Necho at
Carchemish, and this is reflected in Jeremiah's message to
Egypt (46:2–12). In 601 B.C., Nebuchadrezzar was able to turn
his attention to Judah. Jehoiakim was compelled to submit to
Babylon (2 Kings 24:1). Egypt still remained behind the scenes,
however, inciting to rebellion. Three years later Jehoiakim rebelled disastrously.

Jeremiah now began openly to attack the Temple superstition
which the Deuteronomic reform had unfortunately nourished. In
his famous Temple sermon, delivered at the Temple gates and
recorded in chapter 7:1–15, the prophet declared that the possession of Yahweh's Temple was no guarantee of Yahweh's presence.[6] The judgment and destruction of Judah was inevitable.
In 26:1–24 we have a parallel memoir showing how the sermon
was received. The people and leaders alike demanded his death,
but certain elders made a defense by referring to a similar
prophecy by Micah (3:12) one century before. Jeremiah was ac-
quitted but became more and more isolated from his people by
the burden of his message.

In this period, Jeremiah's message of judgment became more
evident. It even took the form of symbolic acts. On one occasion
he publicly broke an earthenware flask, declaring symbolically
that God who had made Judah would also break it because of its
sin. The act took place above the Valley of Hinnom, driving home
still more the point of the message. For even that defiled valley
would have to be used for burial of the dead from the coming
slaughter (19). When the prophet repeated his message in the
Temple courts, he was beaten and put in the stocks (20:1–6). He
was convinced that God would make Babylon the tool of his
judgment on Judah and counseled political quietism. His unpopular message served but to isolate him from his fellows.

To this period undoubtedly belong many of the confessions already referred to and to be studied later. Jeremiah was driven
in upon his own loneliness and so back upon God. This situation
was made more acute by the fact that false prophets abounded,
promising peace and not judgment. Jeremiah had to examine the
basis and authority of his own message (23:9–33).

Another scene marks the passage of Hebrew prophecy from
speech to literature. Isaiah had written down some of his oracles
and bound them up among his disciples. More than a century
later (604 B.C.), Jeremiah was told to write down his prophecies

(chap. 36), the reason being the hope that the written word would succeed where the oral word had failed. Baruch copied down the prophecies at the prophet's dictation. The roll was to be read in the Temple on a fast day. It was read again to the princes in the palace and to the king as he sat by the fire in his winter house. Jehoiakim slashed the roll as it was read and cast it on the fire. The specific prophecy was that Nebuchadrezzar would successfully invade and lay waste the land. A second edition of the roll was dictated with additions. Undoubtedly at this point some of Jeremiah's earlier oracles interpreting the Scythian menace were now transferred to the Babylonian "foe from the north." It is probable that a large proportion of the oracles in chapters 1–25 would have been included in the second edition of Baruch's roll.

After three years of submission to Egypt, Jehoiakim rebelled. Nebuchadrezzar moved against him, but, before action could be joined, Jehoiakim died a natural death, and his young son Jehoiachin (eighteen years old) reigned in his stead. Nebuchadrezzar invested Jerusalem and deported the young king, his family, and the leaders of the nation. So in 597 B.C., we have the first deportation to Babylon of the more influential people in the Jewish community. Although Jeremiah proclaimed an oracle condemning Jehoiakim (22:13–19), he also uttered a lament about him (13: 15–19).

Before long we find the prophet writing a letter to the deportees in Babylon advising them to settle down in the land, since their exile was in God's will. They must accept it as the judgment of God, but God would finally restore them (29:1–32). He warned, however, against false prophets who declared a speedy return. His letter evidently stirred up resentment among them, and yet it is clear, from other oracles, that Jeremiah believed that the future lay with the exiles and not with those who were left in Judah. In an oracle, he portrayed the two groups as good and bad figs respectively, declaring his belief in judgment and yet his hope in the future (24). The future lay with those who had gone into exile with Jehoiachin. Even at the prudential level this made sense, for these deportees included the religious, intellectual, and political leadership of Judah.

Those who remained proved themselves to be bad figs. Pro-Babylonian and pro-Egyptian parties struggled against one another. Jehoiachin's uncle, Zedekiah, was set on the throne by Babylon, but played politics with Egypt which continued to be the *âme damnée* of Palestine. In 593 B.C. the surrounding states (Moab, Ammon, Tyre, and Sidon) sent messengers to Judah to secure support for an insurrection against Babylon. They were met by Jeremiah and presented with symbols of their own captivity, yokes and bands (27:1–11). The prophet was convinced that Nebuchadrezzar's overlordship and even destruction of Judah was

serving God's purpose. All western Asia would be given to Babylon. This was in God's plan, and Judah must accept its judgment
at God's hand. The action of Jeremiah stimulated attacks by the
false prophets. His symbolic act of wearing a wooden yoke to
signify Judah's destiny under Babylon provoked Hananiah to
break the yoke and refute Jeremiah's message. The prophet's
conviction and authority were thus again tested, and he emerged
from quiet reflection authorized to make the yoke so that it could
not be broken, of iron and not of wood (28).

We must not think of Jeremiah as a pessimist, for he was
a prophet of hope as well as of judgment. The prophet found
the ground of his hope, however, in the wilderness tradition and
not in the royal theology. Hope there was but only when God's
moral claims had been met. Hence the judgment must come first.
It was inevitable. Yet beyond this God would provide a new
covenant in which men would do his will because his law was
written on their inward parts. The wilderness tradition and the
exodus covenant thus provide the pattern for his hope. As John
Bright puts it, "The very exodus theology that had condemned the
nation became the foundation of its hope." [7] Jeremiah remained
in this wilderness tradition although he included in his hope
the messianic element derived from the royal theology and the
Jerusalem tradition and dared to hope that God would finally
tabernacle with his people.

The judgment came as the prophet predicted. Zedekiah played
with Egypt once too often. Nebuchadrezzar marched on Judah
and besieged Jerusalem. At the height of the invasion, Jeremiah,
still proclaiming submission, was regarded by many as a pro-
Babylonian. Zedekiah protected Jeremiah who continued to prophesy until the patriots forced the king to grant them their desires. Jeremiah was cast into a cistern and rescued by a foreigner
(37, 38). Jerusalem fell in 586 B.C. (39:1-14).

Sometime in this period of siege the prophet of judgment showed
himself also to be prophet of hope. While in prison, Jeremiah
purchased from a kinsman a plot of land in Anathoth, open to
his redemption. This land was now occupied by the besieging
army, but the prophet's act of purchase was symbolic of his
faith that one day Judah would be free again and prosperous
(32:1-15).

It would appear that a Deuteronomist group provided the leadership of Judah under Babylonian appointment, after the second
group of exiles had departed in 586 B.C. Jeremiah supported
them and their governor, Gedaliah. When the latter was treacherously assassinated by Ishmael, a prince of Davidic blood, this
group of Deuteronomists fled to Egypt, compulsively taking the
prophet with them. The last we hear of Jeremiah is his denunciation of Jewish idolatry in Egypt (40-44). We have suggested
that down in Egypt some of his oracles may have been edited and

given a Deuteronomic flavor. Jeremiah's judgment in his oracle of the good and bad figs was sound. Ishmael's act confirms that. The future lay with the exiles in Babylon.

THE NATURE AND AUTHORITY OF THE PROPHETIC CONSCIOUSNESS—TRUE AND FALSE PROPHECY

For Jeremiah the problem of false prophets became an acute one. Perhaps of all the canonical prophets he comes nearest to exposing the grounds of authority for his prophetic utterance and the nature of his consciousness.

Jeremiah stands in the great prophetic tradition, but he evidently realizes that there can be no marks of behavior by which he is to be differentiated from his false opponents. It is significant that in opposing them he suggests no psychological test. We have already suggested that the difference between the reform prophets and the general class of prophets (n^{e}vi'im) is not to be found at this level. It would appear that the ecstatic element is present in the experience of the canonical prophets as in the professional group which opposed them. This is true of Jeremiah. His message was sometimes mediated through visions grounded in objects like the watchful almond tree and the seething cauldron (1:11–13). He understood the future destiny of the exiles in Babylon through the vision of the good and bad figs (24). Yahweh showed him, and he beheld. He was prepared to admit that his opponents also saw visions, but contended that they were lying visions (23:26 ff.). But how did he know they were delusions?

Again, the ecstatic element in Jeremiah is seen in his employment of symbolic acts. He is told to take a loin cloth, wear it, and hide it in a hole in the rocks. After many days, he is told to recover it, soiled and useless. This is a symbol of the divine judgment on Judah, originally chosen to cling like a loin cloth to Yahweh, but destined to be cast off, marred and profitable for nothing (13:1–14). Again he is told to break an earthenware flask as a sign that God, who has fashioned Judah as his chosen vessel, can also break it and will surely do so (19). He presented the envoys from neighboring states with yokes and bands, signs of servitude, indicating that God had handed over western Asia to Nebuchadrezzar (27:1–11). Finally, we find him wearing a wooden yoke himself as a sign that Judah will go into captivity under Babylon. When challenged by the false prophet Hananiah, who breaks the yoke, Jeremiah is driven again to consider the inspiration and authority of his message. As with his visions, so with his symbolic acts he has to reflect upon the ground of his prophetic consciousness.

Finally, we have the sense of abnormal inner compulsion. Amos could cry: "The Lord God has spoken; who can but prophesy?" (Amos 3:8, RSV). Jeremiah records the same psychological pressure. When he refuses to prophesy any more, God's Word becomes an explosive, burning fire shut up within him, and he has to speak (20:9).

Evidently we cannot differentiate true from false prophecy at the level of the form or pattern of the experience, and it is significant that Jeremiah does not attempt to do so. The insincerity of the false prophets was not demonstrable by the fact that they used the same media as the true prophet. They imitated the prophetic form of utterance (23:31); they palmed off lying visions (23:32). They did at least show little originality in their message; they plagiarized their false oracles, stealing each man from his neighbor (23:30). Here we move beyond psychological media to content, and it is here that the tests must be applied.

One objective test seems to have been formulated about this time by the Deuteronomic school of thinkers. A true oracle will be confirmed by historical events. We find this test used by Micaiah ben Imlah, when confronted by the false testimony of Ahab's four hundred court prophets: "If thou return at all in peace, Yahweh has not spoken by me" (1 Kings 22:28). The Code of Deuteronomy, contemporary with Jeremiah, was confronted by the same problem, and also took refuge in historical validification: "When a prophet speaks in the name of Yahweh, if the thing follow not, nor come to pass, that is the thing which Yahweh hath not spoken" (Deut. 18:22).

Jeremiah does not seem to have relied so much upon this test as upon a consideration of the content of the prophet's message and the quality of his life. First of all, he emphasizes the substance of the prophets' utterance. The content of their message is "Yahweh hath said: 'Ye shall have peace ' " (23:17, ASV), and that despite Israel's manifest sin. In some sense it is true that the preexilic reform prophets were preachers of woe and judgment, prophets of doom. But they were so because of the sin and obduracy of Israel. We have already seen that they were not without hope and that it would be wrong to describe them as pessimists. On the other hand, they were not shallow optimists, and this was the charge which Jeremiah applied to the false prophets. We have noted the superficial trust in the existence of the Temple as a guarantee that Yahweh was with his people, irrespective of their iniquity. This is of one piece with the shallowness that promised *peace,* a term which here for the first time in the Old Testament seems to be used of "peace with God." [8] The false prophets were endeavoring to preserve a sense of security at the price of moral rectitude. They accepted the royal theology and forgot the wilderness tradition. So opposed was Jeremiah to this shallow message that he tended to press his message of judgment to the point of the utter destruction of Judah.[9] Hence he defines the true prophet as one who declares war, evil, and pestilence (28:8). He adds the note that a prophet of peace will be proved to be a true prophet if history validates his oracle (28:9). In our estimate of this extreme position, we need to remember that Jeremiah was himself offering hope, but hope beyond and after judgment. His real concern was with the absence of this latter note in the message that he opposed.

As with the message so with the prophet himself. A prophet who declared smooth things without moral concern would show lack of moral integrity in his own life. His judgment would reflect his character. Hence Jeremiah declared that a false prophet could be identified by the immoral character of his own life. The false prophets in Jerusalem and among the deportees in Babylon alike committed adultery (23:13, 14; 29:23). Furthermore, their contagion influenced their hearers, for whom they were evil examples (23:15). Indifferent to the vice around them, they were loose in their own lives. By their words, they flattered their hearers and confirmed them in their sin (5:7 ff.). By their example, they helped to perpetuate a moral situation which spelled doom for Judah.

Finally, however, Jeremiah has to take refuge in his own innermost conviction. The inner compulsion which Jeremiah described by the figure of "coals of fire shut up within his heart" had its ground in the deep encounter with God. Even when all the other tests failed, he had to fall back upon this deep-seated experience. The authority for his message lay finally in the testimony of the Spirit in his heart. He had the word of Yahweh, and his opponents had but lying visions and dreams (23:28). The basis of his message was most obviously not what he himself had desired to utter. If he had followed his own impulses, he would have said other things. He had stood apart because of Yahweh's Word. Only a fool would have uttered words that invoked such disastrous consequences in his life. If he had given the people what they wanted, his loneliness would never have occurred. But there was a compulsion in him other than the natural inclinations of his heart. His authority was from beyond himself.

Jeremiah variously described the ground for his authority. Perhaps the most fundamental description is that of standing in the council of Yahweh (23:18, 22). Up in the heavenly courts Yahweh, surrounded by his heavenly council, issues his judgments and decrees. Jeremiah, in some sense, believes that he shares in God's council's and knows his counsel (*sodh* means both council and counsel), and that God has sent him forth to declare the divine sentence (23:21, 32). The true prophet has been sent by Yahweh, and the false prophets have not (14:14). He has been addressed by Yahweh (14:14). So the differentiating characteristic of the true prophet is the possession of the Word. He has the Spirit, but his opponents might falsely claim this. The difference

is what the Spirit has put in his heart. His message has not
resulted from human imagination, but it has been given him
by God.

It is here that we enter upon the spiritual depths of Jeremiah's
experience. His possession of the divine Word drove him into
isolation from his fellows, but also opened up to him a way to
the divine heart. Upon Yahweh he lavished all the affections of
which he was starved at the human level. So, in the deep places
of his soul, Jeremiah knew a personal communion with God
which pervaded all his prophetic activity. It was into this personal communion that he withdrew when challenged by Hananiah.
His message was not wholly conveyed to him by ecstatic vision
or audition, though these occur at the outer edge of his consciousness. Undoubtedly some of his symbolic acts were impul-
sive, and he only reflected upon their significance later. There
was an ecstatic element in his visions and in the inward compulsion to prophesy. But all these media have been gathered up
into the center of the prophetic consciousness, reflected upon,
understood, acted upon by a rational and volitional process which
removes them from the level where the false prophets and the
pure ecstatics remained. In the center of Jeremiah's life was a
movement of God in his rational and volitional life. God spoke
to him in his reflective thinking and moved him to intelligent
and decisive action. Finally, however, the truth or falsehood
does not lie in any way in the psychology. As H. W. Robinson
has put it: ". . . whatever the psychological process by which we
explain the experience, the explanation does not in any way detract from the truth of the content, or the reality of the inspiration." [10]

JEREMIAH'S PERSONAL FELLOWSHIP WITH YAHWEH

Jeremiah's prophetic message centered in his prayer life. No
other prophet has so opened up the inner recesses of his soul
and disclosed his wrestling with God. In him, for the first time
in Israel, we have the revelation of the depths of religious devotion and communion with God. In the midst of the collection
of his oracles, we have a series of confessions in which the
prayers of the prophet are recorded. We find them in 11:18–23,
12:1–6, 15:10–20, 17:14–18, 18:18–23, 20:7–11. They disclose
the dialogue between himself and his God, the inner places of his
soul. Yet they serve more than to disclose the prophet's own
inner life. In thus laying bare the spiritual deeps of his communion, the prophet is opening a window by which we ourselves
may see God.

The exact period in Jeremiah's life to which these confessions
apply is a matter of debate. H. W. Robinson [11] and J. Skinner [12]
would place them in the early period of his ministry during the
reign of Josiah. They contend that they belong to the time when
the prophet was gaining inner assurance and a sense of divine

authority for his ministry. They argue that they came before Jeremiah became an active figure on the political scene. It is pointed out that the confessions refer not to public persecution, but to private scoffing, to attempts to inveigle him into treacherous talk. Such would take place when the prophet was sharing his message with a small intimate circle of friends rather than in a public ministry. The courage and self-possession with which the prophet exercised that public ministry in later years, confronting kings of Judah, religious and political leaders, seem hardly consonant with the hesitancy and inner agony found in the confessions. The confessions mark the stages by which Jeremiah arrived at the deep inner conviction, courageous spirit, and assured composure that showed in the days of his nation's agony.

Other scholars believe that the confessions refer to the days when, under Jehoiakim, Jeremiah was an object of public persecution as well as private scoffing and scorn. It is indeed true that some of the greatest and most courageous prophetic figures and religious leaders have, at the same time, had moments of inner agony of spirit and passed through moments of heart searching and questioning such as these confessions disclose. Gottwald cites Luther as an outstanding example.[13] Further, it might be contended that the pattern of frustration and suffering disclosed in these remarkable poems would demand the 'cross without' which the persecution of Jehoiakim's reign could provide.[14] The 'cross within' surely became a deeper experience as the 'cross without' became a significant accompaniment.

It would appear from the records that under Josiah the prophet was not subject to such public attacks as resulted later from his Temple sermon and as were manifested when he was put in the stocks. Outwardly courageous and unflinching, the sensitive spirit of the prophet reflected increasingly the cross which his message publicly laid upon him. Under his composure and boldness was a torment of soul which thrust him ever back on that communion with God which was the source of his strength.

The common word for prayer (tephillah) in Jeremiah's utterances may also be used of legal procedure. The latter usage is related to the defense of some party or to the giving of a verdict (1 Sam. 2:25; Isa. 16:3; Ezek. 16:52). These legal overtones have undoubtedly colored the religious usage. A man is pleading his case before the divine judge and putting forth his plea. It is in this sense that the psalmist demands of God that when his adversary is judged, he come forth quietly and that his prayer become sin (Ps. 109:7). The prophet likewise envisages himself as making his plea in the divine court and arguing his case before the divine tribunal. This is, of course, of one piece with his understanding of himself as a prophet. He claims to have stood in the heavenly council and to have been sent by Yahweh as his messenger. Hence when his message is rejected and he himself is persecuted, he must appear once more before Yahweh to plead his cause and justify his mission. Failure and frustration drive him back for that divine acquittal and confirmation which shall enable him to stand in the evil day.

Sheldon Blank [15] points out that Jeremiah's confessions fall into a fixed pattern: the address to Yahweh, the expression of confidence, a narrative in which the prophet defends his own conduct or disparages his adversaries, and a plea for Yahweh's forbearance and mercy and/or for his vengeance on the prophet's enemies. The form undoubtedly helped in the oral period of transmission, and it certainly enables us to differentiate these prayers and divine dialogues from the prophetic oracles.

One other important element in the oral transmission must, however, be noted, namely the poetic form of Jeremiah's utterances. He was essentially a poet. Indeed he was the lyrical poet *par excellence* of the Old Testament period. There seems little doubt that the *final* form of many of the Psalms owes much to the spreading influence of Jeremiah in and after the Exile. The prophet's favorite meter is the *qinah* or dirge, so called because it is often used in lamentations for the dead. Some of his most impressive lyrics are in this style, for example, the lament on Death the Reaper in 9:21, 22. Even where poetry gives place to prose or where the two are mingled (as in the call experience, 1:3 ff.), the prose retains a rhythmic quality. The rhythm of Jeremiah's soul, in tune with the harmonies of heaven, was reflected in his speech, and this was true of his prayers.

The confessions reveal both a poetical structure and a formal pattern through which the unseen and eternal God becomes visible as he acts in a man's soul. As H. W. Robinson has put it: ". . . to the prophetic consciousness there came some ray of light from the unseen, some ineffable, unanalyzable contact with Him who is Spirit, some communication not in human speech or human thought of new life, . . . necessarily translated, if they were ever to be understood by the prophet or his fellows, into the poetry or prose now before us." [16]

Let us look at Jeremiah pleading his case. It is true that prayer is sharing our life with God. God knows already, and the sharing is really a means to deeper communion, a lining up of our will with God's will, a putting of ourselves at God's disposal. Yet prayer is also a seeking for assurance, and this is why Jeremiah prayed. Outwardly the object of scoffing and obloquy, of persecution and scorn, this man took his case to the heavenly court. Of course Yahweh knew, but Jeremiah is now pleading his case with him. So the center of his confessions consists of a narration of his own condition and of the tactics of his adversaries. He is marshaling his facts, laying bare his motives, seeking for the vindication that God alone can give his servant.

This is one of the deepest aspects of prayer. Man stands before God craving acquittal, the divine word which vindicates his life and assures him of the divine presence. Blank points out [17] that the form and content of Jeremiah's prayers evoke the image of the law court. The prophet refers to God as the righteous judge (11:20), speaks of his adversaries as antagonists (18:19), and employs the legal word *mishpatim*, "cases for judgment" (12:1). So he can cry: "Righteous art Thou, O Yahweh, when I plead with thee: Yet would I bring *mishpatim* to thee."

The Book of Deuteronomy describes indeed the very legal form that Jeremiah's pleading takes (Deut. 19:16–19). We might almost picture the prophet as standing, in his imagination, before the divine council over which Yahweh presides, and arraigning those who, as false witnesses, bear their testimony against him. To God he has revealed his cause (20:12).

We find Jeremiah telling of his helplessness before the brutal situation that surrounds him (11:18, 19). He pleads his innocence. He has prayed for his enemies and defended them before Yahweh (18:20). He has been cut to the heart by the very message of woe that he has to proclaim (17:16). He has not offended against his adversaries and he has not offended against God. Indeed, because of his faithfulness to Yahweh and his Word, he was set apart in lonely isolation (15:17; 20:7–11). Yet this very loneliness drove him back upon God. As H. W. Robinson puts it: "His affectionate and sympathetic heart, his intensely human interests, his need for companionship, and the clinging instincts of self-distrust are all checked in their ordinary social satisfaction by the force of circumstances, which made him a lonely and misunderstood man—but with the result that the treasures of a loving heart were lavished upon God, to the permanent enrichment of the whole conception of religion." [18]

The center of these confessions is the struggle between the natural affections of the man and his commitment to his prophetic task.[19] On the one hand, we have a love for his people, an anguish of soul at their suffering. On the other hand, we have a sense of divine compulsion, an obligation to utter a word of judgment and destruction when all his natural inclination is in the other direction. He is full of the fury of Yahweh (6:11), and yet there is also an identification with the agony and suffering of Judah (14:19–21). The struggle is portrayed most of all in 20:7–18, where the prophet curses the day he was born and complains, in his anguish, at the divine pressure in his soul which he cannot withstand and which sends him out to deliver the Word.

In all this struggle the weakness of the man breaks through, for he curses his enemies and calls down the divine vengeance on his adversaries. He tells of their treachery and hypocrisy (18:18; 20:10), but that is not enough. They must be punished. One of the vexed issues in his moments of torment is the seeming prosperity of the wicked (12:1–3; 18:18–23), and so he arraigns them before the heavenly court, that God, the righteous judge, may act. We find little of that insight into God's heart which in the Song of the Servant (Isa. 53) transforms undeserved suffering into a means of redeeming the guilty. The Spirit of Calvary has not broken fully into Jeremiah's soul.

In the dialogue with God the divine assurance comes home to the prophet's heart. The prophet is torn by doubt and anxious fear. He even accuses God of being like a deceitful brook, like waters that fail. The figure is borrowed from the desert experience of a mirage (15:18). He has been deceived and misguided. Yahweh comes to his prophet in the deep places of the soul. All Jeremiah's confessions show him reasoning his case, and here God comes through, maybe in some reflective insight, maybe in some inner criticism, to confirm his servant. He accuses Jeremiah of self-pity and calls on him to examine his motives. He must repent as well as Israel (15:19). In the innermost struggle of his soul between his own thoughts and inclination and his vision of God's purpose, he must follow Yahweh whatever be the cost. Indeed, to his anxious query about the prosperity of the wicked, the divine movement in his soul is to challenge him to face yet harsher antagonism (12:5). He will be tempted by those nearest to him to betray his trust. But he must stand firm and bear his cross for God's sake (12:6). Here we touch the heights of personal devotion.

Jeremiah's communion with God made him a great intercessor. We have suggested that the prophet was also a specialist in intercessory prayer. This is manifest in the case of Jeremiah. His intense love for his people breaks through his imprecations against his enemies. He denounces Judah and proclaims the destruction of Jerusalem, but he does so with a breaking heart. He is hurt for the hurt of the daughter of his people, and cries for some balm in Gilead (8:18–23). He pours out a divine lament as he sees Israel scattered among the nations (9:16–21). His tears fall unceasingly as he sees the terrible slaughter that is imminent (14:17 ff.). These come as oracles, for here the sorrow of Jeremiah is also the *pathos* of God. His intimate fellowship with Yahweh discloses in God's heart the same love for this covenant people as that which burns in his own.

We are given little indication of what the content of his intercessions was. But, in his own confessions he reminds Yahweh that he has been forbidden to pray for Judah (14:11; cf. 7:16), and that he has stood before God to intercede for his people (18:20). He has pleaded their cause before the heavenly court. Zedekiah and the leaders beseech him to pray to Yahweh on their behalf as the Babylonian menace draws near (21:2). After the fall of Jerusalem, the faithful band around the slain Gedaliah ask that Jeremiah pray for guidance as to their future action

(42:1 ff.). Here we have a man who, because he was near to God himself, was able to draw others into the orbit of the divine compassion. Vengeance and retribution were not the sole elements in his make-up, and, as he looked into the heart of God, he saw there also grace and mercy.

JEREMIAH'S UNDERSTANDING OF GOD AS LORD OF HISTORY

Jeremiah's inaugural vision shows God as the Lord of history. He is the 'watcher' who moves to judgment in history and the cauldron of whose wrath is boiling over on Judah. The prophet early in his ministry associated this judgment with the Scythian menace from the north. As the years rolled on and the Babylonian power came to ascendancy, it was to this imperial power that he turned as the instrument of Yahweh's wrath. God had appointed Nebuchadrezzar as the agent of his judgment and had delivered the land of Judah into his hands (27:6). The prophet reflects in one oracle upon the past mercies of God to his people and their obdurate rejection of every approach through his prophets. Now the time had come and the cup of Yahweh's wrath was full (25:15). He would send Nebuchadrezzar as his servant against Judah and all the nations round about (25:9).

It is true that Nebuchadrezzar's power was temporary, for, as with Isaiah, so with Jeremiah he was but a rod in God's hand. But he was a powerful rod and the judgment would mean the destruction of Jerusalem and its Temple, the end of Judah as a nation, and the desolation of its land. Nebuchadrezzar would so serve God's purpose until his time too should come (27:7). Hence we have the symbolic act of the wooden yoke, the challenge of Hananiah, and the command to make an iron yoke that could not be broken (28). Judah would have to put its neck under the yoke of the king of Babylon (27:1–11).

Technically Jeremiah's oracles here bordered on treason, and yet, in the time of the siege, Zedekiah sought to protect him. His policy was not pacifism. It grew out of the conviction that God was the Lord of history and that history would move according to his purpose. In Yahweh's council the decree had gone forth. Judah's doom at the hand of Babylon was divinely decided, and all opposition would be vain. Jeremiah declared this to both Zedekiah and the Judean leaders, and to the latter this appeared open treachery, a weakening factor in the public morale (37:17–38:4). Yet the prophet defended himself on the ground that this was no deviation from his previous oracles. Indeed, from the moment of his inaugural vision he had declared violence and spoil in Yahweh's name, often against the tender inclinations of his heart (20:7–12).

The prophetic conviction of Yahweh's sovereign purpose is reflected in his call experience when he sees himself as a thought in God's mind before he is born. The same understanding of God's omniscient and omnipotent way is seen also in the oracle of the potter's house (18:1–10). Yahweh deals with Israel as the potter with his clay, dealing with it accordingly as it does or does not respond to him. So obdurate is Israel indeed that Jeremiah sees no alternative but its destruction. Hence we have the symbolic act of the shattered earthenware flask (19:1–13).

As Yahweh is Lord over Israel, so he is Lord of all nations. Jeremiah is called to be a prophet to the nations (1:5, 10). He is a prophet to Judah, but he cannot proclaim the divine Word to God's people without drawing in their neighbors. Judah's destiny is bound up with that of the surrounding nations. Alliances and political machinations relate them to God's purpose. Hence to them also the prophet is called to speak. Yahweh has delivered them into the hands of the king of Babylon and upon them also the judgment will fall (25:15; 27:6 ff.).

Bound up with Jeremiah's understanding of God's control over history is his faith in God the Creator. The One who made the earth and all things in it can dispose of the destinies of the people (27:5 ff.). God's creative power has formed a world in which there is order. He has decreed the statutes which shall be obeyed by all created things, including the heavenly bodies (cf. 33:25; 31:35). So the stork, the turtle, the swallow, and the crane have their appointed times (8:7). And just as God's ordinances hold at the level of nature, so they hold in the realm of human life. His ordinances are set for man's obedience. When Judah breaks his laws, it pays the price. Yet he will abide as sure as the foundations of the world he has made (10:12 ff.). Hence Jeremiah sees hope beyond judgment and grace beyond wrath. He who is Lord of history will not fail his people, just as his statutes for the heavenly bodies shall not fail (31:36).

God is not only righteous judge, however; he is love and grace. Jeremiah so shares in the *pathos* of God that he reflects the divine agony in his own sympathy for Israel. Just as Yahweh has been gracious of old time to the people in the wilderness, so he will abide gracious. He has loved Israel with an everlasting love and drawn it with steadfast convenant love, *ḥesedh* (3:12 ff.). The prophet therefore could call on Israel to repent and could declare that Yahweh was merciful (3:12). Was he not the covenant God and would he not remain loyal to his people? Beyond the judgment lay hope and restoration. He would not keep his anger forever. The agony of God at the waywardness of his people is reflected in an oracle in which Jeremiah asks: "Can a maid forget her ornaments, or a bride her attire? yet my people have forgotten me days without number (2:32, British RV).

The suffering that is wrung from the divine heart and that is shared by the prophet is expressed in the words:

Is Ephraim my dear son?
Is he a pleasant child?
For as often as I do speak against him
I do earnestly remember him still:
Therefore my bowels are troubled for him;
I will surely have mercy upon him, saith Yahweh (31:20).

One other figure of God which Jeremiah uses conveys the sense of divine graciousness. Yahweh is described as the fountain of living waters (2:13). He is the creative and invigorative center of his world. From him there flows the healing stream. Judah has forgotten this and turned to cisterns of its own construction. Its judgment is sure, and yet the very figure that Jeremiah uses here of Yahweh carries with it the basic thought of God's love and mercy.

The Inwardness of Israel's Sin and Individual Responsibility

Jeremiah's emphasis on God as judge was concomitant with his understanding of the gravity of Israel's sin. Israel was God's people and its rebellion was all the more grievous. It was related to him by his gracious covenant, his beloved which yet wrought evil in his house (11:15; 12:7). Jeremiah uses the image from the vineyard, describing Israel as a noble vine gone degenerate (2:21), and arraigning the shepherds who have destroyed God's vineyard (12:10). The first deportees of 597 B.C. can be described as Yahweh's flock (13:17), a figure which again recurs throughout the Old Testament witness and is gathered up in the consciousness of our Lord.

So the prophet recounts the mercy of God to his elected people in the wilderness and in Canaan, only to arraign them more bitterly because of their manifest rebellion (2:1–28). Yahweh has been faithful to them, but they have proved faithless to him. In the early days of the siege of Jerusalem in 597 B.C., the prophet praises the faithfulness of the Rechabites who refuse to drink the wine that he offers and contrasts this faithfulness with the faithlessness of Judah (35:1–19).

This faithlessness of Israel was manifest in the moral and social evils which the prophet condemns. Just as the city's cistern preserves fresh cool water, so Jerusalem preserves rapine and outrage in her midst (6:6, 7). The prophet attacks the injustice shown to the defenseless widow and orphan and the prosperity through ill-gotten gain (5:26–29). He protests against the reenslavement of those Hebrew bondmen who have been set free during the siege of Jerusalem in 588 B.C. (34:8 ff.). He does not show so manifestly the concern for social justice that is present in the message of his predecessors, but this is because he knows that social ills are but the outward sign of an inner malady. Two moral and social evils come in for special attack—lying and sexual looseness. The first with its attendant ills of slander and treachery is such that Yahweh cannot endure to look upon it (5: 1–3). The second is so widespread that prostitution, adultery, and lust abound (5:7 ff.). Both evils mar the relations of man with man and tear society apart.

Judah's rebellion was also evident at the deeper level of religion. In the earlier years of his ministry, Jeremiah attacked the apostasy which baalized Yahwism and turned it into a fertility cult, with all the accompanying sensuality (2:20, 26, 27). According to the number of its cities was the number of Judah's gods (2:28). With the Deuteronomic reform the situation changed, and yet the faithlessness of Judah remained. The baalistic elements and the foreign deities were largely eliminated, and the worship was centralized in the Jerusalem Temple, but a false faith was still very evident. Now, however, it was not directed on the baalim and pagan deities, it was directed on aspects of Yahwistic worship and ritual.

First and foremost here was the Temple superstition, a view which had its basis in the royal theology and which had been fostered by a materialistic misunderstanding of Isaiah's prophecy about the inviolability of Zion. There was a false dependence on the Temple rather than a true obedience to Yahweh. Zion's hill was the place of Yahweh's special abode, and it had been confirmed as such by the Deuteronomic reformation. This was the place which he was pleased to make his habitation and where he was pleased to cause his name to dwell (Deut. 12:5, 11). Yahweh's presence was in his Temple, and therefore the Temple was secure. It could not be shaken and hence Judah could not be destroyed. Bereft of all spiritual response and moral obligation on the part of Israel, this idea was thoroughly materialized. People trusted in the Temple rather than in the God of the Temple (7:4).

Jeremiah countered this false trust by pointing out in his famous Temple sermon (chaps. 7, 26) that the divine Presence was not bound to any location. He dwelt where he chose to put his Name. In the past he had tabernacled in Shiloh, but when Israel had profaned his sanctuary, he had moved his Presence elsewhere. The people had to learn that if the Temple were profaned, God could and would remove his Presence. The Temple and Judah could be destroyed. The Temple was God's house only so long as they made it so by the quality of their response to him in worship and moral behavior.

This must not be taken to mean that Jeremiah dismissed all thought of a tabernacling presence and that he taught a purely spiritual religion. It is true that he emphasized the omnipresence of Yahweh who filled heaven and earth with his presence (23:24).

Yet he was also aware of the need of an incarnational principle. He can praise God that he has set his throne on Zion's hill (17:12). He pleads on behalf of Israel that God will not withdraw his Presence from his sanctuary (14:9, 21). God does choose a place as the throne for his Glory, for his manifest Presence. God may be found wherever men seek him, and we can be grateful for this deep insight of the prophet. Even in the Exile men may seek and find him (29:13, 14). Yet, even when he has cast out his people and destroyed his vineyard, Yahweh still is specially present in Canaan. He does not leave his land, and he will bring his people back to it, while he will also visit with his wrath the surrounding nations who take advantage of the judgment on Judah (12:14).[20] When the day of restoration comes, the northern Israelites will also go up to Zion unto Yahweh (31:6).

Jeremiah also attacks a false confidence in the sacrificial system, so much so that he denies that these were commanded by God at the deliverance from Egypt (7:22). Again, it is difficult to believe that he is advocating a purely spiritual religion, however much we may be tempted to do so.[21] All religion needs external media by which the worshipful spirit may be expressed, and central in such media is the element of sacrifice. An alternative interpretation of the passage in question would be that God did not specifically require sacrifices of Israel, since these were part of the common stock of worship which they shared with all peoples. Rather, God was concerned with the inner attitude of the worshipers, and it is precisely here that Jeremiah places his emphasis (7:8–10). What God commanded was that Israel should walk in his way (7:23). This Judah showed no inclination to do, and so its ritual of worship was a vain and empty thing.

False confidence in circumcision comes in for attack. It is no good claiming circumcision as a basis for security, since this is of no avail when it has no inward accompaniment of faithfulness to Yahweh. Israel has to be circumcised in heart (9:25, 26). Finally they should find no security in the fact that they dwelled in Palestine, as if that land was God's and he would not let his people go (29:1–14). God could still keep Palestine and send them into exile, for the whole world was open to his presence (23:23, 24). In some sense, going into exile would be to go out of his sight (15:1, 2), yet even in exile he would be found of them (29: 11–14).

So we come to the inwardness of sin. Jeremiah moves down into the depths of the human heart. In so doing, Jeremiah is concerned with the individual rather than with the nation. His own experience of personal communion with Yahweh gave him an understanding of individual responsibility before God. The popular proverb "The fathers have eaten sour grapes and the children's teeth are set on edge" is denied by the prophet. Responsibility cannot be laid on the shoulders of the fathers. Every man shall die for his own iniquity. He who eats sour grapes shall set his own teeth on edge (31:29 ff.). It is true that this passage is in the prophet's vision of the future restoration, but this is a projection into future days of his own present conviction. Every man is a responsible individual, and sin must be traced down into the recesses of his heart, not back to his fathers.

In Hebrew psychology the heart was the seat of volition, and Jeremiah can ascribe Israel's condition to a stubbornness of heart. They have an evil and corrupt heart (7:24; 13:10; cf. 4:14). Israel has a rebellious heart (5:23). Its sin is graven on its heart (17:1). The heart indeed is deceitful and desperately sick (17:9). Thus the tragedy of man and of Israel, in particular, is a fatal stubbornness of heart, an obdurate will which is set against God, a heart that is filled with evil thought. So demonic is man's state that he is accustomed to evil and cannot do good. He can no more change the set of his heart than the Ethiopian can change his skin or the leopard its spots (13:23). Hence we have the symbolic act in which Jeremiah buries a loin cloth and digs it up soiled and useless. So it is with Judah (13:1–11). Even the people themselves seem aware of it, for they cry: "The harvest is past, the summer is ended, and we are not saved" (8:20, ASV).

The only hope for Israel is a change of heart, repentance. In the early years of his ministry, Jeremiah was hopeful that Israel would repent and called for it (3:12–14). The word for repentance, *shuv,* means an active turning of the will. The prophet can describe it as an act of inner circumcision (4:4), a washing of the heart from wickedness (4:14).[22] Even late in his ministry he could call for repentance (18:11), but increasingly he realized that this inner change of heart was something that Israel could not produce itself. If change there was to be, it must be the work of God, not of man. Furthermore, because it was an inward change, this work of God must be an individualizing process. Jeremiah was sure that the true barrier lay not in Yahweh's willingness to forgive but in the hardness of the human heart (4:22).

The Hope of a New Covenant and of a Restored Israel

Despite his present pessimism and his conviction of inevitable judgment, Jeremiah was still a man of hope. Yahweh had loved Israel with an everlasting love, and his steadfast covenant-love could not fail (31:3). He would rebuild Judah and restore both her and her northern sister Israel to a land once more prosperous (31:4–6).[23] The prophet saw Rachel weeping for her children and refusing to be comforted. He addressed to her an oracle of hope. God would bring again the captivity of Zion (31:15–23). Such a hope was expressed in the symbolic act of the purchase of the land in Anathoth (32). Houses, fields, and vineyards would again be bought in the land of Judah (32:15).

Yet let us note that Jeremiah does not promise immediate restoration. In his letter to the exiles of the first deportation, he warns his readers to settle down in the land and be prepared for a long stay (29:4–7). The real point is that they should remain faithful to Yahweh and seek him even in Babylon, for he is to be found even there. He is not so bound up with the Temple or Palestine that they shall not find him if they seek him with all their heart (29:12–14). The prophet declares that the exile will last for seventy years, even though Yahweh's thoughts to them are thoughts of peace. In the end, they will return (29:10, 11; cf. 25:11–12). Indeed, in his prophecy of the good and bad figs, Jeremiah sees that the future lies with the exiles. The choice of seventy years is most likely to have been Jeremiah's own, since it is different from the actual period of the exile and could not have resulted from a later reading back of the facts.

Clearly Jeremiah's eschatology has not taken the postexilic form. The restoration will be within history and have a historical setting in Palestine. The restored people will be ruled over by a messianic figure, a king of the Davidic line (23:5 ff.; 33:15–16).[24] This king can be described as the "righteous Branch." Because, in Hebrew thought, the king represents the people in his own person and because the people is an "extension" of his own personality, a righteous king means a righteous people and vice versa. The righteousness of the ideal future king is bound up with his personal relation to Yahweh. His name, which stands for him and participates in his nature, will be "Yahweh is our righteousness." Because God is with him, he will execute justice and his reign will be marked by prosperity. We note, however, that Jeremiah portrays a purely earthly king. There is none of the semidivine aura that is cast around Isaiah's Messiah one century earlier. Also we have no supernatural figure who comes forth to conquer the world, but a man of David's line who shall establish the kingdom, a man of piety and righteousness. By virtue of his relation to Yahweh, he becomes a medium of the divine presence and thus a center of security.

Yet Jeremiah does have an eschatology. This is no prophetic hope. He knows too much about the human heart to believe that man can repent of his own accord. He declares that Ephraim shall repent in the latter day (31:18, 19), and he calls on her to return (3:21, 22). But the reason will be a redemptive act of God himself in which the heart of the individual exile will be created anew and in which a new and individual covenant shall be cut (31:31–34).[25] This Yahweh, and Yahweh alone, can do. He will ransom Jacob (31:11). The nature of the new covenant is bound up with its individualistic and internal character (31:31–34). As ever, God initiates the covenant with his people, but this will be a new covenant. The old covenant was external and made with the nation as a whole. Jeremiah is careful to stress the national character of the new covenant, but it will be made with the individual Israelite. The latter's reshaping from within will constitute him a member of the new remnant. Thus the covenant will be with the house of Israel, but it will be individualized and internalized. It will be marked by inwardness.[26]

God will write his law, his *torah*, on their inward part, so that men will be internally motivated. They will fear and obey the Lord because this is the natural inclination of their hearts. No compulsive methods or external constraints will apply to this newly restored people, for they will act from a right heart within. Further, the new covenant will be an individual one. Each man shall know Yahweh for himself. Personal and individual religion will be at the heart of the new community. Finally, such fellowship with God shall be possible because the new covenant will bring forgiveness of sins.

How this re-creation of man from within was to be achieved by God, Jeremiah does not say. Despite his outward suffering and the accompanying inner agony of spirit which threw him back upon Yahweh, he had not learned as his successor did that suffering borne vicariously may be redemptive (Isa. 53). Instead he harbored at times the vengeful spirit, even though God's grace won and kept him a prophet of hope. It was left for history to show that the eschatological inbreak that would create a new covenant, reconcile man to God, and transform him from within, must be one in which God so identified himself with sinners as to suffer redemptively for man in the humanity of his Son. So our Lord applied to his own sacrifice the hope of Jeremiah: "This cup is the new covenant in my blood" (1 Cor. 11:25, ASV). The day has come when Jeremiah's inner fellowship with God is available for *all* men.

How far Jeremiah's hope was extended to *all* men is another question. His limited vision would seem to have confined the new covenant to Israel. Yet there are glimpses in his oracles of the higher and more universal vision. Indeed, it is implicit in his hope of a new covenant. It is true that the prophet declares the destruction of those who devour Israel (30:16). But he also speaks of the restoration of Israel's neighbors. Those evil nations which have touched Judah's inheritance will be plucked up like Judah, but Yahweh will restore them in the last day. The condition of such restoration will be the acknowledgement of Yahweh and the learning of the ways of his people (12:14-17). They will be built up among God's people, and in the midst Yahweh will dwell because he will be in their hearts.

NOTES

1. So James Phillip Hyatt, "The Book of Jeremiah: Introduction

and Exegesis," *Interpreter's Bible*, 12 vols. (Nashville: Abingdon Press, 1956), 5: 797 ff.

2. Herodotus, *Annals*, 103–107; iv, 1. The identification of the foe from the north with the Scythians is far more reasonable than any identification of it with the neo-Babylonians, if we accept the early date 626 B.C. for the call. There was as yet no sign on the political horizon of such a group arising within the Assyrian Empire to bring about a dynastic change. Prophecy is usually conditioned by current historical events or by possible future ones which can be discerned in the present situation. James Phillip Hyatt would identify the invading foe from the north with the Chaldeans and Medes who destroyed Nineveh in 612 B.C. in *Journal of Biblical Literature* 59 (1940):499–513. The volume by Adam C. Welch, *Jeremiah: His Time and His Work* (New York: Macmillan Co., 1951), pp. 97–131, sees in the vision of a foe from the north the beginning of the like ideas associated with postexilic prophetic eschatology: Ezekiel's Gog from Magog, Joel 2:20, and Daniel 11. This chapter contains an excellent analysis of the case for and against the Scythians.

3. John Skinner, *Prophecy and Religion* (Cambridge: University Press, 1930), p. 28.

4. Welch, *Jeremiah*, pp. 146–47, holds that Jeremiah did not support the Deuteronomic reformation. Hyatt, "The Book of Jeremiah," pp. 779–80, holds that no single passage among the genuine oracles of the prophet gives an indication that Jeremiah advocated Josiah's reforms. Johannes Lindblom, *Prophecy in Ancient Israel* (Oxford: Basil Blackwell, 1962), p. 359, holds that the references to "the words of the covenant" in chapter 11 apply to the Sinai covenant, not Deuteronomy.

5. The absence of many oracles that refer to the period 621–608 B.C. may well be due to the fact that there was no great event on the political horizon through which the prophetic consciousness of Jeremiah could be divinely stimulated. The word of the prophet always matched God's movement in history.

6. Lindblom, *Prophecy in Ancient Israel*, p. 359, writes: "Jeremiah's standpoint is this, the temple is in itself holy and Yahweh's house, but because of the wickedness of the people and the false use made of it by the people it will be destroyed."

7. John Bright, *A History of Israel* (Philadelphia: Westminster Press, 1959), p. 319.

8. The word is a covenant term applied to the relation between parties in covenant relation.

9. Skinner, *Prophecy and Religion*, p. 192.

10. H. Wheeler Robinson, *The Cross in the Old Testament* (Philadelphia: Westminster Press, 1955), p. 134.

11. Ibid., pp. 155 ff.

12. Skinner, *Prophecy and Religion*, pp. 208 ff.

13. Norman Gottwald, *A Light to the Nations* (New York: Harper & Bros., 1959), p. 360.

14. Cf. Sheldon Blank, *Jeremiah: Man and Prophet* (Cincinnati: Hebrew Union College Press, 1961), p. 117.

15. Ibid., pp. 112 ff.

16. Robinson, *Cross in the Old Testament*, p. 134.

17. Blank, *Jeremiah*, pp. 105, 119 ff.

18. Robinson, *Cross in the Old Testament.*

19. Cf. Skinner, *Prophecy and Religion,* p. 210.

20. Cf. W. J. Phythian-Adams, *The People and the Presence* (Oxford: University Press, 1942), pp. 64 ff.

21. Lindblom, *Prophecy in Ancient Israel,* pp. 358–59, points out that Jeremiah repeatedly shows a favorable attitude toward the cult. The prophet can hold that he who enters the Temple stands before Yahweh (7:10 ff., 30; 34:15). Jerusalem with the Temple can be described as Yahweh's throne (14:21; 7:12). The prophet is indignant at the desecration of the Temple (7:11). Hence Lindblom holds that we cannot argue that Jeremiah rejects all cultic practices. Hyatt, "The Book of Jeremiah," pp. 874–75; Skinner, *Prophecy and Religion,* p. 182; and Welch, *Jeremiah,* p. 143, interpret 7:22 as indicating that the sacrificial system played no essential part in true Yahwism. Welch says: "What such an announcement means is that the interests of true religion would be better served if the whole system should disappear . . . thus, the prophet repudiated the sacrificial system of his nation in principle" (p. 143).

22. Robinson, *Cross in the Old Testament,* p. 178, describes this as an "inner consecration of the will."

23. I have refused to regard this passage as a later addition.

24. Many critics dismiss 33:15–16 as secondary, but there seems no satisfactory reason for this dismissal on objective grounds. So much seems to turn on whether or not the critic concerned believes that the preexilic canonical prophets held messianic ideas.

25. Cf. Bright, *History of Israel,* p. 319: "The awful chasm between the demands of Yahweh's covenant, by which the nation had been judged, and his sure promises, which faith could not surrender, was bridged from the side of the divine grace."

26. I follow the analysis of Skinner, *Prophecy and Religion,* p. 329.

Chapter Six

The Divine Presence
and the
Re-creating Spirit

The prophet Ezekiel was both prophet and priest, and his prophetic
writings bring us back to the Temple and its cultus. The book
of the prophet was regarded as a literary unity until quite recent
times when it has been called in question from many directions.
No one would dispute that, as we have it, the book is a unity,
but the suggestion is made that it comes to us through editorial
hands which have welded together disparate elements and created
out of them the prophetic figure of Ezekiel. It is argued that the
theme of judgment in the early chapters contrasts oddly with the
hope of restoration in the closing ones, that the apocalyptic section of chapters 38 and 39 is out of place with the main body
of thought, that the prophecies to Jerusalem could hardly have
been made from Babylon, that the suggestion of a trance state in
which the prophet was transported in vision from the Babylonian
Exile to the condemned city was a literary device, that the mingling of a priestly emphasis with a prophetic message implies
multiple authorship, and that the chronology which is so plenti-
fully sprinkled through the book is artificial.

The more sober of such critics suggest that Ezekiel exercised
his ministry in two parts, the first in Jerusalem and the second
in Babylon. Thereby they are endeavoring to remove the difficulty
of the trance state just referred to.[1] Others suggest that his
authentic oracles were uttered in Jerusalem where he remained
until the final exilic deportation of 586 B.C., that his oracles were
later edited, adapted to exilic conditions, and augmented by the
addition of the last chapters.[2] More extreme critics transfer his
ministry to the preceding century in the reign of Manasseh and
even associate him with the exiles of northern Israel.[3]

The wide disparity between the various theories offered and the

121

mysterious lack of unanimity should warn against acceptance of any single theory. I prefer to support the traditional unity theory of the book. As Skinner points out, the whole book carries "the stamp of a single mind." It presents us with the picture of a remarkable personality who combined in his own person prophetic, priestly, and even apocalyptic elements. Rather than speculating about hypothetical authors, it would seem better to assume that behind the book we have such a personality as it portrays, a man who, while he had ecstatic traits, could also be rational and statesmanlike in his planning, a man who could be a prophet and yet show a concern for cultic and priestly matters. It is true, of course, that scholars will vary in their response to some of the evident difficulties, but there would seem no need to exaggerate them into the basis for some critical theory which the text as a whole does not warrant.[4]

We have still, however, the problem of how the book came to be compiled. It is such a literary unity, at first sight, that it would seem to be different from the edited collections of oracles which we find in the other prophetic books. Yet this is only a superficial judgment. It would seem that Ezekiel actually committed some of his oracles to writing for there is a literary style about them.[5] This would account for oracles against Jerusalem in chapters 8–11, which may have been sent there from Babylon in literary form. It would also account in part for the preponderance of prose rather than poetry in this book, although, as we shall see later, Ezekiel apparently uttered his oracles in poetic form and was capable of true originality at this level. The best solution appears to be that the oracles of Ezekiel were in part transmitted from the prophet in literary form and in part remembered by his circle and committed often to parchment in condensed or even expanded prose. As the book took shape it was subject to a considerable process of editing which, occurring much longer after the prophet's death than in the case of other prophets, gave the opportunity of imposing a more homogeneous structure on the whole. This superficial unity does not, however, hide to the practiced eye the complicated processes of oral and literary transmission, of collection and redaction to which the material has been subjected. That the book appears to have been written by the prophet himself may be due to the fact that considerable autobiographical material was available in literary form. The collector sought to perpetuate this by the formal style he adopted, for in truth the traditions do present to us the living figure of the prophet himself.

The Historical Background of Ezekiel's Ministry and the Course of His Life

Ezekiel grew up in Jerusalem during the generation when Jeremiah was the great religious figure. He lived through the period of political unrest and religious tension which preceded the exile. According to the record (Ezek. 1:2), he began his ministry in Babylon in the fifth year of the captivity of King Jehoiachin. The young king, his family, and the leaders of the Judean state were deported into exile in the year 597 B.C. This first deportation left Jerusalem and Judah sadly bereft of leadership. It had been preceded by the reigns of Jehoahaz and Jehoiakim when the Jewish state had dallied with Egypt and ignored the warnings of Jeremiah.

Many of the teachings of Jeremiah were in the religious atmosphere that Ezekiel breathed, and it is evident that they left their mark upon his personality. Indeed, the two prophets were contemporaries during the closing years of Judah's existence as an independent kingdom, and there is sufficient evidence of correspondence between the survivors in Judah and the first deportees in Babylon for us to understand that Jeremiah's teaching was not unknown in Ezekiel's environment. We can believe that the prophet in exile was not unfamiliar with the letters which Jeremiah wrote to the deportees (Jer. 29:1–32), and thus that the quietism of the Judaean prophet and his individualism affected Ezekiel.

Yet there is a contrast between the two men. Jeremiah wears his heart upon his sleeve. He is frank and even daring in his self-disclosure. His inner experience is portrayed unashamedly in his confessions. Ezekiel, on the other hand, is a man of studied reserve, who lets little of himself peep through his messages. We never really penetrate into the inner deeps of the man's spirit. Jeremiah is warm-hearted and sympathetic. He shares in the agony of the people to whom he declares his oracles of judgment. If he stands apart and is isolated from them, it is because of the Word of Yahweh shut up within his heart. Often he struggles against declaring his oracles because of his feeling for his people, and his messages are born out of the agony of his own spirit, an agony which he knows that he shares with his God. For Yahweh, too, agonized with his people, even while he gave them up to judgment. We have little or none of this in Ezekiel. He stands apart from his hearers, whether they be deportees in Babylon or survivors in Jerusalem. He is stern in his denunciation and shows little compassion in his declaration of judgment. Human affections are suppressed, even to the point of refusing to mourn over his wife's death and using such a refusal as a prophetic sign. His is an iron strength which will allow no emotional element or human weakness to turn him from the declaration of God's purpose.

In literary style Jeremiah was a poet whose prophetic oracles have the poetic quality of the psalms. Ezekiel used much more of a prose style than his contemporary, although poetry comes breaking through. Some critics deny that such poetic elements are original, but there is often an originality in the imaginative use of figures and in the quality of his poetic oracles that belies this judgment. One example is the lament over Tyre in chapter 27.

Both men had contacts with the priesthood. Jeremiah came of the priestly family of Anathoth, and we have seen that despite his attack on a false trust in the Temple and the misuse of the sacrificial system, he still was concerned with the worship of Yahweh. Ezekiel was a prophet with a real concern for the priestly office, and the last part of his ministry was concerned with the restoration of the Temple and its priesthood and with the new ordering of the priestly ritual. Jeremiah had rejected the old but not denied the necessity of such an approach to God. Ezekiel portrayed the new approach to the divine presence. While Jeremiah turned away from the old Temple because of its misuse, Ezekiel saw a more glorious Temple in which a chastened people would glorify God. The Deuteronomic Reformation had placed a new emphasis on the old Temple, and offered a religion which was obedience to the written commandments of God. Jeremiah had rejected the materialistic interpretation of the Deuteronomic concern with the Temple and had spoken of an inner and spiritual law written on man's heart. Ezekiel's call is indicative of the combination of the two. He eats the roll with its written message, *torah,* from God. In his ministry there is the spiritual interest of Jeremiah together with the material manifestation for which Deuteronomy stands.

We shall assume that the datings given in the prophecy are essentially correct, even though they may raise a problem here and there. Ezekiel was deported with the young King Jehoiachin and the Judaean leaders in 597 B.C. It is quite clear that both he and Jeremiah believed that the future lay with this group. They both spoke scornfully of those who were left in Jerusalem. The deportees do not appear to have had too hard a lot. Ezekiel's prophecy discloses much about their life, as do Jeremiah's letters to them (Jer. 29:1–3). They governed themselves and owned their own homes. Jeremiah's letter reveals that they retained the same rights of property and the same family life as in Jerusalem (Jer. 29:4–7). Ezekiel owned his own home (Ezek. 12:1 ff.), and to this home the elders came freely. Evidently the exiled community retained something of the same social system and governmental order as in Palestine and had their elders to represent them. In this environment Ezekiel received his call.

The record tells us that it came to him in the fifth year of the captivity, 592 B.C. The fact that two dates are mentioned and that 1:1 speaks indefinitely of a thirtieth year has led some critics to suggest that Ezekiel received two calls, one in Palestine and one in Babylon, and that the two have been combined into the complex experience recorded in the first three chapters of the prophecy. I prefer to accept the inaugural vision as recorded and interpret the thirtieth year as possibly a reference to the prophet's own age, and thus as coming from some autobiographic form of tradition. Other suggestions are that the thirtieth year is a reference to Ezekiel's completion of the written edition of his oracles. "Thirtieth year" would then mean thirty years after the call, or 562 B.C. It is, however, difficult to believe that this could be the case, since, as we have seen, it is very doubtful whether the book, with all its actual complexity of structure, could have been the original work of the prophet.

The dual dating is an indication that the book has undergone some complex editing before attaining the form which we now have. Probably the editor was a disciple, and he has evidently preserved the remarkable personality of his master. His hand would, however, account for the way in which doublets of speeches and events have been clumsily introduced into the material, and the way in which dated oracles have become focal points for others which do not appear to have been delivered at the same time.

The historical setting for Ezekiel's vision was undoubtedly a new surge of political unrest. There was a new Egyptian king in 594 B.C., and the Syrian states hoped by his aid for release from Babylon. Jeremiah witnesses to this in Jerusalem, and we learn from him that two exiles were burned in Babylon for attempts at insurrection (Jer. 29:21 ff.). Such a man wrote a letter to Jerusalem attacking Jeremiah's religious quietism (Jer. 29:24–32).

The natural occasion for the prophet's call was an impressive thunderstorm over the Mesopotamian plain. The thundercloud was driven by the wind with the lightning flashing around it. For the prophet this was transformed into Yahweh's chariot, attended by winged living creatures of serpentine form. The involved description of the chariot, its wheels, and its winged attendants, reveals the magnificence of Yahweh who sits enthroned upon it. The theophany is described in elaborate, even grandiose, terms, but we should not allow this to obscure the genuine religious encounter which underlies it. The prophet felt the presence of a holy God and knew his own creatureliness. Indeed the complex figures and symbolisms involved in this description of God's traveling throne convey a sense of his effortless mobility and omnipresence. Here in symbolic terms we have a portrayal of the swiftness of the divine activity. There is also the impression of the divine power. It is a majestic king of swift-moving presence and effortless power who appears to Ezekiel seated on his throne, and even the regal chariot and its attendants are portrayed in terms redolent of the glory they bear and attend.

The vision of God himself, pictured with his burning splendor in human form, brings home to the prophet a sense of the divine otherness and holiness. God is other than man and even the human form is presented in such resplendent glory that it con-

veys the sense of distance between God and man. Before this
vision the prophet falls prostrate as a frail 'son of man', a mortal
who cannot stand in the divine presence. It is the transcendence
of God that is central in the prophet's call, his majestic holiness.
He is King, but there is a holiness and remoteness about his
presence that sets him apart from the mortal men whose history
he controls.

The mortal and frail son of man stands on his feet at the
divine word, and eats, at the divine command, the roll of prophecies
which he is to utter. Like Isaiah 150 years earlier, he is warned
that his words will not receive a hearing, but this must not
prevent their delivery (2:5; 3:4–11). Israel will know that there
has been a prophet in their midst, for God's Word through his
prophets has an objective reality. Once uttered into a situation,
it will re-create that situation and set in motion those divine
forces that will bring about its fulfillment. Apparently the prophet
then fell into a trance state for seven days (3:15).

The editorial hand has not always preserved Ezekiel's datings
in an orderly way. Actually the order is broken in the prophecies
to foreign nations where often the oracles are grouped around
specific peoples. Thus two oracles against Pharaoh, dated in 586
B.C. (30:20; 31:1), occur after the prophecy of Nebuchadrezzar's
conquest of Egypt, dated in 570 B.C. (29:17). We have to remember too that recorded dates only apply to the oracle or event
to which they are immediately attached.

The main outlines of Ezekiel's background and life come clear,
however. One year after his call, the prophet was transferred in a
trance state to Jerusalem, and there was granted to him a clairvoyant vision of affairs in Jerusalem. It is true that such a visionary experience does not appear to have occurred again, but we are
dealing here with a complex personality, and such an experience
is by no means beyond the bounds of possibility. Some scholars
find the idea of trancelike clairvoyance so difficult that they prefer
to speak of a separate ministry in Jerusalem. But Ezekiel had
lived in Jerusalem, and there was sufficient communication between
the city and the exiles for him to be appraised of the current
state of affairs. Thus all the material would be present upon
which his highly charged imagination could feed and produce the
background for his clairvoyant state.

It is significant that Ezekiel does not speak as one living in
Palestine. In 12:10–16, Ezekiel addresses the oracle to the Jerusalem survivors, but evidently does so from exile. Hence he addresses
the Judaean community as *them* not *you*, for he is speaking
in Babylon. His immediate hearers are the deportees, and he can
offer his prophecy to them as *your sign* (v. 11). Yahweh will do
to *them* (in Jerusalem) what he has done to *you* (in Babylon).
Again, in 11:14–17, we have a passage in which the prophet
is evidently telling the exiles what the Jerusalem survivors say

about them, and what Yahweh will do for them and others still to be deported. The oscillation between *them* of Jerusalem and *you* in Babylon indicates that the prophetic oracles are being given in exile. The change of subjects in verse 16 arises from the oracle being addressed to the Jerusalem survivors. It is difficult to believe that Ezekiel's prophecies could have been so discerningly rewritten to convey the impression of presence in Babylon when actually he was in Jerusalem.

If it be argued that his message would not be meaningful unless it was delivered to those to whom it was directed, we have to remember that there was a greater sense of corporate oneness among the Hebrews than we possess. A word uttered to a group within the whole people would be effective for the whole. Actually Ezekiel's ministry seems to have been more private than public, although there were occasions when he addressed the public at large. The elders came to his house to consult him, and to them he seems to have uttered his innermost thoughts as Yahweh laid them on him. But in uttering these oracles to them, he was uttering them to the Israel whom they represented. He may even have sent them to Jerusalem in literary form.

We have glimpses of Ezekiel's private life, but these are mainly related to his public ministry. He had a home and was ordered, in one symbolic act, to break down its wall (12:1 ff.). He was married, but even the death of his wife becomes for this stern, proud man, not an occasion for outward grief, but rather a sign to be associated with his prophetic utterance (24:15 ff.).

The siege and fall of Jerusalem seem to mark the changing point in Ezekiel's ministry. He who has been a prophet of judgment and destruction to Judah now becomes a prophet of hope and restoration to the exiles. The fiery denunciations give place to pastoral comfort.

This change of emphasis is seen in the structure of the book itself. The first twenty-four chapters belong to the earlier period of ministry and are mainly directed to those remaining in Jerusalem under Zedekiah as king. These oracles are unsparing in their condemnation of the apostasy and idolatry of these people and declare, in no uncertain terms, their judgment and the destruction of their city. Chapter 24, verse 1, is dated in 588 B.C., and the following sign and oracle evidently relate to the beginning of the siege of Jerusalem.

In chapters 25–32 we have a series of foreign oracles, those dated belonging mostly to the period of the siege and directed against nations which, in various ways, helped in or rejoiced over the downfall of Judah: Moab, Ammon, Edom, Philistia, Tyre, Sidon, and above all, Egypt. One oracle in this section is dated late 570 B.C., and represents the latest recorded moment in the prophet's ministry.

In chapter 33, dated in 585 B.C., we learn of the fall of Jerusalem, and the note changes in chapters 34–48 to one of hope. Visions of a new Israel are brought to a climax in the closing nine chapters with their elaborate description of the ordering of the restored community. We may assume that this change of message is no literary device. In his understanding of God's covenant relation to Israel, Ezekiel stood, like Jeremiah, in the exodus tradition. The moral reprobation of Judah must inevitably mean judgment. Yet the promise was also certain. Furthermore, as a priest, enough of the Jerusalem theology was in Ezekiel's make-up for him to be sure that any future hope must be bound up with Yahweh's presence among his people on Zion's hill. This thought comes uppermost as he becomes a prophet of hope. Yet for him, as for Jeremiah, this must come only after judgment had supervened, and it could come only when, by a divine act, Yahweh had made Israel into an obedient people.

The wilderness tradition and the royal theology thus both contribute to the prophet's theology. Ezekiel rejects the popular hope with its ignoring of Yahweh's moral claim, but he grounds his hope in the belief that Yahweh will find a way to restore his people at the moral level and tabernacle once more on Zion's hill. At the time when he is prophet of judgment, he rejects the popular shallow hope. He likens the prophets who declare it to those who daub a bulging wall with whitewash and say it will not fall (13:1–16). But he comes back with a stronger hope grounded in the moral foundations on which the judgment rests.

THE PERSONALITY OF EZEKIEL AND HIS PROPHETIC CONSCIOUSNESS

As we have already indicated, in the case of Ezekiel we are concerned with a complex prophetic figure, as stern and proud as the Yahweh whom he served and presented to his people. He was a man subject to unusual psychological and physiological traits. From the physiological side, he appears to have been a cataleptic, liable to trance states in which he was dumb and "astonied" for long periods of time. Lapses into aphasia are evident, and he was a man who, as we have suggested, was the subject of visionary experience, even apparently possessing some clairvoyant gift. Despite the view of some critics, he had poetic gifts and a great measure of imagination. His oracles are full of moving imagery and involve some impressive parables.

We find accompanying this sensitive and imaginative aspect of his personality an abnormal concern with prophetic symbolism. Whereas the other great prophets took occasion at times to act out their message, with Ezekiel the occasional becomes the normal. Hence we find him miming the siege of Jerusalem with a brick (4), shaving his head and disposing of his hair to portray the fate of the inhabitants of Judah (5), breaking down a wall of his home and carrying out his furniture to declare the imminent deportation (12:1–13), putting together two sticks to prophesy the reunion of the southern and northern kingdoms (37:15 ff.), marking out two roads and setting up signposts to indicate that the king of Babylon was at the parting of the ways and would be directed by divination against Jerusalem (21:18–23), manipulating a sword to symbolize the divine fury (21:8–17), and refusing to mourn at his wife's death as a sign of what would happen in Jerusalem when Yahweh profaned his sanctuary and wrought his judgment in the city (24:16–27).

The imaginative insight and creative aspect of the prophet's consciousness is evident in the large number of allegories that he employs. A worthless vine, no good for timber for fuel (15), and a faithless wife, giving favors to pagan gods (16:1–43), provide the basic figures for two attacks on the people of Judah. The prophet can portray Judah as a lioness whose whelps, representing Jehoahaz and Jehoiachin, have been carried off respectively to Egypt and Babylon. The judgment of Judah is also presented in the parable of a boiling cauldron in which the choice ones of the flock will be consumed (24:1–4). Again, the familiar vineyard figure supplies the basis for the description of Judah as initially a fruitful vine in a fertile vineyard but now plucked up, her strong rods burned, and planted in the wilderness where she puts forth "no strong rod to be a sceptre to rule" (19:10–14). The fates of the northern kingdom of Israel and the southern kingdom of Judah are pictured in a vivid story of Yahweh's two wives, Oholah and Oholibah, with their harlotry and destruction at the hands of their lovers (23). Finally, we have the allegory of an eagle which takes away the top of the cedar of Lebanon and plants a seed of the land which grows as a vine and yet shall perish (17:1–21). This is interpreted as the king of Babylon taking away Jehoiachin and replacing him by Zedekiah who shall come to nought.

The prophet also employs vivid imagery in his foreign oracles. In his attacks on Tyre, Ezekiel pictures that state as a stately ship bent on commercial adventure and success which will be sunk at sea. He can employ a version of the Paradise story of Genesis 3 to present the king of Tyre in the dress of the first man in Eden. He has been so successful in the greatness of his trade and so arrogant in it that, like Adam, he must be cast out of his paradise (28:11–19). Egypt comes in for its share of figurative representation. It is like an exalted cedar of Lebanon which will be toppled to its doom (31), and the familiar image of the chaos dragon which is defeated by God is also employed (29:1–15; 32:1–9).

This man with so many facets to his complex personality had a lonely path to pursue. As proud and stern as the God in whose name he spoke, he shut himself off from his fellows in the early years of his ministry. Isolated by his message of sure judgment for Jerusalem, unheeded or mocked at by his contemporaries, he was largely driven in upon himself and a comparatively small circle of friends. Other prophets were capturing attention by a more favorable message, and Ezekiel can liken them to white-wash. The prophet escaped physical suffering, but he suffered in spirit from the utter incredulity and indifference of those around him. They could cry, "The vision that he seeth is for many days to come" (Ezek. 12:27). We can imagine that the news of the fall of Jerusalem (33:22) brought a change in circumstances and brought uppermost the pastor and the priest in his involved make-up.

Ezekiel's loneliness and isolation were only made worse by his bodily condition if he was, as seems indicated, a cataleptic. His physical torpor, his temporary spells of aphasia, and his abnormal auditions yet became media for his experience of God. We ought not to allow this to detract from the significance and authority of the prophet's message. The intermittent pathological conditions were traced by the prophet directly to the divine intervention. In the typical Hebrew way of thinking, he had no place for secondary causes even if they be physiological. All things leaned directly back upon the activity of God, and the vertical dimension of ontological cause was more significant than the horizontal plane of creaturely causation. Hence his physiological and psychological states were for him media whereby Yahweh himself drew near and whereby the prophet could derive his message and his resources from his God. It may well be indeed that these media became the major way in which the prophet was brought into contact with God. H. W. Robinson has reminded us that we must use the power of faith to interpret affliction and transform it into a means of grace.

Ezekiel has his characteristic vocabulary to describe this activity of God in his consciousness. He was essentially a prophet of the Spirit. His predecessors had preferred to use the category 'the Word of Yahweh' in describing their prophetic inspiration. He returned to the idea of the Spirit which had earlier been associated with the prophetic consciousness. For him the divine activity in his life is best expressed as the activity of the Spirit. Although the word for Spirit, *ruach*, does retain some of its original physical associations, it is now associated with spiritual activity. In the vision of the valley of dry bones it is a windlike Spirit which blows through the valley, but it re-creates the army of dead men and is thus presented as a spiritual force.

The old charismatic associations persist when Ezekiel smites with his hand, stamps with his foot, and manifests excessive physical energy (6:11; 21:14 ff.). The quasi-physical idea of energy still lingers in the description of spirit as the directive energy of the moving throne bearing the divine Presence (1:12, 20, 21; 10:16 ff.). The prophet has not yet arrived at the understanding of the Spirit as a personal and spiritual presence.

The Spirit is, however, associated more with the more spiritual aspects of Ezekiel's task. The Spirit mediates his visions. Thus the Spirit sets him above the valley of dry bones (37:1), transfers him in trance state to Jerusalem that he may better exercise his ministry of judgment (8:3), brings him back again (11:24), and transports him to the inner court in his vision of the restored Temple (43:3). Further, the Spirit sets him on his feet so that he, the frail son of man, may commune with God (2:2) and falls upon him so that, under its compulsion, he denounces idolators (11:5).

An indication that a more spiritual and personal understanding of Spirit is present is to be seen in the fact that the word *Spirit* can also be used to describe a permanent aspect of human personality. Now it becomes akin to heart and soul, and thus already we have that postexilic usage which can ascribe the higher spiritual, rational, and volitional aspects of man to the human spirit. Ezekiel undoubtedly marks the transition from the idea of Spirit as a windlike invasive divine power of quasi-physical nature to a more personal understanding of it. In this personal understanding, Spirit is retained to describe a personal spiritual power from Yahweh. But the word also describes the upper aspects of human personality, that aspect of man where there is real encounter with God.

Hence Ezekiel can look forward in vision to the day when Yahweh will give men a heart of flesh and put a new spirit in them (11:19; 18:31, 36:26). Significantly this divine re-creating activity in the human spirit is associated with the divine Spirit: "I will put *my* spirit in you" (36:27). Here the Spirit of Yahweh becomes a personal re-creative presence through which man himself receives a new spirit. So God will pour out his Spirit on the house of Israel (39:29).

One other phrase is used by Ezekiel to describe his extraordinary experiences—"the hand of Yahweh." The phrase is significantly used whenever some abnormal experience attends the prophet, and evidently signifies that he has passed under the divine control. In his inaugural vision, the hand of Yahweh is upon him as he sees the divine Presence on the storm chariot, and it comes upon him again at the close of the vision (1:3; 3:22). Ezekiel's transition in trance state to Jerusalem is initiated when the hand of Yahweh is laid on him (8:1), and it comes again when the city falls to the Babylonians (33:22). It is the hand of Yahweh which, with the Spirit of Yahweh, makes possible the vision of the valley of dry bones (37:1) and which also initiates the vision of the restored community (40:1). In a way the phrase is synonymous with the Spirit in activity. It is associated especially with visions and in one case with a period of dumbness (33:22). It thus seems particularly applicable to the abnormal elements in the psychical and physiological make-up of the prophet.

Clearly Ezekiel, like his predecessors, believed himself to have stood in the counsels of Yahweh. The Spirit stood him upon his feet that Yahweh might address him. In his visionary experience the Word that he was to deliver was received by him objectively from God as a roll which he had to devour. The hand of Yahweh was laid upon him that he might see visions and receive auditions that God would not grant to other men. The prophet manifests a developed form of the prophetic consciousness. His message carries signs that prophetic testimony was reaching the peak of its disclosure of the divine order. Already in it we find signs of that new emphasis which later was to develop into apocalypticism and to free itself from the moral vision and historical framework of its prophetic forebears. To the prophetic message we must now turn our attention.

THE DIVINE HONOR AND ITS VINDICATION

It is a transcendent holy God who confronts us in the testimony of Ezekiel. There is an overwhelming sense of the majestic greatness of Yahweh. The weak and mortal son of man falls on his face before this holy everlasting God. Because God is so exalted, he has a concern for his honor. Again and again, the prophet uses the phrase, "(You) (They) shall know that I am Yahweh" (6:7, 13, 14, and others.).

Perhaps in no oracle more than that in 20:1–44 do we find this persistent refrain. In a detailed discussion of the vicissitudes of Israel's history, its experiences of Yahweh in judgment and in mercy, the prophetic testimony points continually to the disclosure of the divine name. God acts always for his name's sake. The aim of his judgment is to establish the knowledge that he is Yahweh. Israel profaned his name among the nations, and so, again and again, he shut them up in his wrath and laid his hand upon them. So God has scattered and will scatter them among the nations for his name's sake. But this is not the sum total of his purpose. He will purge them of their rebels and gather them together out of their dispersion, that they may know that he is Yahweh. His last act for his name's sake will be one of grace beyond their deserving. "And ye shall know that I am Yahweh, when I have wrought with you for my name's sake, not according to your evil ways, nor according to your corrupt doings, O ye house of Israel" (20:44). God shows a zeal for his own honor lest his name should be profaned in the drama of history. He is concerned to vindicate his honor and his name.

This might seem to imply that Ezekiel's God is a supreme egoist, and yet this would be to misunderstand the phrase "for my name's sake." We might argue that for a man to act on behalf of God in order to vindicate the divine honor would be a noble motive, but that the idea is less attractive when it becomes the motive of God himself. We have, however, to grasp the true significance of the word for *name* in Hebrew thought. The name is a revelation of the inner being of a thing, its true essence. For a man to give his name to someone is for him to disclose himself. Thus a name is a disclosure of the true nature of that to which it belongs. When God gives his name, he is revealing himself. His name is Yahweh. For Israel to know that he is Yahweh means for Israel to know him as he really is. When God acts for his name's sake, he acts that the integrity of his being may be preserved. A God who did not vindicate himself in the arena of history which he had created and sustains would be no God at all. The real issue is what is the true content of his name. If the name Yahweh is God's inner personal being disclosed to Israel, then when he is acting for his name's sake, he is acting in a way consonant with and revelatory of his true being. The name of God is God in action, God disclosing himself, and he will act in history in a way befitting his nature as Yahweh. Cries Isaiah: "Behold, the name of Yahweh cometh from afar, burning with his anger, and in thick rising smoke: his lips are full of indignation, and his tongue is a devouring fire . . ." (30:27).

We have to remember that Israel, as God's people, also bore his name. In Hebrew thought this implied that, in some sense, Yahweh's being and nature were extended over them. Now if the Israelites behaved in a way that belied the divine name, they were putting Yahweh to an open shame among the nations. Equally, if other nations offended Israel, their offence was also directed against Yahweh. Both these attitudes lie deep in the thinking of Ezekiel and should help us better to understand his testimony to the divine honor and his analysis of the divine motivation.

Another expression that Ezekiel uses of God's activity in history is his jealousy or envy. At the human level the Hebrew word (*gin'ah*) can express an ignoble human passion, but it can also describe zeal and have around it an aura of nobility. God's jealousy then becomes his zeal to express his innermost being and to accomplish his purpose which is consonant with his nature. It is in this sense that the word is used by Isaiah in 9:7, 59:17, and 63:15, and it would appear to be basic in the thought of Ezekiel. God is righteous and holy. He cannot live with iniquity, and his jealousy for his name is his zeal to fulfill his righteous will in judgment and in mercy. Hence he will show his anger both against Israel (23:25) and against her neighbors who rejoice at her fall (36:5, 6). H. W. Robinson describes the divine jealousy as "the proper indignation of a righteous God against all unrighteousness." [6]

The emphasis on God's honor is thus an appeal to his innermost nature, and its true significance turns upon how that innermost nature is understood. What we regard as essential to God's honor gives meaning to our interpretation of a phrase like "for my name's sake." It is here, perhaps, that Ezekiel tends to fall short. God's honor should be vindicated in the arena of history, but what is essential in his honor? What is the content of his name? In his discussion of God's judgment upon the foreign nations, Ezekiel shows a different emphasis from Amos. The latter arraigns each nation before the divine tribunal at the level of moral righteousness. They are judged for their own moral evils and not for their relations to Israel. Ezekiel, on the other hand, places the judgment on a different basis. In ill-treating Israel, the foreign nations had cast dishonor on Yahweh. Their relation to God's people was the ground of their condemnation. There would seem to be here a less exalted understanding of the divine judgment. Yet we have to remember that God is righteous and that judgment in Amos's sense vindicates his name as the righteous God. Further, in giving Israel his name God was in some sense bringing the nation within the orbit of his being, so that offense against it could call in question his own righteousness.

The deeper moral implications in Ezekiel's message become clear when we note that Israel too is under judgment. Israel also has offended the divine honor, rebelled against God's manifest nature. They have not known his name, and therefore his name must be vindicated among them. Jerusalem is guilty as well as other nations, and the Temple is contaminated by evil worship. In his condemnation of sin and his declaration of judgment, Ezekiel shows that Yahweh's name is essentially moral righteousness. When he defends his honor and acts for his name's sake, he does so because righteousness cannot live with moral evil and sinful rebellion.

Nor is this righteousness the whole content of the divine name. Grace as well as wrath springs from his name. When Israel went into captivity, Yahweh's honor was satisfied. Yet in this act of vindication, he also opened up another attack on his honor. For the captivity of God's people incurred the stigma of feebleness on his part. The other nations misunderstood the exile and blamed it on Yahweh's weakness. And so, once more, Yahweh must act for his name's sake (36:21 ff.). The restoration will thus vindicate the divine honor.

Again, it might seem that the vindication of the divine honor as the motive of salvation is of a lower order than the gracious message of Hosea. If God is essentially love, however, if his righteousness is grounded in his love, if his name is love, most of all is his name vindicated when he acts graciously. Salvation is the most natural expression of his righteousness, not judgment. Yet Ezekiel is careful to suggest that the motive for God's gracious act is not Israel's need but God's honor (36:22). Thus, we might allow that Ezekiel tends to make God an unfeeling egoist concerned only with his own honor. We need, however, to modify such a judgment in the light of Ezekiel's final message of comfort and restoration. The God of judgment is a God of grace.

To preserve his honor, to act for his name's sake, means to act in covenant love and faithfulness, to be gracious. So in 33:11 we have an evangelical call to repentance and a promise of mercy which matches that of any of the other prophets.

THE TABERNACLING PRESENCE

The gracious aspect of God is seen in Ezekiel's picture of the tabernacling divine presence. Phythian-Adams [7] holds that this constitutes the essential element in the prophet's message. Ezekiel envisaged the Temple as God's house but realized, like Jeremiah, that the Temple and Jerusalem must fall. He faced, like his contemporary in Judah, the unpopular task of convincing the people that such a divine judgment would be a reality. Yet, for him more than for Jeremiah, the Temple was the focal point of the divine presence among the people. It is probable that Jeremiah's view was influenced by his connection with the priestly family of Anathoth so that for him the divine presence would not necessarily be focalized in the sanctuary of Zion. On the other hand, Ezekiel would seem to have strong connections with the Jerusalem priesthood and may well himself have been a Zadokite. As a result, the tabernacling presence on the hill of Zion was a living reality. If he sees the glory of Yahweh departing from this place of his habitation, his hope is bound up with the return of the divine presence when the land and the people are restored (9:3, 10:18; 43:2; 44:1, 2). God's presence among his people is thus connected with the Temple for Ezekiel, where this thought is not central in the message of Jeremiah. Yet it was not so bound up with Zion that Zion was necessary for it. Yahweh could withdraw his presence, and that withdrawal would mean the judgment of Judah.

The inaugural vision of the prophet makes it clear that, though the Temple is God's house, yet his presence is all pervasive. So, above the plains of Babylon, the glory of Yahweh, his manifest presence, confronts the prophet in the storm chariot. God is not bound to a place made by hands. He walked with Israel long before David's seed erected a house for his name (2 Sam. 7:7), and even though he chooses to dwell especially in that house, he is not tied to it. When his presence departs and the judgment descends, he will still abide with his people even in their exile, as he is even now with the frail son of man in Babylon. The Glory of Yahweh talks with Ezekiel by the river Chebar (3:23).

When Ezekiel is transported in a trance to Jerusalem, he sees the Glory of Yahweh leave the holy of holies, the place of his chosen dwelling, move to the outer walls of the place of worship, and finally depart (10, 11). As this takes place, the prophet is called on to declare the judgment of Jerusalem. At the same time, there comes the assurance that God's presence will dwell with the exiles and that he will be "to them a sanctuary *for a little while*

in the countries where they are come" (11:16, ASV, italics mine).
Ultimately God will restore them to their land, re-creating them
from within by a miraculous act (11:19).

Thus, the prophet's eschatological hope centers in the restored
Temple with its tabernacling presence. God will renew his covenant by renewing his people, and they evidently will be his people
by his everlasting presence in their midst. Ezekiel, in a vision,
sees the Glory of Yahweh return to the restored Temple and is
told that the gate by which the divine presence has entered the
sanctuary shall never again be opened (44:2). The presence of
Yahweh is now enthroned among his people. He has set his
sanctuary in the midst of them forever, and his everlasting covenant is ratified by his presence (37:26–28).

Jeremiah had tended to emphasize the spiritual aspect of religion and the divine omnipresence. We cannot say that Ezekiel
ignored this, but it is evident that he desired to maintain the
Israelite understanding of a tabernacling presence. Nor must we
regard this as a primitive survival in his thought, for it expressed
a deep principle which ultimately was actualized fully in history
in the Incarnation. While it is true that God fills the whole earth
with his glory, it is also true that he is to be known most of all
only in the place which he has chosen, where he has set his name.
For old Israel this was the Temple, for the new Israel it was the
Incarnation and the continuing indwelling by the Spirit in Christ's
body, the Church. For the Christian, Immanuel, God with us, is
not a truth confined to a temple made with hands. The divine
presence is in the living Body of Christ, and the new covenant is
ratified because Christ dwells in the hearts of his people.

JUDGMENT AND INDIVIDUAL RESPONSIBILITY

Ezekiel was a prophet of judgment in the broadest sense. For
him God was the God of all nations, and all peoples were subject
to his judgment. The focal point of the divine wrath was Judah,
and with this the prophetic oracles are particularly concerned.
The trance vision discloses the withdrawal of the divine Glory,
the inner side of that event which is the destruction of Jerusalem
and the depopulation of Judah. Judgment means that God has
forsaken his people and taken from them his tabernacling presence. In his parable of the two sisters, Oholah and Oholibah,
Ezekiel makes it clear that the doom which has overtaken the
faithless northern kingdom and its capital city of Samaria must
come also upon apostate Judah and Jerusalem (23). Judah has
indeed proved a faithless wife, it has gone awhoring after the
idols and shared in their abominations, and the judgment of God
is sure (16).

Ezekiel places great emphasis on the sin of idolatry, for it
above all others impugns God's honor. Hence he arraigns the
various alien cults which have found a home in the Jerusalem

Temple (chap. 8): the animal cults of Egypt (8:10); the fertility cult of weeping for Tammuz, probably due to Babylonian influence (8:14); the sun worship with its roots in Babylonian practice (8:16); and the image of jealousy (8:3), which is so styled because it provoked the wrath of Yahweh (cf. Deut. 32:16, 21) and which may have been a survival of the Canaanite cult of Astarte, associated with the sacred tree or *ashera'* (cf. 2 Kings 21:7). In thus attacking idolatry, Ezekiel was helping to preserve the essentially spiritual nature of Israel's religion, while at the same time emphasizing the incarnational aspect by his particularizing and focalizing of the divine presence. Sexual immorality was also attacked by Ezekiel, but chiefly in connection with ritual observance and the profanation of the sabbath. The prophet's concern for the honor of Yahweh made him emphasize most of all apostasy and idolatry.

The judgment which the prophet sees overtaking Judah was corporate and national, but it was also individualized. In chapter 9 he is given a vision of the slaughter of Jerusalem, and in the vision the seventh angel names those not falling into idolatry, setting a mark upon their foreheads and thereby saving them from the massacre. Thus the judgment is a purging and an individualizing process which is completed in the Exile. Indeed, even for those in Babylon there was a purging which was to be accomplished in the wilderness as in former days. When the exiles returned to Palestine, all would leave Babylon, but all would not reach the homeland (20:34–38).

This individualizing of the judgment on Judah is of one piece with Ezekiel's emphasis on individual responsibility. Even more than Jeremiah, Ezekiel was a strong individualist, and, in one of his oracles, this is spelled out in detail (chap. 18). Like Jeremiah, the prophet rejects the current proverb about sour grapes. He refuses to accept the fact that judgment falls on the innocent because of the guilty and verges on a strong individualism which denies the complementary truth of our strong interrelatedness. He argues that each man is rewarded for his obedience (18:5–9, 14–17) and punished for his sin (18:10–13). He clarifies his point by building his argument around a righteous father, an erring son, and a good grandson. Each will be rewarded according to his deeds, to the first and third a good and long life, to the second, death. The good or evil of one generation will not accrue to the merit or guilt of the next. Ezekiel quite boldly states the responsibility of each man for his own destiny. "The soul that sinneth, it shall die" (18:4, ASV).

So extreme, however, does his individualism become that he atomizes the individual life and ignores its wholeness, its integral set and character. Thus the consequences of a life lived in sin may be wiped out by the repentance of the present moment (18:21–23), while a past life of obedience and faithfulness may be undone by the sin of the present moment (18:24; cf. 3:20). The sinner is thereby both freed from all responsibility for others and from the burden of his own past. This is so manifestly untrue that it needs no refuting. Neither physically nor psychologically can we escape the consequences of our past wrongdoing, even when we are redeemed in Christ. Our guilt is removed and we are reconciled, but the physical and psychological scars remain.

This extreme position did, however, serve to bring into sharp relief the responsibility of the individual in an age when the mass deportations were raising questions about the divine justice. It was easy to blame their troubles on their fathers and to evade personal responsibility. The fathers had eaten sour grapes, so the children's teeth had been set on edge. But the finer souls of Israel were already feeling an element of injustice about this understanding of the divine activity. Ezekiel's extreme individualism needs to be balanced by an accompanying sense of our membership one of another. It waited on Second Isaiah to see, also in the Exile with its doubts and disillusionment, that the innocent might bear redemptively the sins of the guilty and their consequences.

We note that Ezekiel had no sense of a real after-life, without which his doctrine of individual responsibility and retribution raises difficult questions. His picture of Sheol, in his portrayal of the end of the king of Egypt, is the presentation of a meaningless nonexistence which has its own degree of persistence, but where all moral and social distinctions cease to count (32:17-32). It was left for postexilic eschatology with its doctrine of personal resurrection to make Ezekiel's emphasis fully acceptable.

Ezekiel's list of sins for which a man may be arraigned is an interesting mixture of moral and ceremonial trespasses. The sin of idolatry finds a central place, for this most of all touches the intimate relation of man to God. Yet it is listed alongside of both moral and ritual offences. Even at this stage of his ministry Ezekiel manifests enough of the priest and of the priest's concern with ritual obligation to stand apart to some degree from his great prophetic predecessors.

INDIVIDUAL REGENERATION AND NATIONAL RESTORATION—
THE SUPERNATURAL WORK OF GOD'S SPIRIT

Ezekiel's eschatology is both corporate and individual, like his understanding of judgment. For him the future is bound up with a miraculous act of renewal in which God will make Israel truly his people. In the early part of his ministry as prophet of judgment and watchman over Israel (3:16-21; 33:1-20), he refers occasionally to the future hope. But after the fall of Jerusalem and the completion of the deportation, he becomes prophet of hope and pastor to his people. Restoration there will be, but it will be God's act, not man's.

Like Hosea before him, Ezekiel uses the figure of resurrection, and he uses it nationally, not individually.[8] In the vision of the valley of dry bones, the prophet sees a vast living army resurrected from the dry bones, which alone remain on the site of its ancient battlefield (37:1–14). The difference between the dead, mouldering dust and the living group of men is the Spirit of Yahweh which blows through the valley at the prophetic behest. Thus the Spirit here is represented as a quasi-physical re-creative force issuing from God, and the national resurrection is God's act.

Like Hosea also, Ezekiel returns to the wilderness tradition for imagery. There will be a new deliverance akin to the old exodus out of Egypt, and furthermore there will be a new purging process in "the wilderness of the peoples" (20:33–38). There will be an individual purging out of which the nation will be reconstituted, but out of the purging will come a regenerate people.

Thus, the national restoration, like the national judgment, is individualized. The people were stubborn and would not listen to the divine Word. As with Jeremiah, so with Ezekiel, Israel has hardened its heart against Yahweh. The prophet describes it often as a "rebellious house," and, at the outset of his ministry, he is warned that they may not hear (2:4 ff.). Thus, only God, by a supernatural act, can effect a change in them. Ezekiel dares to believe that God will accomplish this through his Spirit. He will give them a right heart and a new spirit when he gathers them from their dispersion among the nations (11:17 ff.). In 36:26 ff. this promise is repeated, and the prophet declares that God will put his Spirit in them.

In 18:31, Ezekiel calls on Israel to repent and to produce a new heart and a new spirit. Clearly we have here the human aspect of that divine-human encounter in which man is made anew. In some sense, faith will always be both God's act and ours. It is we who respond, but we respond within God's all-embracing grace. Thus the new heart, the new capacity for response, is God's act and yet our response makes it ours too. Finally, however, it is God who takes the initiative, and Ezekiel belongs to that great company of Paul, Augustine, Luther, Calvin, and Jonathan Edwards who knew that all regeneration springs from God and that even our response of faith is his gift to our needy souls.

God would restore his people to their land and restore them as people who would gladly do his will because they were newly created within. They would become aware of their past ingratitude and faithlessness, as Yahweh established his covenant with them (16:62–63). Furthermore, they would truly be his covenant people for they would walk in his statutes and keep his ordinances and do them (11:20). Activated from within, possessing a new spirit, they would fulfill Yahweh's purpose when first he brought up a rebellious people from Egypt.

The mode of restoration which God would employ to restore his people is not discussed by Ezekiel. He lacked the contemporary historical situation which later made it possible for Second Isaiah to see Cyrus the Persian conqueror as Yahweh's shepherd. It was sufficient for the prophet that God would act and that, by his miraculous intervention, Judah would be restored to its home. Furthermore, not only Judah but also the northern kingdom of Israel was involved in this restoration. Ezekiel sets two sticks together as symbolic testimony to God's intention in this matter (37:16 ff.). Earlier in his ministry, he lay on his side to symbolize the same hope (4:4–6). Yahweh would himself seek out his sheep, and, like a good shepherd, he would gather them together (34:12 ff.).

In describing the restored land, Ezekiel begins with an elaborate description of the new temple with its inner sanctuary made ready for the tabernacling presence (40–42). In a vision he sees the Glory of Yahweh returning from the East whither the presence had departed when Judah was given up to destruction (43:1–9). The Glory now fills the house and promises to abide among his people forever. So God has fulfilled and maintained his everlasting covenant in the midst of a people who have been renewed within by his Spirit.

It is significant that, in the subsequent vision, the prophet is dominated by the priest. Israel is indeed to be a kingdom of priests, and the Temple and its ritual are the true end of its existence. It is shown to be God's people because his presence tabernacles in its midst in his house (37:26–28). Hence we find the cultus taking over. Elaborate directions are given with regard to the priesthood, which is to be purely Zadokite (43:19; 44:15). The other Levites, evidently constituted of the non-Jerusalem priests left over by the Josianic reformation, are to be the temple servants and to exercise no priestly role (44:10 ff.). The whole temple worship is to center in the sacrifices, of which the two most significant are the sin offering and the guilt offering, both innovations so far as preexilic practice was concerned (44: 29; 40:39, 42). Just as the preexilic burnt offering and peace offering have been relegated into the background, so also the priesthood now has, as its central task, the offering of the sacrifices rather than the giving of the *torah*. We now have a community centering in the indwelling presence whose chief task is the offering of sacrifices and who, to do this correctly, must observe many ordinances of ritual purity.

This encompassing of the divine presence by an insulating wall of ritual purity is amplified by the allotment of the living space around the Temple. Zion is perfectly insulated by the Zadokites, the priestly section of the people. To the north the land is given to the Levites, and to the south, completely cut off from the Temple by the insulating dwelling space of the priests, lies the city of Jerusalem (45:1–6).

The land to the east and west of the insulated holiness of Zion is given to the Davidic prince (45:7 ff.). It is noteworthy that here too the priestly emphasis has taken preeminence. The righteous messianic ruler of Isaiah's eschatology is replaced by a civil ruler whose major task is to preserve peace and order that the worship of the sanctuary may be performed in tranquility. H. W. Robinson [9] describes him as a kind of "ecclesiastical commissioner" whose main task is to oversee the provision of the sacrifices (45:17 ff.). Ezekiel had little room for the Davidic kings whom he regarded as bad shepherds bent on their own concerns. Only God is the good shepherd who will gather his scattered people (34), and the Temple is his and his alone. Here his presence is pleased to dwell. Ezekiel is careful to disassociate the Temple from any description of it as a royal chapel (43:7 ff.). It is significant that the prophet uses the title *prince* and not *king*, but he does clearly regard the restored state as a return to the glorious age of David and thinks of the Davidic ruler as a "prince for ever." Thus another strand of the royal theology and Jerusalem tradition is woven into his hope.

From the altar of sacrifice a stream of healing water flows out through the Temple gates, getting deeper as it moves through the city, out through the land, to the water of the Dead Sea. Everywhere it flows fertility abounds. The waters of the Dead Sea are cleansed of their salt, and fish are found in them. Only certain marshes on its shores are given over to salt, and they provide this necessary element for the sacrificial ritual (47). This picture of a healing stream and of the renewal of the land is a significant part of Ezekiel's eschatology. We find the hope that the land will become fruitful echoed also in 36:30.

Jeremiah could describe Yahweh as the "fountain of living waters" (Jer. 2:13), and after Ezekiel, we find Joel referring to the fountain which shall flow forth from the house of Yahweh in the last day (Joel 3:18). Deutero-Zechariah also includes in his eschatological message the promise of living waters that go out from Jerusalem (Zech. 14:8), while a postexilic oracle in Isaiah speaks of drawing water from the wells of salvation in the coming day (Isa. 12:3).

It is noteworthy that all such passages are bound up with the thought of the tabernacling presence among his people. Behind the hope there may well lie the belief that Zion was built on a sacred rock which was the center of the world and that under it were imprisoned the living waters of the deep. These waters were originally ordered at Yahweh's creative Word and could be reordered and released in life-giving streams at his pleasure.[10] As the sacrifices were offered and the divine presence was known, the healing waters were released. Here was the renewal center of all spring water, that is to say, living water. It was no accident that the seer of Revelation wrote a *midrash* around this passage in Ezekiel and saw that the true healing stream must flow from the throne of God and the Lamb.

In a highly Utopian way, Ezekiel describes the division of the land in strips among the twelve restored tribes. The strips are planned to the north and south of the central insulated Temple area, and the concubine tribes are made to occupy those furthest from the tabernacling presence. Other nations have no place in this scheme of things. We are left with the picture of a redeemed remnant in a restored land, with the divine presence tabernacling in its midst. Everything politically and socially gathers around the Temple worship, its statutes and ordinances. There is no thought of Israel being a redeeming remnant by which the other nations shall be brought to God. Here is an exclusiveness which has little room for evangelical appeal.

This constitutes the bulk of Ezekiel's eschatology, except for one element which is not definitely related to the rest.

APOCALYPTIC CONFLICT—GOG FROM MAGOG

In chapters 38 and 39 we are told of a mysterious figure, Gog from the land of Magog, who makes war on God's people.[11] He would seem to sum up in his own person all the pagan nations which had attacked Israel in the course of its history and against which the prophet directs his foreign oracles. He is thus the quintessence of heathenism. In attacking God's people he is attacking God, and it is God himself who comes to the rescue of Israel. Gog is not defeated by human historical forces, but by the supernatural powers which Yahweh hurls at him. He is slain in battle, and Israel is left victorious. The setting would appear to be after the restoration, and we may describe it as the last and climacteric attempt of paganism and idolatrous power to overthrow Israel and drive out the Presence. Thus here we have the beginning of what later developed into apocalypticism, and it is to be noted that the vision of Gog reappears in the picture of a final conflict in the Johannine Apocalypse.

We have here the first indication of the tendency in postexilic prophecy to transcendentalize the end and separate it from the historical. This process was never completed within the biblical revelation. Even in the Book of Daniel, the final consummation takes place on this earth, and there is no pessimism about history as the scene for the actualization of the divine purpose. Yet after the Exile, the Day of Yahweh is itself more and more attributed to a direct and supernatural divine intervention, and Yahweh is no longer envisaged as using the normal processes of history to accomplish his End and usher in his Day.

Ezekiel was prophet and priest, apocalyptist and legalist. All were combined in his complex personality. From him stemmed many streams of development in the postexilic period, and it has been said of him that he was the "father of Judaism." It is certainly true of him that he influenced the subsequent history of Judaism more than any other prophet. He heightened the element of the miraculous and the transcendent in the eschatological hope. He gave a legalistic and ritual coloring to the way of life of postexilic Judaism. He emphasized the responsibility of the individual, and, at the same time, paradoxically stressed the transcendence of God. Both these emphases left their marks on subsequent theological thought. Individual responsibility led to a new concern with life after death and the problem of suffering. Divine transcendence led to a new understanding of mediating conceptions and hastened the development of a theology of wisdom. So this complex prophet, with his psychological and pathological problem, left his mark on the movement of the divine revelation. His exclusiveness and his concern with a saved remnant raised real problems for those who knew, in the tradition of the patriarchs, that Israel was to be a source of blessing to all peoples. It is here that Second Isaiah brought a new vision.

NOTES

1. See Alfred Bertholet, *Hesekiel: Handbuch zum Alten Testament* (Tübingen: J.C.B. Mohr, 1936); H. Wheeler Robinson, *Two Hebrew Prophets* (London: Lutterworth, 1948).
2. Cf. Volkmar Herntrich, *Ezechielprobleme* (Giessen: A. Töpelmann, 1932).
3. See Charles C. Torrey, *Pseudo Ezekiel and the Original Prophecy* (New Haven: Yale University Press, 1930); J. Smith, *The Book of the Prophet Ezekiel: A New Interpretation* (New York: Macmillan Co., 1931).
4. This older view is defended by Carl G. Howie, *The Date and Composition of Ezekiel* (Philadelphia: Society of Biblical Literature, 1950); George Fohrer, *Eziekel: Handbuch zum Alten Testament* (Tübingen: J.C.B. Mohr, 1955).
5. Cf. Johannes Lindblom, *Prophecy in Ancient Israel* (Oxford: Basil Blackwell, 1962), p. 263: "My own conclusion from the evidence is that the literary history of the book of Ezekiel is substantially analogous to that of other prophetic books in the Old Testament. The only difference is that in this book the distance of the original sayings of the prophet is for the most part greater than in other prophetic books."
6. Robinson, *Two Hebrew Prophets*, p. 98.
7. W. J. Phythian-Adams, *The People and the Presence* (London: Oxford University Press, 1942), pp. 77 ff.
8. Harald Riesenfeld, *The Resurrection in Ezekiel*, xxxvii (Uppsala:

A.B. Lundequistska Botzhandeln, 1948), traces this resurrection motif in Hosea and Ezekiel to the royal cult and the king's miming of the descent into Sheol. He is careful to suggest that the thought of Hosea does not necessarily have any immediate connection with the cult but that the latter supplied the terminology (p. 7). He endeavors to show that Ezekiel 37 has modes of expression which "must go back to the conceptions of re-generation of life bound up with the ritual of the yearly festival in the classic Israelite Kingdom" (p. 13). His discussion of the influence of the passage on later Jewish and Christian thought and liturgy is worth consulting.

9. Robinson, *Two Hebrew Prophets*, p. 123.

10. Cf. Phythian-Adams, *People and the Presence*, p. 99. Psalm 33:7 may echo the same idea.

11. Chapters 38 and 39 appear to contain two versions of the invasion of Gog, derived from separate traditions. Chapter 39 describes the beginning of the invasion of Israel by Gog and his forces, whereas their destruction has already been described at the end of chapter 38. According to Bertholet, *Hesekiel*, one version makes Yahweh himself the one who leads Gog to invade and so to his destruction, while the other version sees the invasion as initiated by Gog himself with the same end result.

Chapter Seven

The Redeemer
of Israel and the
Suffering Servant

Toward the end of the Exile in Babylon a new prophetic voice was heard. The oracles are preserved in Isaiah 40–55 with possibly some of the oracles in the last ten chapters of the roll of Isaiah. In these prophetic oracles the poetic gifts of the prophets reach their climax. Jeremiah had perfected the Hebrew lyrical form, but in Deutero-Isaiah there is a sustained poetical style which is replete with rich imagery and many dramatic figures of speech.

The prophet draws from the realm of nature and the depths of human personality in the figures that he employs. Mountains and plains play their part in his eschatological imagery (for example, chap. 40). He speaks of the way of Yahweh and pictures the transformation of the wilderness. The "arm of Yahweh" is a favorite expression. He pictures God as a travailing woman in 42:14 and as a compassionate mother in 49:14 ff.

His poetic forms vary from hymns like the hymn to creation in 40:12–26 to laments like 53:1–9, from ecstatic hymns like 42:10–13 to confessions like 50:4–9 (in the style of Jeremiah), from mocking songs like 47 to compassionate lyrics like 43:1–4 and 49:14–16. Dramatic imagery is borrowed from the law court (41:1–42:4) and from the Babylonian New Year Festival, as when he describes the pagan deities leaving Babylon (46:1–13) and the triumphant coming of Yahweh as king (52:7–10).

The prophet knows how to plumb the deeps of grief and compassion, but he knows also how to reach the heights of joy. The series of oracles begins with the prophet as a proclaimer of comfort (40:1 ff.), and it finishes with a triumphant note of rejoicing in 54:1–7. Unlike his predecessors, we find in him little invective and threat. Perhaps 45:9–13 might be cited as an instance of this type of oracle.

The prophet is concerned with redemption. Oracles of salvation are addressed in Israel (40:1-2, 43:1-7), and messages of judgment are generally reserved for the pagan nations and their gods (41:1-29, 47:1-15), although the element of judgment is not absent from oracles on Israel, like 48:1-11. Yet there is a redemptive note even in the message to the nations, for this prophet, above all his predecessors, sees the reconciliation of all peoples to Israel's God and sounds a universalistic note. He is a prophet of comfort not only to Israel, but also to the nations. His deep compassion becomes, like that of Hosea before him, a window into the heart of God.

THE COMPOSITION OF THE ORACLES OF DEUTERO-ISAIAH

Questions about the unity of this book have been raised by many scholars. Chapters 40–55 often appear to be a string of detached oracles, hymns, laments, and other elements, of high poetical quality but with no order in their assemblage. Thus, Mowinckel [1] suggests that they are mechanically linked together by certain catch words which are recurrent. There is no doubt about the number of separate units in this section of the roll, units which may be differentiated in the basis of their form.[2] It is true that they seem logically unrelated. Furthermore, the distinction between the divine oracle and the prophet's plea is not always as clear as it is in the literary predecessors of Deutero-Isaiah. Muilenburg points out that the fixed forms of preexilic prophecy begin to break up. He holds, however, that these units are incorporated in a larger whole which is a unity. The individual poetical forms are subordinate elements within a continuing whole. This whole is not, however, of epic type. The extravagance of the poet within the prophetic consciousness takes Deutero-Isaiah off in flights which seem to have no direct relation to their actual place in the literary context but which are relevant to the developing theme of the whole. Gottwald [3] suggests that Deutero-Isaiah combines the orderliness of the thinker with the caprice of the poet.

It would seem probable that we have in this section of the prophetic roll the ordered thought of the prophet, but it is also probable that the oracles were not delivered in the order given. When at last they were committed to literary expression, the prophet's mind, dominated by the general theme of his message, directs the general movement, but his memory is alive with many remembered utterances tumbling over into the movement of his thought. In consequence, we have verses and short lyrical forms which burst into the main development and seem irrelevant at the point of their entry. Yet they help to carry forward the general theme of the whole.

This theme is redemptive and eschatological. It begins with the heraldic message of Yahweh's coming to redeem his people in 40:1–11 and ends in the paean of joy over the fulfillment of the divine purpose in 55:1–13. In between, the theme moves in recurrent cycles as the prophetic mind takes off in flight after flight of poetic vision and as his rich memory yields up its treasures.

The book seems to fall into two sections. In chapters 40–48 there is a message of comfort to exiled Israel and of judgment on the nations. The prophet comes forth to announce a message of comfort from the heavenly council, for Yahweh is coming to visit and redeem his people. Within the setting of God's creative act and his control over nature, the prophet presents Yahweh as the Lord of history before whom the nations are arraigned in judgment. The dramatic picture of the trial scene or *rîv* is recurrent (41:21–29; 43:8–13). The downfall of Babylon and the exodus of its gods is declared (47:1–15; 46:1–13). With majestic repetition of the word *behold* we are told that Yahweh is coming as Redeemer (40:9–10, 15; cf. 42:1). In the midst it is declared that Cyrus, the Persian conqueror, will be the historical agent of Yahweh's redemptive purpose (44:24–45:13). Already the Servant theme is lifting its head (41:8–20; 42:1–9; 44:1–13).

In chapters 49–55, we have a change of pace. Cyrus is no longer mentioned. The coming of Yahweh moves forward to its triumphal consummation, but now the Servant and his suffering come to occupy the stage. Yahweh as Lord of history vindicates the sufferings of his Servant. The issues of the identity of the Servant will have to be discussed later. He seems at times to be identified with Israel, especially in chapters 40–48, and at other times to be almost an individual figure. This is eschatology, and the Servant is a central figure of the *eschaton*. Maybe the prophet saw that the restoration to Palestine under Cyrus would not be enough. For Israel and for the world, redemptive suffering was essential, and the sufferings of Israel in Exile, seemingly with an overplus that was undeserved (40:2), might be focalized in an eschatological figure through whom all nations should be brought near and a true covenant made possible. In this second section of the book we are getting nearer the return and there is, if anything, a more triumphant affirmation that Yahweh is coming as King and will lead his people home (52:7–12). Through the eschatological imagery of moving hills and departing mountains, all Israel and nature are summoned to a paean of praise (54:1–10), and the section closes with the tender evangelical appeal of chapter 55. Maybe this section was written after Cyrus's policy of restoration to Palestine had become clear.

THE HISTORICAL BACKGROUND, RELIGIOUS ENVIRONMENT, AND SPIRITUAL RESOURCES OF THE PROPHETIC MESSAGE

The historical background of this section of Isaiah is very

evidently the Exile, but at a later period than the ministry of Ezekiel. Babylon is the dominant power, but its fall is imminent. Just as Judah had to reckon with Babylon, so now Babylon must reckon with the Medo-Persian power under the leadership of Cyrus. This brilliant young Mede had overthrown his Persian overlord and welded the Persian peoples into a menacing force bent on world conquest. His striking figure must have caught the eye of the Jewish exiles long before the fall of Babylon. When in 546 b.c. Asia Minor became subject to him, it must have been clear that he was a strong rival to the king of Babylon. His tolerant policy was probably known, and so it was felt that a change in the fortunes of the Jewish people was at hand. Cyrus would appear, like Sennacherib and Nebuchadrezzar, as an instrument of Yahweh.

A man who had sat at the feet of Isaiah and Jeremiah and who was at unity with them in his faith in the divine control over history would see the Persian conqueror as a servant of God. He would look beyond the brilliant warrior and see the hand of Yahweh. Cyrus was the chosen instrument of God even though he did not know it (45:4, 5). So in a succession of oracles, Deutero-Isaiah interprets the divine meaning in the tremendous events of his time. Cyrus has been raised up by God to subdue the nations (41:2-4), to shepherd Israel home, and to rebuild Jerusalem (44:28; 45:13). In one oracle the prophet even suggests that the culmination of Cyrus's career will be his conversion to the worship of Yahweh (41:25).

The hopes were actually fulfilled in large part. The city of Babylon was taken at night. Nabonidus, the Babylonian king, had neglected the worship of Marduk, and Cyrus was welcomed by the Babylonian priests. He made Babylon his center and showed a spirit of toleration toward the people of the Empire. He restored various subject peoples to their homelands, including the Jews, and allowed them to worship their own gods.

The exiles in Babylon had apparently been fairly free, but their religious faith was bound to suffer by continued contact with their pagan environment. The dramatic elements in Babylonian worship, especially its New Year Festival, must have left a mark upon people who were exiled from the Temple at Jerusalem and its ritual. The many gods of the Babylonian pantheon, with all their rich mythological background, would influence the thoughts of a people long exiled from the land of promise. Some of this background is reflected in the prophet's thought. He undertakes a vigorous attack upon the pagan deities, portraying their procession out of fallen Babylon. His portrayal reflects the dramatic ritual processions of the gods in the Babylonian New Year Festival (46:1-13). His acquaintance with idol making comes out in the passage in which he vividly describes the fashioning of an idol

(44:6–20). He is aware of the elements of magic and divination in his religious environment and of the astrological aspects of Babylonian religion (47:12–13). Over against the annual recital of the creation myth at the New Year Festival (the *enuma elis*) the prophet sets forth the Hebrew picture of God as sole and absolute creator with its consequent effects upon the understanding of nature and history.

When we turn from this background of historical events and environment of paganism and mythology into the depths of the prophet's own religious consciousness, we find the rich spiritual resources from which he drew in meeting the situation he faced. The great movement of revelation in Israel's history lay behind him. He continually points back to the former things (43:9; 46:9), and these undoubtedly embrace all the dealings of God with his people in Israel's past. He is familiar with the traditions preserved in JE. He reminds the people that they are the heirs of Abraham, God's friend (41:8; 51:1, 2). He even takes them back behind the patriarch to the universal covenant made with Noah (54:9, 10). The rich traditions of the exodus from Egypt dominate his thinking, as we shall see shortly. Israel was God's chosen people, and the deliverance that he had wrought he would work again in still loftier ways. The glory of the end would echo the fertility of Eden in the beginning (51:3).

Still closer to his own time, the prophet reflects again and again the teaching of Isaiah of Jerusalem. Granted that the group of disciples around this prophet was perpetuated through history, we may imagine that Deutero-Isaiah claimed to be explicitly of this group. He describes the Servant as a disciple in 50:4, and this passage may well reflect his conviction about his own mission. As Martin Buber [4] suggests, he has received the disciple's tongue and can uncover the master's words.

This same servant song (50:4–9) reflects the confessions of Jeremiah. There is little doubt that in his intense insight into the heart of God, in his capacity to understand suffering, and in his poetical expression, Deutero-Isaiah shows the influence of the prophet of the new covenant. Nor can we miss some knowledge of Hosea. That prophet's picture of Yahweh leading Israel into the wilderness, wooing it again, and ultimately restoring it to the land has strong connections with Deutero-Isaiah's hope of a 'new exodus.'

The images and vocabulary of Isaiah, Jeremiah, and Hosea are all reflected. Indeed, the shepherd image of Yahweh and other figures may show acquaintance with the work of Ezekiel. The anonymous prophet of Isaiah 40–55 stood in the midst of the stream of Israel's spiritual heritage, and his own prophetic genius used it to the full. Volz [5] has even suggested that the prophet was the spiritual leader at the end of the exilic period and that he helped in founding the synagogues. It was in such synagogue assemblies that his message of comfort and oracles of salvation were first delivered.

The Holy One of Israel—Creator and Redeemer

Out of this rich heritage, Deutero-Isaiah drew many images to express his own vision of God. With his master and predecessor, Isaiah of Jerusalem, he shared a burning conviction of the divine holiness. This holiness represented for the first Isaiah God's otherness and uniqueness. He was other than man, who was flesh and not spirit. Furthermore, this divine transcendence was moral in essence. Yahweh as the Holy One was unique in his righteousness, the transcendent Lord of history whose moral will exercised judgment. The same note is sounded by Deutero-Isaiah. God's holiness is exclusively his alone, and all created things can be holy only as their holiness is derived from him. Yahweh alone is absolutely holy, and Israel can be hallowed only because it is his chosen. God can therefore be likened to no other (40:25). He stands apart in his transcendent majesty. Indeed, his holiness can be an awesome power before which all nations must bow. He is the mighty one (41:10).

The holiness of God is one way in which the prophet expresses his lofty monotheism. He who is the Holy One of Israel is the unique and sole deity among all peoples. Again and again, the prophetic oracles assert that there is none other beside or equal to Yahweh (44:6, 8; 45:5, 6, 18). He will not give his glory to another (48:11). He is Yahweh and affirms this through his messenger, "I am He" (41:4; 45:18; 46:4; 48:12). What is implicit in the message of his prophetic predecessors becomes explicit in the thought of Deutero-Isaiah. Yahweh was so supreme that, for the preexilic prophets, there was no room for another God. But they never carried this faith to the point of declared monotheism as did the exilic prophet. For him God is indeed the unique and only One who inhabits eternity.

In the light of this, Deutero-Isaiah undertakes a vigorous campaign against the pagan deities. We understand this more when we remember the polytheism of his Babylonian environment. The heathen gods are confidently challenged to competition. The prophet asserts that they are mere nonentities who can achieve and predict nothing. In a tremendous trial scene, the gods are arraigned before the heavenly court (41:21–29). They are declared to be nothing on two counts. They are able neither to carry their pronounced purpose into historical actuality nor to predict the future (41:23). Yahweh alone is wise and powerful. He and he alone is the prime mover of all events. All of Israel's past history testifies to his power and his wisdom. He has foretold the end from the beginning. With his foreknowledge he has seen the course of history. But more, he has willed that course and carried his purpose into effect. In the past of Israel Yahweh's predictions have been validated by the events in which his purpose has been actualized (44:6–8; 48:14; cf. 42:9). Beside him there is no god (46:9–10). The nations are challenged to put their testimony to their gods alongside of that of Israel to Yahweh. Their gods neither can predict nor have they any power to control events (43:8–13; 45:20–21).

The prophet also adopts another line of attack upon the pagan deities. He describes derisively the materials from which the idols are made and shows thereby their impotence and nonbeing (44:9–20; cf. 41:6, 7; 40:19, 20). The gods have no essence. They are made by men, so that any claim they may have over the peoples has only the authority of those who make them. Buber [6] points out that the prophet must have been aware that the idols were only material representations of the cosmic forces which the pagan nations worshiped. He suggests that the prophet attacked them in such concrete language because he was really concerned to show that the actual gods were "not beings but configurations of the human soul." The pagan gods know nothing. They can neither interpret the past nor predict the future. Only Yahweh can inspire prophecy and move history in the direction of his will.

The uniqueness of God is seen in his power as Creator. Because he alone is God, Yahweh is the absolute Lord both of nature and of history. Deutero-Isaiah is the first to use the distinctive verb *bara'*, "to create." This verb is used only with God as subject and never with man. It would appear to carry the connotation of a transcendent divine act and to imply absoluteness. Man may make (*yatsar*), but he cannot create (*bara'*). The word is used frequently in Deutero-Isaiah and occurs in the P story of creation of Genesis 1, a story probably written down about this time.

Babylonian astrology can associate its deities with the heavenly bodies, but for this prophet they are the hosts of heaven which God himself has created and which God controls (40:26). In a wonderful cosmic creation hymn (40:12–26), the uniqueness of the Creator is declared as he is portrayed sitting above the circle of the earth and stretching out the heavens like a curtain (40:22). Yahweh has created the heavens and formed the earth (42:5; 44:24; 45:12, 18; 48:13).

Undoubtedly the annual recitation of the *enuma elis* creation epic in the Babylonian New Year Festival challenged the prophet at this point, but he is not concerned fundamentally with nature. His concern is with history. Although God is creator and the prophet sees the cosmic order as a manifestation of the divine power and wisdom (40:12–14), yet the natural order is but the setting for God's purpose in history.

The two orders interpenetrate in the thought of Deutero-Isaiah, and he can use the verb *to create* of Israel as well as of its cosmic setting (43:1, 7, 15; 45:11). God has made man and the nations as he has created the heavens and the earth (42:5), and among the nations he has formed Israel. Before him who in his absoluteness controls nature and before whom the isles are a little thing, the nations are a drop in a bucket, and princes and judges are brought to nought (42:15, 23, 24). Indeed, it is God who creates righteousness and salvation in history. Creation is continued in the achieving of his purpose for historical man (45:8). He creates the new within human history and actualizes his intention (48:6 ff.). As in the opening chapters of Genesis, God's creative work moves from nature to the peoples and from the peoples to Israel. The cosmic framework of nature declares God's greatness and majesty and manifests man's frailty. Yet it is for man that the world was made (45:18), and nature exists to be the scene of redemption. Creation is, for Deutero-Isaiah, the prelude to the actualization of the divine purpose. God the Creator is Yahweh the Redeemer. What was begun when he established the earth and formed the heavens reaches its consummation when he saves Israel and all the nations of the earth turn to him.

So the Creator is also Redeemer. God's uniqueness and holiness are manifested most of all in his action as redeemer. Then it is seen that he is essentially love. It is here that Deutero-Isaiah makes the same emphasis as Hosea. He is a prophet of grace. His concern with creation and with the cosmic theme is but to associate them with the divine love. God's control over nature means that he can transform the wilderness and make it subserve the return of his people from exile. He will place oases in the desert for the pilgrims who come back from Babylon, and topographical changes will take place to serve his purpose. We must take such passages literally (40:3, 4; 49:9–11), for they show that creation is subservient to redemption.

The central word in the prophet's description of God as redeemer is go'el (41:14; 43:14; 44:6; 48:17, and others). This may be rendered "kinsman-vindicator" as well as "redeemer." It signifies the act under Hebrew law whereby a man may, in some sense, act as savior for his blood kin. If his kin has been murdered, he may avenge the blood; if the kin has been enslaved, he may pay the ransom price. There is here a deep sense of corporate solidarity and belongingness which characterizes Hebrew thought. A covenant establishes a kinship as close as blood kinship. Yahweh is bound to Israel by a covenant of his own origination, and the prophet daringly declares that God will play the part of kinsman-vindicator to his people. His freely self-conferred obligation to Israel is expressed when he becomes the nation's redeemer. It is he who will pay the ransom price and set the exiles free (43:3). Those who have opposed Israel will be winnowed like the chaff (41:14 ff.). He will strike down Babylon (43:14; 47:14 ff.). God will redeem Israel as a husband seeks a wife who has been cast off (54:5 ff.), and here we may see the influence of Hosea.

Yahweh can also be described as "savior" (43:3). He is the

author of salvation, and his salvation will not tarry (46:13). He is a righteous God, and Deutero-Isaiah sees him as a God of judgment. As judge he acts chiefly on Babylon and Israel's adversaries (40:10, 17), for Israel has paid double for her sins (40:2). But his righteousness means that he will abide true to himself, and he is love. His glory, his manifest appearance, is the glory of saviorhood. His righteousness is manifested in his salvation (51:6, 8). He is a just God and therefore a savior (45:21). Indeed, he has appeared to hide himself, and Israel has doubted his love, but even his hiddenness and wrath have been part of his saving purpose (45:15).

Because God is creator of all men, his lordship is universal and his salvation is ultimately for all people. Here for the first time we have an explicit declaration of a noble universalism. All the ends of the earth are to see the salvation of God (52:10; cf. 49:6), and the divine decree of salvation shall go forth for a light to the nations (51:4 ff.). Yahweh is the redeemer of all men. He is universal Lord.

God transcends all space, and before him all nations are but as grasshoppers. But he also transcends time. He is the Eternal One, the everlasting God (40:28). Hence Deutero-Isaiah can describe him as the first and the last (44:6). He is the primordial source of all history and its transcendent goal. He is the whole who embraces all history within his eternity. Yet he transcends it, and history is the scene for the fulfillment of his purpose. Thus, his eternity is not timeless being. History is time acquiring meaning, and such meaning is related to God's eternity. He can declare the end from the beginning as impotent pagan deities cannot (46:10), and he controls history by his word through the prophets (55:10 ff.).

The last reference, with its emphasis on the objectivity of the prophetic word, is a reminder that through the prophetic oracle God initiates in history that which shall surely come to pass. As with Jeremiah and Ezekiel, so with Deutero-Isaiah, the divine Word is creative when it is flung into a situation. The creative word of Genesis 1 turns chaos into order. So the prophetic word transforms the disorder of human sinfulness and alienation into the realm of God's redemption.

THE NEW EXODUS AND THE PEOPLE OF GOD

The predominant motif with Deutero-Isaiah is eschatological. He gathers up the hope of his predecessors in all its diversity, and many of the strands become integrated in his thought. The Jerusalem tradition, preserved in Isaiah of Jerusalem, still finds its place as the prophet speaks of God giving salvation to Zion (46:13). He sees Jerusalem being rebuilt and the foundation of the Temple laid once more (44:28; 45:13). There may even be a reflection of Ezekiel's hope of a tabernacling presence when it is declared that Yahweh will return to Zion (52:8). So the prophetic herald is called on to declare to Zion that its God reigns (52:7). The messianic theme might seem to be absent in a specific sense unless we associate it with the image of the suffering servant to which we shall turn later. Yet the prophetic oracle declares that God will make an everlasting covenant on the basis of that which he made with David (55:3). This at least is a reflection of the royal theology. The long vista which looks back to Abraham and to the primordial past (22:11) finds its echo in the specific references to Abraham's seed (41:8) and the challenge to look to Abraham their father (51:2). We have also the continually recurring emphasis on the former things (41:22; 42:9; 43:9; 46:9).

But these former things evidently refer also to the Exodus and its accompanying events, so central in the wilderness and exodus tradition. Here the message of Hosea and the hopes of Jeremiah are brought into fusion with the Isaianic tradition. Indeed there is little doubt that the Exodus motif is dominant in the thought of Deutero-Isaiah. The end time will reflect God's activity in the past not only in the primordial time of creation, but also in that creative act when Israel was made the people of God in covenant relationship to him. Gunkel's emphasis on *Urzeit und Endzeit* finds particular exemplification in this prophet. Hosea sees that the restoration of Israel must be understood as a reenactment of the Exodus motif (Hos. 2:14–18). Deutero-Isaiah makes it central in his understanding of eschatology.

We must not dismiss this as allegorization, for it is grounded in history. Allegory tends to dissolve away the historical foundations and leave us with a universal truth not dependent ultimately upon any specific historical act. But God acts in history, and we are concerned here rather with the typical patterns of his activity. This is the basis of a true biblical typology. What God has done he may do again in the same pattern or he may act in such a way that the fundamental pattern is repeated in a higher way so that out of it a 'new thing' emerges. This is a constituent element in the vision of Deutero-Isaiah.

Hence the prophet pictures the return as a new exodus, so heightened, however, that it is a unique event, a new thing. The eschatological hope is shaped upon the event by which Israel was first created as God's people. The pattern of the Exodus is reflected in the new promises offered by the prophet, in the description of the deliverance from Babylon, in the journey through the desert, and in the reentry into Palestine. The prophetic oracles promise fertility and prosperity to the restored people (48:19–21; 54:1–3). The promise to Abraham that through him and his seed the nations shall evoke blessing is echoed in 42:6 ff.

Israel is summoned to go forth out of Babylon with joy (48:20; 55:12), not in haste as in the days of the first Exodus (52:12; cf. Exod. 12:11). The accompanying presence of Yahweh in the cloud and the fire is to be traced in the revelation of the divine glory as the wilderness is made ready before the returning exiles (40:3-5), and Yahweh himself can be described as a mighty warrior doing battle for his people (42:13; 49:24–26). The imagery of the creation epic in which God defeats and orders the chaos becomes the basis for a picture of Yahweh cutting Rahab in pieces that his ransomed may return (51:9–10). The Red Sea crossing is undoubtedly also reflected in this picture and explicitly employed in 43:16–17.

What Yahweh did in the former things he will do again as he creates the new things. Like the pillar of cloud and the pillar of fire in the former things, Yahweh will go before and behind his people. He will be their advance guard and their rearward (52:12). So God prepares a highway in the desert (40:3–5; 43:19; 49:11), supplying water and food on the way (41:17–20; 43:19–21; 48:21; 49:9, 10). The covenant theme finds its place as the prophet promises a covenant of peace that shall be everlasting, although the basis here would appear to be the Davidic rather than the Sinai covenant (54:10; 55:3). Yahweh will lead his people in (42:14–16) and will gather his tribes together once more (52:1; 54:7). Jerusalem shall be restored, and Israel shall become a light to all peoples (44:28; 42:6; 49:6, 7).

We note that although the prophet portrays the End in the symbolism of the former things, he so transforms the latter that he evidently believes the End to be a new and unique event. God will surpass himself and perform by his strong arm more than Israel deserves. It would seem that the covenant of the end time is portrayed in terms of the Davidic covenant rather than of that at Sinai, because the former was more obviously open to the understanding of free unmerited grace (55:3). It is noteworthy that former things supply a background also in the remembrance of God's covenant with Noah (54:9, 10; cf. Gen. 9:8–17).

The hope was evidently triggered by the advent of Cyrus, and Deutero-Isaiah follows Isaiah of Jerusalem in his understanding of the divine lordship over history. God sits on his throne amid his heavenly council and decrees that Cyrus shall be his shepherd (44:28), and the prophet comes as his messenger to initiate the new movement of history by the utterance of the divine Word. As events declared in the past have already come to pass, so Yahweh's choice of Cyrus as the deliverer of his people shall be validated in history (41:25–27; 42:9; 48:3–5). Cyrus is no contingent happening in history. He is within God's purpose from the beginning (41:4), and the whole movement of Israel's history has its setting within the divine plan.

Deutero-Isaiah does not set alternatives before man as did Isaiah. The call to repent, to turn, and the dialectic of sin and grace are almost absent (read 44:22, however). His vision is completely eschatological. God's grace has triumphed over rebellious Israel and its sin is forgiven. Now history moves toward its divinely ordained consummation. God has made his decision, and the new things shall surely come to pass. He has set the time and agent for the accomplishment of his purpose.

We might almost see in this the determinism of the later apocalyptic, yet this would be a mistake. Deutero-Isaiah recognizes the human element, but he believes that God's decision overrules history in spite of this. Cyrus is his anointed one (45:1), anointed by Yahweh even though he has not known Him, called by the name for the sake of the divine purpose (45:4, 5). The Persian conqueror will let the exiles go free and rebuild Jerusalem, for God has raised him up in righteousness and will make straight his ways (45:13).

God moves and acts in history, even though in his transcendent holiness he is other than and beyond history, and man serves the divine purpose in spite of himself. This is a recognition of human autonomy, and at the same time an affirmation of divine omnipotence. Deutero-Isaiah can no more solve this paradoxical mystery than we moderns. In the first section of the prophecy, the prophet even dares to hope for Cyrus's conversion (45:2–5). The emphasis in the prophetic message may well have arisen in the polemic against the Babylonian deities. The pagan New Year Festival included a casting of the fates, for the gods were supposed to determine the world's destiny. So the prophet declares that the latter is in God's hands alone.

Like Ezekiel, Deutero-Isaiah marks the transition from preexilic eschatology with its emphasis on the continuity between history and the end time (*eschaton*) to postexilic eschatology and its understanding of a discontinuity with the end time as a transcendent divine act. Yahweh is still the God who acts within history, and there is a continuity between historical movements associated with Cyrus and the descent of the end time. Yet the end comes with God's own coming in his manifest glory, transforming the desert and making a highway for his people. We even find the heightening of language associated with a transcendent and theophanic inbreak when we are told that the heavens will vanish like smoke and the earth grow old like a garment (51:6). There is transcendence and also discontinuity here, even though the historical Cyrus be the advance guard of the Day of Yahweh. Thus the end time is a direct theophany, and yet it is within the historical scene. A new thing is created, and yet it is in some way continuous with the former things. We do not yet hear of a new heaven and a new earth.

Central in this end time is God's glory. God acts for his name's sake (48:9, 11). God will not give his glory to another. He will not share his name with other deities (42:8). God redeems to glorify his name, that is to say, to manifest his innermost being, for his name is his revealed nature. In giving his name God is giving himself. This might seem at first to reflect the same ego-

tistical pride as does, in part, Ezekiel's vision of God. Yet we need
to remember that from the beginning to the end of Deutero-Isaiah's
message, God shows himself as self-giving love, as grace, and as
compassion upon the undeserving. We have a more profound
plumbing of the deeps of the divine being. It is God's transcendent,
holy love that is active in the movement of redemption. A message
that begins with comfort ends with a joyful note of restoration
and sounds throughout the theme of the divine compassion. God
is the comforter of Israel (40:1; 49:13; 51:3, 19; 54:11). The
redemptive end (*eschaton*) of history is thus motivated by love.
Israel has done nothing to deserve it, and God's purpose is thus
sheer grace. He has blotted out its transgressions and forgiven
its sins (43:25; 44:22; 54:8). He has created Israel for his glory
and called it by his name, but his name is love, and his glory is
to manifest compassion (43:7). It is such divine glory which initiates the end time by its coming (40:5).

Because God's glory is a garb of compassion, the ultimate
consummation (the *eschaton*) will be one of universal love. The
God before whom all pagan deities are nonentities and who is the
God of the whole earth (54:5) will have mercy upon all peoples.
For the first time explicitly we have the affirmation that all the
ends of the earth may see and share in the salvation of Israel's
God. God is pleased to make great and glorious his *torah*, his
revelation (42:21). Such purpose is steadfast, and its consummation involves a universal appeal to all peoples. The prophetic herald
calls on all the ends of the earth to look to the one God and be
saved (45:22).

In the end time, however, this universal hope is bound up with
God's particular activity in and through Israel. The scandal of
particularity is in the center. The redeemer is the King of Israel
(44:6), and it shall be Israel's task to witness to his compassion.
It must testify that he alone is God and that beside him there is
no savior. Israel is Yahweh's witness to his mighty acts (43:8–13),
and through that witness the nations shall be gathered. Chapter
45, verse 20 and 49:12 may well refer to far more than the
dispersed of Israel. They should be read in conjunction with
55:4, 5. It is Israel's special task to show forth the glory of its
God and to declare his praise in the islands (42:10–12). They
themselves will return with a rejoicing that shall echo to the ends
of the earth and testify to the mercy of God (48:20). The glory
of Yahweh has come and their testimony to his presence will
ring the earth. So the prophet declares that the representatives of
the nations shall be liberated and come in their chains to pass
under the service of Yahweh along with Israel. The call of
God through Israel will bring the recognition that "God is in
thee" (45:14). This brings us to the place and function of the
Servant figure.

THE SERVANT OF YAHWEH

This enigmatic figure is brought to a focus in four 'servant songs': (42:1-4; 49:1-6; 50:4-9; 52:13-53:12), although the description also appears elsewhere in the prophecy (41:8-10; 42:19, 20; 43:8-13; 44:1-8; 44:21-22; 44:24-28; 45:1-8). In the latter passages the Servant is clearly identified with Israel and is thus a corporate figure. The Hebrew consciousness was so aware of corporate solidarity that it did regard groups in this individualizing way, and Deutero-Isaiah was no exception to the line of his prophetic predecessors in this matter. Israel is Yahweh's wife (54:5), and Babylon can be described as a virgin daughter, a lady forever (47:1-8). Our difficulty arises in the fact that, in the servant songs, the identification of the Servant with Israel is by no means so clear. Thus in 49:3, the Servant is declared to be Israel, but in 49:5 ff. he is distinct from the nation with the task of raising up and restoring the nation. Again, the figure portrayed in 53:8-12 is far too individual in the delineation to be totally identified with a corporate whole.

For this reason, and because the poems are not always seen as playing their role within the general movement of the whole prophecy, many scholars have regarded them as extraneous insertions. Some would still regard them as by the same prophet. Others would even question this. In an acute analysis James Muilenburg [7] has shown that the motifs in the servant songs reflect those in the rest of the prophetic oracles. Thus the Servant is to set judgment on the earth and the isles are to wait for his *torah*, his revelation (42:4), but the themes of judgment and *torah* are reflected also in 40:27, 42:21, 24, and 51:4. There is the same concern with the witnessing to the peoples of a universally available salvation (49:6; cf. 51:5 ff.). The theme of salvation which is dominant in the other oracles is dominant in the servant songs also. The birth of the Servant and the formation of Israel are described in similar terms (49:1, 5; cf. 44:21, 24). Muilenburg contends that all this militates against the songs being the work of another hand.

Nor can we regard the songs as later interpolations. As Muilenburg points out, the fourth song (52:13-53:12) does preserve the continuity between 51:17-52:12 and 54:1 ff. We must recognize that the dominant theme of the whole section is contained in essence within this song. The redemption and restoration declared in the other oracles is brought to a focus in the redemptive suffering of the Servant. So also with the other songs. They fit into their context not as interpolations, but as elements in the development of the theme.

Once we have admitted this, however, we still have the problem of the identity of the Servant. The vast number of attempts at such identification in all their multivariety makes us aware of the magnitude of the mystery that we face. Interpretations vary from various corporate views, through identification with various historical individuals, to a purely messianic understanding.[8] The lack of agreement may well indicate that there is some aspect of truth in all the views. There are first of all those who take the approach that is indicated by those oracles not included in the servant songs. They take a corporate view of the Servant and identify him with either the actual Israel or the ideal Israel or the faithful remnant within Israel. One difficulty with this view is that there are passages in the songs themselves which demand a more individualistic interpretation. Such passages as 53:8–12 are best understood in individual and personal terms.

Hence there are others who identify the Servant with some historical personage. The choice of the latter varies from Moses [9] through Jeremiah [10] to the prophet himself.[11] Even the tragic figure of the young king Jehoiachin [12] has been included. The presence of the exodus theme and a covenant motif might lead us to the idea of Moses. The obvious influence of the Jeremianic literary form and the presence in the songs of elements akin to Jeremiah's confessions and laments (50:4–9; 52:13–53:12) might support the identification with Jeremiah. We know so little of Deutero-Isaiah himself that the equating of him with the Servant leaves us in a field of open speculation. Again we may say that elements from all these historical figures, including the prophet's own experience, may be present in the image of the Servant. Yet the difficulty remains that there are parts of the songs where a more corporate image of the Servant seems demanded.

The influences of the Babylonian New Year Festival, of the Tammuz ritual, and even of a possible preexilic Hebrew Enthronement Festival are held by others to be the key.[13] In varying ways in such festivals the king was held to be both the representative of the god and the representative of the people. In the case of the Babylonian festival and of the Tammuz ritual we have the naturalistic theme of the god dying and rising again, such death and resurrection being reenacted by the monarch who was his representative. We find it very difficult to believe that such ideas could have directly influenced Deutero-Isaiah whose historical understanding of Yahweh, of his abiding steadfastness and covenant relationship with Israel, would eliminate such an understanding of either Yahweh or his royal representative. Aubrey Johnson's [14] reconstruction of a possible preexilic Hebrew ceremony is more acceptable. Here the king as representative passes through an annual ritual of death and resurrection in order that, in his person, the life of the nation and its righteousness or moral health may be renewed. Undoubtedly, if we accept the very plausible view that such a ceremony was held, the memory of it would linger on and would even be stimulated by the pomp and ritual of the pagan Babylonian festival.[15] This may well, therefore, have contributed to some degree to Deutero-Isaiah's picture of the sufferings of the Servant in the fourth servant song. We have the emphasis on the creation epic, already noted, and its association with the exodus motif. We have also the presence of the tradition of the Jerusalem royal theology and the motif of the Davidic covenant. Both of these are bound up with such a festival, so the idea of influence from the ritualistic past is not strange. The point is that the Servant, so understood, may well then have been a royal figure.

This brings us to another line of identification, the view that the Servant is specifically messianic. One difficulty here is the fact that the Servant was not generally identified with the Davidic Messiah in Jewish tradition and interpretation until the Christian era.[16] It could be pointed out that just as Yahweh's Spirit is possessed by the Davidic Messiah of Isaiah 11, so the Spirit rests upon the Servant (42:1). Yet this charismatic aspect is not peculiar to the Messiah, any more than the use of the phrase, the "anointed one," applies specifically only to Israel's king. Again, we might point to the association of the Servant with a covenant that seems generally conceived along lines of the Davidic covenant (49:8; cf. 55:3). It would seem that there is some truth in this identification of the Servant also.

The real understanding of the servant figure probably turns upon our insight into the Hebrew way of thinking. H. W. Robinson would have us remember the corporate aspect of Hebrew thought, whereby it was easy for the men of the Old Testament to move from the individual to the group of which he was a member, and vice versa. Indeed, in the early days, as we have already seen, the emphasis tended to fall first upon the group and then upon the individual whose personality was in some sense also merged with the corporate personality of the whole. Although with the Exile and in the ministries of Jeremiah and Ezekiel the emphasis upon the individual had become far more central, this does not mean that we must dismiss at this point the corporate aspect of man's consciousness. It was still far more natural for him than for us twentieth-century westerners with our individualism to move easily from the group to some individual within the group. This individual could incorporate the group in his own personality and represent it.

If we understand the servant image in this fluid way, we can see how easy it would be for the prophet to hold together both a corporate and an individual conception of the Servant. The Servant could be Israel, but he could also be an individual person who gathered up in himself in a representative way all of Israel. In portraying this person, the prophet called upon the rich resources of Israel's past, for these too were gathered up in the

Servant. Thus, we should not be surprised to find traces of Moses and Jeremiah, aspects drawn from the ritual of the Enthronement Festival and the royal theology, even elements derived from the prophet's own experience. So the Servant would come to embody the spiritual riches and experiences of Israel's history and individual men of God. He could be both personal and corporate, Israel as a whole and yet a person who in a representative capacity gathered up all Israel and its historical past.

It has been pointed out that no Hebrew man of the prophet's own time could actually embody the vision which Deutero-Isaiah puts into this image. The Servant is a figure of the end time, a focal point of that redemption which is brought to Israel by the coming of Yahweh in his glory. Thus he may well have been for the prophet the Davidic Messiah. Yet his task was one of sacrificial death and redemptive suffering. He appears to have been for Deutero-Isaiah the central figure in whom God was to achieve the redemption of Israel and the proclamation of his *torah* to the nations. If in the first part of Deutero-Isaiah the interest centers in Cyrus, in the second part it centers in the Servant. Cyrus is the historical agent who ushers in the coming of Yahweh. The Servant is the central figure through whom God consummates his purpose. We may even see, with Buber,[17] the prophet deliberately contrasting the two in God's purpose, if we compare the statement on Cyrus in 41:1–3 with that of the Servant in 42:1–4.

So we come to the task of the Servant himself in the time of the end. In the fourth song the Servant becomes the innocent sufferer, despised and rejected by his fellows. At this point evidently the image is not corporate, but individual. Despite his message of comfort, the prophet does not spare Israel for its sin and shortcoming. It has been spiritually blind and deaf, and the Exile has been its judgment (42:18–25). Even in the Exile it has been querulous (40:27; 45:9). It has continued obdurate and hardhearted (46:12; 50:2). But God will not reject his servant Israel. He will redeem it, and its center will be the representative figure in whom Israel will be gathered representatively and whose innocence will cover the nation's guilt. His innocent suffering at the hands of his fellows—and the songs echo the laments of Jeremiah—will become a guilt offering (53:10) whereby men shall draw near to Yahweh. Here we have the deep revelatory insight that God's redemption can be wrought only when one man vicariously lays down his life for his fellows and in his righteousness justifies the many. The Servant will bear men's sins and intercede through his sacrifice for the transgressors. His offering is thus within God's purpose, indeed is the focal point of the ultimate consummation. It pleased Yahweh to bruise him, but in his pouring out his life to death, redemption would be accomplished. So the Servant would bring Jacob to Yahweh and restore the preserved of Israel (49:5, 6). But as Israel is gathered up in this representative act of redemption, the image of the Servant expands from the individual sufferer to the corporate whole, and he becomes, through his sufferings and the testimony of Israel, a light to the nations (49:6; 42:6). So 52:13–53:12 is a collective lament in which Israel and the nations read their own guilt and sin in the sufferings of the Servant and become the many who are justified by God. To them, at the end of the lament, the divine oracle of promise is given.

The Servant is the focal point of the covenant of the ultimate consummation, a covenant extending beyond Israel to the Gentiles (42:6). Its models are the steadfast graciousness of God shown in the covenant with all men in the days of Noah and in the covenant with the house of David, both very evidently sheer acts of grace to the rebellious and undeserving (54:9; 55:3–5). The universal motif returns as the prophet sees in the restoration of Israel the reconciliation of the nations. Yet the universal hope comes through historical particularity. God approaches men through his Servant who is both the individual and yet representative sufferer, and through Israel which is redeemed in the sufferer. So the Servant will bring a new world order among men. He will establish judgment (*mishpat*), (42:1, 4).

The magnificent hope of the prophet remained unfulfilled promise until the Christ-event dawned. All the patterns of the ultimate consummation as the prophets saw it became actualized in the person and sacrifice of Jesus of Nazareth. In him, the true people of God became a reality and through his mighty act and the testimony of his body, the Church, all men may draw near.

NOTES

1. Sigmund Mowinckel, *Studien zu Deuterojesaja* (Stuttgart: W. Kohlhammer, 1938), p. 5.
2. In this matter James Muilenburg has done an outstanding study in "The Book of Isaiah, Chapters 40–66: Introduction and Exegesis," *Interpreter's Bible*, 12 vols. (Nashville: Abingdon Press, 1956), 5: 381–418; 422 ff.
3. Norman Gottwald, *A Light to the Nations* (New York: Harper & Bros., 1959), p. 403.
4. See Martin Buber, *The Prophetic Faith* (New York: Macmillan, 1949), pp. 203 ff.
5. Paul Volz, *Jesaia II: Kommentar zum Alten Testament* (Leipzig: P. Deichert, 1932).
6. Buber, *Prophetic Faith*, p. 209.
7. See Muilenburg, "The Book of Isaiah," pp. 406 ff.
8. For a full discussion of these views see Christopher R. North, *The Suffering Servant in Deutero-Isaiah* (London: Oxford University

Press, 1948), *passim*; H. H. Rowley, *The Servant of the Lord* (London: Lutterworth Press, 1952).

9. Ernst Sellin, *Mose und seine Bedeutung für die Israelitisch-Jüdische Religionsgeschichte* (Leipzig: A. Deichertsche Verlagsbuchhandlung, 1922).

10. Sheldon Blank, "Studies on Deutero-Isaiah," *Hebrew Union College Annual* 15 (1940): 18 ff.

11. So Sigmund Mowinckel, *Der Knecht Yahwäs*, 1921.

12. Also see Ernst Sellin, *Das rätsel des Deuterojesajanischen buches* (Leipzig: A. Deichert, 1908), pp. 131 ff.

13. See Hugo Gressmann, *Der ursprung der israelitisch-jüdaischen eschatologie* (Göttingen: Vandenhoeck und Ruprecht, 1905), pp. 326 ff. Mowinckel argues that the fourth song was contributed by a disciple of Deutero-Isaiah and describes the prophet's sufferings. Ivan Engnell, "The Ebed Yahweh Songs and the Suffering Messiah in 'Deutero-Isaiah,'" *Bulletin of John Rylands Library* 31 (January 1948): 1–42, contends that the sufferings of the Servant are to be understood in the light of the Tammuz liturgy.

14. See Aubrey Johnson, *Sacral Kingship in Ancient Israel* (Cardiff: University of Wales Press, 1955), *passim*.

15. We have already noted that the prophet was influenced by processional features of this festival, as seen in 46:1 ff.

16. Cf. Rowley, *Servant of the Lord*, pp. 59–88.

17. Buber, *Prophetic Faith*, pp. 219. ff.

Chapter Eight

The Descent of the Spirit
and the Figure of
the Son of Man

Deutero-Isaiah marks the high point of Israel's prophetical tradi-
tion. Those who came after him showed a superficial optimism or an increasing pessimism about the historical scene.
The high notes of the message of the great predecessors are
sounded, but some associate the ultimate consummation, the
eschaton, too closely with the contemporary scene, and others
despair of the historical order altogether. We are on the verge
of thoroughgoing apocalypticism, and this kind of thought characterizes postexilic prophetic eschatology. By apocalypticism
we mean an increasing despair of history, a belief that the End
will come by direct divine intervention and not by the agency
of historical forces, a view of the present as a scene of judgment
in which the faithful wait for the divine deliverance which God
will bring. Yet we need to remember that apocalypticism did add
a cosmic and universal dimension to the final consummation.
It brought in all the nations and embraced all history within its
perspective. We have seen that as early as Isaiah of Jerusalem
there is a transcendent reference in the End, however much
historical agents may also be mentioned. The miraculous element
of a divine intervention appears in Ezekiel's hope of a re-created
spirit in man and in the mysterious figure of the Suffering Servant
who is central in Deutero-Isaiah's vision of the End. The postexilic prophets accentuate what is already present, but tend increasingly to sever the End from history. In the Book of Daniel
we have almost attained a genuine apocalypticism.

The prophetic figures that we are now concerned with cover
the period from the returns of 538 B.C. and 520 B.C. to the time
of the Maccabean revolt. They include Haggai and Zechariah,
prophets associated with the return of 520 B.C. under Zerubbabel.

Here we must separate Zechariah 9–14 from the first eight chapters, attributing the latter to the historical Zechariah. The so-called Deutero-Zechariah (9–14) carries a more distinctively transcendent flavor in its understanding of the End. It makes no mention of Zerubbabel and Joshua, so prominent in Zechariah 1–8, and its reference to Greece in 9:13 seems to indicate a period when the Hellenistic Age is dawning. We shall refer it broadly to the period of Alexander the Great and after.

We have also the prophecy of Joel which again carries the marks of a much more transcendent view of the Day of Yahweh and which at least assumes that the Temple and the city of Jerusalem have been restored (1:14; 2:7 ff., 17). There is no reference to a king, the priests are leaders of the society, the northern kingdom of Israel is not referred to, Babylon and Assyria are not mentioned, while 3:6 refers to the Grecians buying Judahites as slaves, a state of affairs much more consonant with the Exile and after. The general indications are toward a postexilic dating, roughly about 450 B.C.

Obadiah has two sections, verses 1–14 and 15–21, which are both compatible with postexilic dating. The second section is an eschatological message with a universal note that suggests the postexilic period.

Malachi is an anonymous book which, because of its concern with the problem of foreign marriages, so crucial in the time of Nehemiah and Ezra (2:11, 12), and its reference to the governor (*pekah*) in 1:8, evidently belongs to the Persian period, around 450 B.C.

Included in the postexilic group of prophecies are two sections of Isaiah, chapters 24–27 and chapters 56–66. Isaiah 24–27 consists of a combination of prophetic oracles with lyrical hymns of praise and thanksgiving. They describe a catastrophic judgment of cosmic proportions, which savors of the same transition from prophecy to apocalyptic as we find in Ezekiel 38 and 39 and Zechariah 9–14. They do not employ the simple view of the End found in preexilic prophecy, and, although the influence of the Isaianic circle is to be found in certain aspects of style and vocabulary, there is far more evidence of dissimilarity. They portray the transcendent and universal emphasis which characterizes postexilic prophecy, but they are not developed apocalyptic.

Isaiah 56–66 is often termed Trito-Isaiah, although the unity of the section is by no means evident. There is sufficient variety of style and subject matter to make this a series of detached oracles, some bearing sufficient similarity to Deutero-Isaiah to have been by his hand or from his immediate circle, for example, 57:14–20, and chapters 60–62. The setting of these oracles is Palestine, after the return from exile. The leadership of the restored community is attacked (56:9–12), and there is a resur-

gence of the syncretism that characterized the last days of
preexilic Jerusalem (58). We find in the closing chapters the
transcendent and cosmic understanding of the End which followed the exile. It is difficult to date the section other than generally after the return and during the next century, the dates of the
individual oracles being various.

Last of all, we have the Book of Daniel. The presence in this
book of both late Hebrew and Aramaic; the fact that it occurs in
the late third section of the Old Testament canon, the Writings,
and not in the Prophets; the lack in it of accurate knowledge of
Babylonian history during the exilic period; the absence of any
mention of Daniel by Ben Sirach in his list of famous men
(Ecclus. 44–50), written about 200 B.C.—all these suggest a
late date for the book. Add to these the fact that correspondence
with actual history in chapter 11 ceases in the time of the
Maccabean revolt and the fairly certain identification of Antiochus
Epiphanes with some of the images and incidents in the visions,
and we may date the book about 165 B.C. It is a "tract for the
times," written when the Jews faced fresh persecution and, in its
first section (chaps. 1–6), drawing on stories with an exilic setting to encourage them. A full critical survey is not within our
purview. We shall satisfy ourselves by suggesting that the book
is a unity, and that the Aramaic sections were fitted for popular
consumption (chaps. 2–6), whereas the visions were written in
late Hebrew as a language more fitted to their lofty and less
popular character (chaps. 8–12). The stories section may well have
been circulated separately at first, and then been incorporated in
the larger book with a Hebrew introduction (chap. 1) and an
Aramaic connecting chapter (7).[1]

THE POSTEXILIC BACKGROUND OF PROPHECY

The Persian rule lasted from 539 B.C. to 321 B.C., and this
period witnesses the decline of the Hebrew prophetic consciousness. Several factors contributed to this but the most important
was the absence of a broad international background in which
great political events and significant historical figures were evident. Israel was reduced in size to a small community, and its
Persian suzerainty remained to a large extent unshaken by great
crisis happenings. The Jews now had little hope of political power,
and no possible deliverance appeared upon the horizon. Until the
time of Alexander the Great, no significant figure crossed the
historical stage, and it is noteworthy that oracles in Obadiah (1–
14) and Malachi (1:2–5) were in a measure stimulated by a comparatively minor event, the fall of Edom at the hands of the Naba-
tean Arabs.

A second element was the increasing emphasis on the divine
transcendence, already evidenced in Ezekiel. As early as the
prophetic work of Zechariah this issue is to the fore. Even

for him, Yahweh was so transcendent that angels had to mediate the divine decrees and counsels. This loss of a sense of direct contact with God must have exercised a profound influence on the prophetic consciousness. It is significant that the postexilic period saw the development of various mediating conceptions and agencies. Angels mediated between God and man. Already present in Ezekiel, they become more central in Zechariah, and by the time of the Book of Daniel have become accepted intermediaries. In the postbiblical period, angels came to play a large part in the machinery of apocalyptic and in Rabbinic teaching as mediators of the law. Again, the concept of Wisdom as a divine intermediary in creation develops in the Wisdom Literature until a poetic personification becomes a full mediating being (Prov. 8; Ecclus. 24; Wisd. of Sol. 9). The prophet tends no longer to feel himself the direct instrument of Yahweh.

A third factor in the situation was closely bound up with the last—the emergence of a written law and a legalistic spirit. Deuteronomy enshrined, to a large extent, the preexilic prophetic emphasis on morals and retribution, within the framework of the original Shechem covenant. Jeremiah had finally opposed it only because he saw the externalism to which it was leading, and it was this externalism which dealt a death blow to prophecy. Ezekiel the prophet turns into priest toward the end of his ministry and legislates for the restored community and its temple. After the Exile, no prophet akin to Jeremiah in spiritual intensity arose to combat the growing legalism and to emphasize the need of a new covenant, the law written in the heart. It was this externalism and legalism which became responsible for the preoccupation of postexilic prophets with the Temple and its worship and with a narrow nationalism and exclusiveness which denied the all-embracing vision of their predecessors.

In addition, we have to remember that the glorious promises of Deutero-Isaiah and of Zechariah remained unfulfilled. The latter prophet had even made the mistake of identifying the Messiah with the historical figure of Zerubbabel. When the latter mysteriously disappeared from the scene, even though Zechariah had declared that Yahweh would use him, there grew up a tendency to distrust the prophetic voice.

Finally, we have to remember that the major task of the prophetic revelation now seemed to be accomplished. The promises had been made, and there was little that could be added to them until the day of fulfillment dawned. The great moral notes had been sounded. Most of the great theological insights had been disclosed already in the prophetic consciousness. All that could be done now was to combine and synthesize what had already been declared. Israel had tasted the bitter dregs of judgment. It had ceased to exist as a political nation and found continuation as a church, which treasured its past and waited for deliverance. So we shall not expect, in this postexilic prophetic consciousness, to find much that is new, although certain new elements in the End become evident.

The effects of all this on the religious life of postexilic Israel are very evident. For one thing we can see a movement from the prophet to the priest. The Temple and its worship with the accompanying structure of the Law increasingly occupy the centre of the stage, and the prophetic voice falls into the background. Ezekiel had emphasized just this state of affairs in his picture of the restored community, and with his postexilic prophetic successors the Temple and its affairs become a preoccupation.[2] For Haggai the bad economic conditions besetting the newly returned exiles are a judgment for their failure to rebuild the Temple (1:1–11; 2:15–20). For Joel, a century later, the greatest calamity is that the worship of the Temple should cease. A plague of locusts has caused the failure of the daily peace and food offerings (1:9, 13), and the prophet sees this as the advance guard of the Day of Yahweh. Even the Day itself is to be characterized by the purification of ritual observance, and the note of moral righteousness is not raised (2:14). There are sections of Trito-Isaiah that major on the ceremonial observance of the Sabbath (56:1–7) and fasting (58:1–12), yet the moral emphasis does appear, while the old prophetic spirit breaks through in oracles that attack the social and economic ills of oppression (57:1), injustice (59:14), falsehood (59:15), and sexual impurity (57:3). This prophet sees that the major issue is man's separation from God (57:11 ff.; 59:1–11), and he attacks the immoral elements in religious practice (57:1–6; 66:1–4).

Zechariah follows his contemporary Haggai in condemning the failure to rebuild the Temple, but he also sounds the moral note in his condemnation, and at times he touches the heights of his great predecessors (for example, 7:8 ff.). He sees sin personified as a woman who is cast into an *ephah* measure, covered with a heavy lid, and transported into Babylon where she is to remain for the future (5:5–11). Yahweh will purge his people of evil, and that evil is moral not ceremonial. In a great passage that is reminiscent of Micah, the prophet enjoins the people to speak the truth and execute justice (8:16, 17). Yet with it all the Temple and its worship have come to occupy a place of far greater importance, and Joshua the high priest is given a prominent position in the prophet's oracles. Yahweh will dwell with his people in a restored community that centers in the Temple (8:3).

Malachi is the last book of the Roll of the Twelve in more senses than mere position. In this unnamed prophet many of the features that mark the decline of the prophetic consciousness are present. Not least is the marked stress upon cultic observance and ritual. The prophet does at times condemn the moral evils of the people. Yet these are attacked, not so much *sui generis,* as because they are hindrances to the religious mission of the nation. The indifference of the priesthood and the laity, the neglect of the cult in the offering of unclean sacrifices, and the remission of tithes are the ills which account for the lack of prosperity and the widespread social injustice and oppression (1:6–2:9; 3:7–12). The prophet stresses the ritual requirements rather than the moral obligation, although he does seem to go deeper when he indicates that his abhorrence of perfunctory ritual is due to the deep-seated indifference to God which underlies it (3:8). Even "Malachi's" denunciation of the divorce of native wives turns not so much upon the worth of human personality as upon the necessity of conserving a pure and undefiled religion, for it is closely bound up with the remarriage with foreigners (2:10–16). Even the eschatology centers in the cult. The Day of Yahweh will be a day of cleansing for the priesthood (3:1–6).

The decline of the prophetic consciousness in this postexilic period is seen also in the fate of the preexilic cultic prophets. Although this group included, as we have seen, many of the false prophets whom the reform or classical prophets attacked, they also included many zealous and devout followers of Yahweh. Some of their work may indeed be preserved in Nahum and Habakkuk. Undoubtedly, they were responsible for units of oracles and prayers preserved in the Temple and the local shrines for cultic use. To such units many of our psalms may well be traced. Thanks to the work of Gunkel and Mowinckel, biblical scholarship has long since ceased to regard the psalms in our Psalter as wholly postexilic in origin.[3] It is evident that in their present form they are shaped to the needs of the postexilic worshiping community. Furthermore, we can trace the influence of Jeremiah and Deutero-Isaiah upon some of the lyrical forms. It is clear, however, that many of the thanksgiving hymns (corporate and individual), the laments (corporate and individual), the imprecatory psalms, and the so-called royal psalms can be traced back, by their form and content, to preexilic usage.

Their transformation into the Psalmody of the Second Temple is better understood when we seek to trace the fate of the preexilic cultic prophets. Aubrey R. Johnson has shown conclusively that in the postexilic period the latter became the Levitical choir guilds. In our Psalter, there are collections of psalms ascribed to such guilds as Asaph, Heman, Jeduthun, and the sons of Korah. The historical Books of Chronicles are a postexilic rewriting of the Deuteronomaic historical writings contained in the Books of Samuel and Kings. Their concern is with the Temple and its ritual, and they show a special interest in the Levitical singers. Evidently they are a rewriting of the history from the point of view of such interest. Johnson has shown how the prophetic figures and functions mentioned in Samuel and Kings are associated with Temple singers in 1 and 2 Chronicles, thereby demonstrating the fate of the cultic prophets. Thus the prophets of 2 Kings 23:2 are replaced by the Levites of 2 Chronicles 34:30. Even the Chronicler describes the two choir leaders, Asaph and Jeduthun, as the king's seers (1 Chron. 15:17–19; 2 Chron. 29:30; 35:15). Heman, the third choir conductor, is described in 1 Chronicles 25:1–7 as "the king's seer in the words of God, to lift up the horn," and the latter phrase is a sign of success or well-being drawn from the animal world (cf. Ps. 92:10; 75:10; 89:17, 24). Thus, he is the one who gives oracles of peace. It is noteworthy that the Chronicler uses the verbal form of *to prophesy* to denote the special function of the Temple singers (1 Chron. 25:1–7). This identification is reinforced when we remember that the early $n^e vi'im$ are described as descending from high places with musical instruments. Perhaps most interesting of all, we find the Chronicler describing a typical prophet in action, but in action as a member of a Temple choir (2 Chron. 20:1–30).

Thus the moral emphasis of the great prophetic tradition found continuing expression in Jewish psalmody and had its place in the Temple worship. Yet the canonical prophetic figures themselves were suffering a decline. The fate that had overtaken the cultic prophets is reflected also in them. They occasionally reached great moral heights, but then only by sounding again the great ethical demands of their predecessors. They too were becoming dominated by the cult. The nation had now become a church. Its life was that of a theocracy in which, because Yahweh was increasingly envisaged as remote and transcendent, the priesthood became the leaders of the community. The land, with its life, its seasons, and its times, was Yahweh's. There were special cultic times and places for approaching God. Man's possessions belonged primarily to his creator, and the theory of property was given a religious base in the enforcement of the tithes. There is a greatness about such a vision, but it suffered from the way in which the ritual and the moral were regarded on the same level. The ritual was often given the preeminence.

The Increasing Emphasis on the Transcendence and Cosmic Proportions of the End Time

For the preexilic prophets, the Day of Yahweh had been the act of God, but it had been ushered in by historical agencies, and there was a sense of continuity between history and the End. Even in Isaiah of Jerusalem there is a recognition of the transcendent dimension in the latter and also an attempt to picture it in cosmic terms, yet the continuity with history is very evident. Jeremiah's emphasis on the miraculous divine inbreak in the creation of the new and inward covenant, Ezekiel's hope that God will create a new heart and a right spirit when the Day dawns and will resurrect the valley of dry bones, Deutero-Isaiah's use of the absolute word *bara'*, "to create," of the end as of the beginning of history, and his vision of the mysterious and divinely ordained figure of the Servant—all these indicate that the transcendent and miraculous aspect was deepening. In addition we have to remember that the mysterious figure of Gog from the land of Magog introduces into the final consummation the idea that God will himself intervene directly in history to deliver his people. Postexilic eschatology was already lifting its head.

With the postexilic prophets, the Day of Yahweh will be ushered in by a world cataclysm in which God himself will intervene directly in human affairs. So for Joel, the Day of Yahweh is ushered in by the advance guard of the plague of locusts and accompanying drought, but the center of the End is portrayed as Yahweh himself sitting in the "valley of decision" and passing judgment upon the nations of the earth. The judgment takes the form of battle in which the heathen nations will be destroyed (3:9–16) and in which God will intervene with cosmic upheaval. The final consummation will also see the exaltation of Jerusalem to a state of prosperity. The royal theology may well find expression in the declaration that Yahweh will himself be a stronghold and refuge for his people in the midst of the cataclysm (3:16). God will come to dwell in his holy mountain and the tabernacling presence will make Jerusalem holy and Judah prosperous (3:17, 20, 21), while the surrounding peoples will be a desolation (3:19). Universality is here, but it is a universality of judgment. God is sovereign over all peoples, and his moral demands extend to all nations.

In Joel's understanding of the End, the outpouring of the Spirit is central. In dealing with the Day of Yahweh, the prophet prefaces the awesome cataclysm by declaring that God will pour out his Spirit upon all the Israelites. This divine intervention is obviously intended to signify a democratization of the prophetic religion. Those who receive the Spirit will be able to see God's will and declare it prophetically. Ezekiel, with his emphasis upon the re-creation of a right heart and a clean spirit in the restored Israel, had already envisaged this hope of the gift of the Spirit to the house of Israel (Ezek. 39:29; cf. Isa. 44:3). Joel adds the evangelical note of grace within this context and declares that all who call upon the name of Yahweh shall be saved. Thereby the remnant of the redeemed will be constituted in Mount Zion and in Jerusalem (2:32). Once more we see how the type of theology manifested in Isaiah and Ezekiel persists in the thought of this prophet.

The Gog-Magog vision of Ezekiel and the idea of a cataclysm of cosmic proportions is reflected again in the oracles of Deutero-Zechariah. We may doubt whether these oracles form a unity, and hence it would be wrong to seek for a systematic picture. We find, however, the constituent elements of such a picture in some of the oracles, especially 12:1–13:6; 13:7–9; and 14:1–20. The emphasis upon a direct divine intervention against the enemies of Israel and in defense of God's covenant people occurs in 9:13 ff. Yahweh will appear over his people, and his arrow will go forth like lightning. The reference to Greece in verse 13 suggests the Hellenistic period, possibly as late as the Maccabean period. The victory is won by God, even though the Jews participate.

The oracle of 10:3–12 attacks the foreign shepherds and leaders who oppress the people. It declares that God will confound them and will gather together the dispersed of Ephraim and Judah. There follows in 11:1–3 a lament over the fall of the tyrants. Chapter 11, verses 15–17, is another oracle which declares the fall of the tyrannical oppressors. In this case the object of attack appears to be a worthless native shepherd.

In 12:1–14 we have a picture of Jerusalem itself beset by the heathen. The prophet emphasizes, like his great predecessor Isaiah, the inviolability of Zion. The country people of Judah, at first onlookers, join in the fray as the strength of Yahweh of hosts is manifested through the stronghold of Jerusalem. The heathen nations shall be overthrown. This theme is repeated in chapter 14 with yet greater emphasis upon direct divine intervention. As the nations gather around Jerusalem, Yahweh himself will go forth to fight for his people. In natural convulsions, his presence will be felt, and his holy ones, his angelic hosts, will appear with him.

In the picture of the End, the cosmic aspect will find expression also in the fertility of the land and the prosperity of the redeemed people. The end will be a time of purifying (13:7–9), and there is a suggestion of the enigmatic figure of the Suffering Servant in 13:7. The same figure also appears in the picture of the martyr who has been pierced in 12:10 ff. The exact purport of this is not clear, although it appears to be an aspect of the divine redemptive activity. Vriezen sums up the situation well when he suggests that Isaiah 53 "hardly found an echo among the people in spite of the fact that the post-exilic prophets now and then revert to this idea (Zechariah may be a case in point)." [4] The theme of the healing stream of Ezekiel 47 recurs in Zechariah 14:8, and again the implication is creative renewal of land and people.

In Obadiah we find an eschatological section (vv. 15–21). The Day of Yahweh is near and will be one of universal judgment on the nations. Again, the Jerusalem theme of Isaiah and Ezekiel is central. Mount Zion will be holy, a place of escape for the righteous and purified Israelites who escape the judgment, and saviors, akin to the judges of old, will deliver the people from the oppressors. It will be the day of God's Kingdom. The developed eschatological note is not so evident.

Not so, however, when we turn to Trito-Isaiah. Here there are oracles which reflect the theophanic and transcendent aspect of postexilic eschatology. In 63:1–6 we have a picture of Yahweh returning from crushing the Edomites, his garments stained in their blood. The choice of Edom was probably typical rather than specific. It may well be that Edom was in the center of the picture at the time of writing, as with Obadiah. This is a theophanic manifestation of the avenging God and is evidently of eschatological form. Coupled with this, we have a picture of the glorious future in Isaiah 60–62. Yahweh will be Israel's savior (60:16), and the processes of nature shall be subservient to the welfare of his people (60:19 ff.). The Day of Yahweh is declared imminent, and then a righteous people shall be manifested in a restored land.

In Isaiah 65–66 a more transcendent note is sounded. God's vengeance on the heathen nations is announced, and it is declared that he will create a new heaven and a new earth in which paradisiacal conditions will prevail. The use of the verb *create* and the emphasis on former things not being remembered (65:17) suggest a divine act akin to the initial act of creation. In 66:10–24, the theophanic intervention of Yahweh with cosmic upheaval, venting his wrath upon the heathen nations, is again described (vv. 15 ff.). In the center of the restored order shall be Jerusalem, God's holy mountain, and all flesh shall worship before him in the Temple (vv. 20–23). Thus the cultic interest and the emphasis on the presence in Jerusalem are both present.

The so-called little Apocalypse of Isaiah (24–27) contains a picture of world upheaval and destruction in which a catastrophic judgment overtakes the nations, including a specific but unnamed heathen city (24, 25). It is clearly set forth as God's act (27:11, 13). Yahweh will come forth from his place to punish the inhabitants of the earth for their iniquity, and the gory details of a conflict are portrayed (for example, 26:21). The struggle of God with the primordial chaos monster becomes an image for this new day of his triumph (27:1). Out of the midst of the cataclysm the Jews will be delivered. The absence of systematic presentation and the piecemeal nature of the complex of oracles mean that we cannot see clearly what the prophet or prophets hoped for.

Yet there is the image of resurrection (26:19). Apparently only the righteous dead are raised, and some scholars doubt whether this is so much individual resurrection as resurrection of the nation (cf. Ezek. 37). If the former be the case then we have for the first time the portrayal of an end time in which membership of the restored and righteous remnant will be through a divine and individualized act of resurrection. Once more the emphasis falls upon divine intervention. The Isaianic theme of the inviolability of Zion and the necessity of faith is very evident (for example, the oracle of 26:1–10).

In the Book of Daniel, the trends of postexilic eschatology find

their fullest expression in a point of view that is passing over
into apocalyptic. This is not the weird apocalypticism and the
esoteric speculation of the period between the Testaments, but it
is sufficiently near to it for many of those traits to be in evidence. It is our contention, however, that Daniel at least retains something of the prophetic note. The canvas is worldwide,
and, in the true prophetic succession, God is represented as the
ruler of all nations. The world empires are all under his sovereignty. It is he who reveals the mysteries of history (2:28), and
his kingdom is everlasting (4:3).

In the stories of the first six chapters and the visions of the
second six chapters, this theme is dominant. The visions convey,
in mounting emphasis, the conviction of the seer that the advent
of the End is near. In the first vision (chap. 7), the four world
empires of Babylon, Media, Persia, and Greece are evidently portrayed in the symbolic figures of the four beasts. In the earlier
dream of chapter 2, they are symbolized in the various metals
constituting the great image. The author's misreading of history
is seen in his emphasis on a historically nonexistent Medean
empire, but his real point is made in the act of God by which
the successive sovereignties of these empires are brought to an
end. A divine intervention overthrows the fourth empire, the
Hellenistic, and God's everlasting kingdom is set up on earth,
symbolized in the figure of the Son of man, to a full understanding of which we must turn later. In the dream of chapter 2, the
mighty image which is built of the successive empires is dashed
to pieces by a stone cut out by no human hand (2:34), again
an indication that the End will come by divine agency. World
dominion now becomes the lot of God's people.

In chapter 8 we have a vision of the conflict between the
Medo-Persian Empire, represented as a ram, and the Hellenistic
Empire of Alexander, represented as a he-goat. The latter prevails,
and its four horns, Alexander's successors, produce in their midst
a fifth small horn, Antiochus Epiphanes. This king ushers in a
period of great tribulation for God's people, and the seer is anxious to emphasize that the end is now imminent. Once more
God will intervene, and Antiochus and his abominations will be
wiped out. The Greek tyrant will be broken, but by no human
hand (8:25).

In chapters 10–12:4 we have a summary of the actual history
of the conflicts and alliances between the Egyptian Ptolemies,
the kings of the south, and the Syrian Seleucids, the kings of
the north. The account conveys the sense of a deterministic view
of the future because of the author's literary device of throwing
back a Maccabean prophecy to the time of the Babylonian exile.
The story culminates in Antiochus Epiphanes and his setting up
of the image of Zeus, the abomination that makes desolate, in
the Temple (11:21–45). Yet he shall be destroyed and none shall

help him. The setting of his destruction will be around Jerusalem, and the typical picture of the last enemy assailing Mount Zion appears again (11:45).[5] The End thus dawning will involve a great tribulation for the Jews, but it will also bring the divine act of resurrection. The latter will be heralded by the archangel Michael, indicating the heavenly intervention by which the time of the End supervenes. The resurrection will be both of the just and the unjust. Thus we have a deeper insight than Isaiah 26: 19. The wicked also will be raised, even though it be "to shame and everlasting contempt" (12:2).

THE DAVIDIC MESSIAH AND THE SON OF MAN

The anticipation of a Davidic Messiah largely disappears after the early postexilic period. This is probably to be explained by the overenthusiastic identification of this figure with Zerubbabel by Haggai and Zechariah (Zech. 1–8). We can understand this in the light of the political background. At the accession of Darius to the Persian throne in 521 B.C., the ancient world was in complete disorder. Darius himself had only succeeded to the kingship by overthrowing other claimants. Thus, at this time there was direct stimulus for the hope of the political independence of Judah. Zerubbabel, the prince appointed by the Persians, was himself of the Davidic line, and Jewish aspirations would easily fix on him as the anointed one under whom the kingdom would be reestablished. A messianic prophet could thus easily find a stimulus for his message from the contemporary situation.

One oracle of Haggai identifies Zerubbabel with the "Signet ring" chosen by Yahweh (2:23). The title signifies that he is to occupy the position originally enjoyed by Jehoiachin (Jer. 22:24–30), and this would indicate accession to the Davidic throne. The same theme is taken up by Zechariah who describes Zerubbabel as the *branch* or the *shoot* (3:8; 6:12). The title itself is a messianic one and was so used by Isaiah (Isa. 11:1; cf. Jer. 23: 5–6; 33:14–16). Joshua as high priest is closely associated with Zerubbabel and is to stand at the right hand of the latter, working in close association with him (6:13). Chapter 6, verse 12, might seem to identify the branch with Joshua, but this is clearly not intended. In 4:9 Zerubbabel is he who is to rebuild the Temple, and the branch is identified by this description in 6:12. Both Zerubbabel and Joshua are anointed ones (4:14), however, working together to restore the kingdom.

After the rebuilding of the Temple, Zerubbabel mysteriously disappears from history, and with this we may imagine that many hopes were dashed. It may well be that Zerubbabel actually participated in a plot to establish Judah as an independent state under his kingship. Certainly in Zechariah 6:9–14 we have a visionary description of a coronation ceremony, possibly in anticipation. Later Nehemiah was accused by Sanballat of attempting to become king of Judah, that is to say, he was accused of making messianic claims (Neh. 6:6).

In Deutero-Zechariah, the oracle of chapter 9 portrays the messianic prince coming to Jerusalem riding upon an ass. He is just, and he will speak peace to the nations. He is lowly, and yet his dominion will be worldwide. He rides no war horse, for it is not his task to bring victory, and so, as A. B. Davidson puts it, he shares "the character of the saved people." It is God himself who brings the End by direct intervention in this group of oracles, and it is he who sets his messiah on the throne. This thought is echoed again in a psalm which probably dates from the same Maccabean period (Ps. 110). "Yahweh saith unto my lord, Sit thou at my right hand, until I make thine enemies thy footstool" (Ps. 110:1). In Psalm 2, also a messianic psalm, the kings of the earth are exhorted to acknowledge the supremacy of God's anointed. The latter is hailed as the newly begotten son of Yahweh himself, and it is Yahweh who sets him on his throne. We have already suggested that the prophetic tradition found expression in the Psalter.

The final consummation is thus seen to embody the figure of the Davidic Messiah as well as the enigmatic figure of the Suffering Servant in the exilic and postexilic periods. In Deutero-Zechariah both such figures appear. There is no evidence of any complete or related pattern here. The whole is shrouded in a mystery that waits upon the historical actualization of the full pattern in Jesus of Nazareth. The mystery is only made more obscure by the appearance of yet another enigmatic figure in the last stages of Old Testament eschatology, the Son of man.

In the first vision of the Book of Daniel (chap. 7) there appears the symbolic image of the Son of man. This figure stands in contrast to the four beasts which represent the successive world empires. The four earthly kingdoms are pictured as rising out of the sea, but the fifth kingdom, which is to shatter all of them and finally prevail, is pictured as one like a son of man coming on the clouds of heaven. Thus, the figure is a transcendent one, strangely in contrast to Ezekiel's use of the same phrase to describe his own frailty and weakness. In an explanation that follows the vision the full meaning of the imagery is made clear. There the Son of man is identified with the Kingdom of the saints of the Most High. It is thus a societary image and represents the true remnant of the end time. Furthermore, the human form of the figure serves to contrast the humane aspect of the divine Kingdom of the end time with the weird beastlike figures of the worldly kingdoms. The latter symbolize in their very form the demonic perversions which characterize man-made empires.

Yet more is involved here than a remnant concept. The image is also messianic. We need to remember that the beasts did not represent people but kingdoms, and that, in the thought world

of the time, the king represented the kingdom in his own person.[6]
Again, the Son of man represents the Kingdom of the saints of
the Most High and may be identified with the anointed king of
the coming kingdom. Thus, the Son of man may well be a messianic as well as a remnant figure. What has been said earlier
of the image of the Suffering Servant may well apply here. We
have an easy oscillation between the corporate and the personal
because it was natural to the Hebrew mind.

In this case we have a completely new understanding of the
Messiah. He becomes a transcendent celestial figure coming on the
clouds of heaven. The Davidic Messiah is of human birth and
descent. The messianic Son of man is 'from above'. Indeed, he
may well be the supervention of the Ancient of Days who is
described as himself coming to deliver his saints in 7:22. Ezekiel
says of the divine glory that it had "the resemblance of a son
of man" (Ezek. 1:26; 8:2 ff.). In Old Testament thought, clouds
accompany that glory, and the seer of Daniel never associates
angelic manifestations in this way. Thus the Son of man may
even be a divine being who takes the form of man. He establishes
and rules over the Kingdom of the End.

We need not regard this as an idea foreign to the Hebrew
traditions. Aage Bentzen [7] has convincingly demonstrated that
the image of a "primordial man" is buried deep in the Hebrew
consciousness. He has even made out a case for the inner unity
of the various messianic images carried in the eschatology of the
Old Testament. In this view the Son of man becomes a syn-
thetic figure which unifies the various strands of the messianic
hope and thus, as E. Jacob puts it, "allowed Judaism to safeguard
certain specifically religious and transcendent values." [8]

Universalism Versus Nationalism

Postexilic prophecy reveals an intense religious nationalism.
This began in a sense with Ezekiel in his ideal picture of the
restored community as centering in the Temple with its ritual
and observance. With him there emerges that religious particularism which served to conserve Judaism during the postexilic
period. So when Ezekiel differentiates between the circumcised
and the uncircumcised in Sheol (Ezek. 32:19, 28–30), we have
the beginning of the separation which is so marked in the era
now being considered. In the postexilic period this spirit is seen
in Nehemiah's condemnation of Jewish labor upon the Sabbath
and in Ezra's prohibition of foreign marriage. It springs from
the proud consciousness of being God's people, his elect nation,
and from the sense of a stewardship in religion.

Yet this nationalism took a religious rather than a political
form. Israel, in the exile, left Palestine as a nation, and it returned as a church or, at least, as a church in process of formation. With the failure of the messianic hope which Haggai and

Zechariah had centered in Zerubbabel, the thought of freedom from foreign domination seemed impossible of realization. The over-lordship of Persia, the presence of a Persian governor, the small-ness of the community of returned exiles, and the lack of natural boundaries which would aid in the formation and defense of an independent state—all these tended toward the formation of a theocracy, a national unit which centered its life in its religious traditions and convictions rather than in political freedom and independence.

This nationalistic spirit is reflected in the oracles of the post-exilic prophets and in the formulation of the eschatological hope. While Haggai and Zechariah do seem to anticipate political as well as religious freedom under the messianic prince Zerubbabel, after them this idea of nationalism fell into the background. Henceforth Israel's nationalism is expressed through its religious life. Israel is Yahweh's, and, as such, it is a holy people. For it to fulfill its holy task, it must keep separate from other peoples. It alone has the true knowledge of Yahweh. Hence freedom from all contaminating foreign influences is a necessary condition for its religious nationhood to be preserved pure and intact. The enemies of Israel are the enemies of Yahweh, and so he will avenge his people upon its adversaries. This narrow nationalism reached the height of social exclusiveness and bitterness in the Book of Esther, but it colors some of the noblest postexilic literature.

We find this idea expressed in the postexilic eschatology. Deutero-Zechariah sees Israel saved by the direct intervention of Yahweh himself. God now makes Jerusalem the metropolis of religion. In this noble prophecy with its apocalyptic trend, it is foretold that "everyone that is left of all the nations which came against Jerusalem shall go up from year to year to worship the King, Yahweh of hosts, and to keep the feast of tabernacles" (14: 16). Later, with all-embracing charity, the prophet declares, "and in that day there shall no more be a Canaanite in the house of Yahweh of hosts" (14:21). Yet in earlier oracles in this section of Zechariah, it is made clear that membership in the coming kingdom will involve abstinence from unclean foods ("having blood in the mouth," 9:7). Thus membership involves keeping ritual, as distinct from moral, laws. The essentially spiritual na-ture of the Kingdom, which is found in the other oracle cited, is thus lost.

The first Zechariah (1–8) paints a picture of the messianic future and describes the influence of Israel among the nations. Once more there is a touch of universalism, as we are told that "many people and strong nations shall come to seek Yahweh of hosts in Jerusalem, and to entreat the favor of Yahweh" (8:22). Yet this too is tainted by a spirit which almost verges on national-ism. The prophet exults that the Jews shall be lifted up and exalted so that "ten men shall take hold out of all languages of the nations, even shall take hold of the skirt of him that is a Jew, saying, We will go with you, for we have heard that God is with you" (8:23, British RV).

In Trito-Isaiah we have passages like chapters 56 and 60–62 which echo the spirit of Deutero-Isaiah and indicate Israel's missionary task. But we also have oracles which express national-ism in their description of the Day of Yahweh (59:18). The theophany of 63:1–6 is one of bitter vengeance, in which God is seen coming back from Edom, his garments dyed in the blood of Israel's adversaries. What a strange contrast to the noble dec-laration that men shall be drawn to Yahweh as they see his glory in Israel (66:18), that Israel shall be a nation of priests among the nations (61:9; 62:2), and that the Temple shall be a house of prayer for all nations (56:7)!

Malachi shows the same spirit of narrow nationalism over the marriage of the Jews with foreign wives. Such marriages contam-inated Israel in its holy and religious stewardship. Yet the glorious universalism, inherent in the great prophetic tradition, bursts through the narrower outlook. Malachi 1:11 is a majestic utter-ance which declares that Yahweh is the God whom all people can worship.

In other postexilic oracles we have a clear and explicit uni-versalism in which the salvation of God is extended to all peoples on the moral and religious basis of grace. In the Isaiah 24–27 passage, it is promised that on his Day Yahweh will make a feast of fat things for all peoples (25:6–8). He will strip away the mourning shrouds and swallow up death forever. The anony-mous prophet of Isaiah 19:19–24 sees an altar to Yahweh in Egypt and the Egyptians returning to God in "that day." Then Israel shall be a third with Egypt and Assyria, a blessing in the midst of the earth. In the Day of Yahweh, Egypt and Assyria shall dwell in peace and worship together. "For that Yahweh of hosts hath blessed them saying, 'Blessed be Egypt my people, and Assyria the work of my hands, and Israel mine inheritance' " (19:25).

The whole is gathered up in the story of Jonah in which the universal gospel of grace is presented in a parabolic form grounded in a historical base. The latter may be difficult to delineate, but the message of the story is clear. Jonah is Israel running away from its task, and that task is to overcome its narrow nationalism and particularism by declaring God's grace even to Nineveh, to the other nations. Like Jonah, God's people had to learn that God's mercy was extended to all peoples. Should God not have pity on Nineveh, that great city, as Jonah had mercy on the gourd (4:10, 11)? Here is the message of Deutero-Isaiah brought to focus in Israel's failure to fulfill its task. Here the emphasis is on moral and not ritual relationship to Yahweh.

Some observations need to be made at this point. It is significant that Zion is so central in all the visions of the new order
and also that the Gentiles are pictured as coming up to Jerusalem
to worship. The tradition associated with the royal theology had,
as we have seen, emphasized the tabernacling presence. In the
Temple Yahweh was especially present, and as long as faith
was tied to material media like the land and the Temple, a
purely spiritual monotheism, severed from these, could find no
place in Jewish thought. We have noted this even in the case of
Jeremiah.

But then if Judaism was tied to Zion, are not we tied to
Christ in whom dwells all the fullness of the Godhead? Judaism
could no more escape the centrality of Zion than we can escape
the centrality of our Lord. Indeed the presence of Yahweh in his
sanctuary and in the midst of his people foreshadows the glory
of his presence in his Incarnate Son and by his Spirit within
his Church. Only in Isaiah 25 do we find any possibility of a
universalism detached from Zion. Since the restoration is centered in Zion, we may expect that the movement of the Gentiles
will be to Jerusalem, where Yahweh is present among his people,
where the *torah* is, and where instruction can be found. The
Gentiles must seek God where most of all he is to be found.

Furthermore, there could be no idea that the Jews should go
out and preach a lofty monotheism which all peoples would
accept without any particular relationship to the Jewish race. Such
a thought would have been far from the Jewish mind, just as
today we cannot preach a nebulous Christianity which may be
accepted and practiced apart from the Church, the New Israel.
God had given himself within the particularity of history, in
certain historical events, to the Hebrew people. It was their task
to show forth the salvation he had wrought in their midst to the
surrounding nations. In so doing they had to bring these people
also to the particularity of their own history. God's nature, purpose, and saving grace were to be understood through those events
in which he had chosen to act and through the people whom
he had elected. Israel had become a Church in the eyes of the
exilic and postexilic prophets.

It was a tragedy that at this point Israel forgot its missionary
vocation in seeking to preserve its religious identity. Hence we
have the attitude to foreign marriages. Hence, also, we find the
emphasis on the ritual requirements of the *torah* alongside the
moral. Israel failed to go to Nineveh, and its finest spirits had to
cherish as an eschatological hope what contemporary history did
not manifest. This at least they saw. Because Yahweh had chosen
it, Israel was more than one nation among many. It had the
characteristics of a Church. It was a spiritual entity. If others
would share in the blessings of salvation, they could not do so
apart from Israel, and, in some sense, they must belong to it.

Here was the real issue. How could the other nations share in the blessing?

In the centuries that followed the exile the Jews of the Dispersion did show an intense missionary spirit. Yet their proselytes had to become Jews and forsake the race of their origin. The Psalmist, in the true prophetic spirit, can rejoice that this one and that from many different Gentile nations shall be incorporated into Israel and be born at Zion (Ps. 87:4–6). What proselytism failed to recognize was a universal salvation that could be separated from Jewish nationality and its ritual laws. But then could such a separation be possible so long as political nationalism and racial blood were marks of the divinely elected race?

Israel was waiting for something. As Phythian-Adams has finely written:

> Already (by the time of our Lord) the prophets had spoken of the resurrection of this people, and though the resurrection had been thought to have taken place at the return from Exile, the plain facts of the last five centuries had shown that it was still to come. The "dry bones" of Ezekiel were dry bones still; the "servant" of Deutero-Isaiah had still to rise from his grave; the Spirit foretold by Joel had still to be poured out; "Jonah" had still to be freed from his three days and nights of darkness. Under whatever prophetic image we put it, it is this truth which stares us in the face when we study the people amongst whom our Lord was born.[9]

Israel could do nothing but wait for the Day of Yahweh. Her prophets had told her so, and their task was now accomplished. Deutero-Zechariah seems to suggest this: "And it shall come to pass that when any shall yet prophesy, then his father and his mother that begat him shall say unto him: 'Thou shalt not live for thou speakest lies in the name of Yahweh'" (13:3). No more could be said, and the authentic voice must be silent until God should raise up another prophet and more than a prophet, the God-man in whom the Day of Yahweh dawned redemptively upon a sinful and broken world.

NOTES

1. So H. H. Rowley, *The Relevance of Apocalyptic,* rev. ed. (New York: Association Press, 1964).

2. For a detailed study of the relation of the postexilic prophets to the cult, consult Theophane Chary, *Les prophètes et le culte à partir de l'exil* (Paris: Desclée & Cic, 1955).

3. Mowinckel's great work is now available in English. See Sigmund Mowinckel, *The Psalms in Israel's Worship,* 2 vols. (Oxford: Basil Blackwell, 1962).

4. Th. C. Vriezen, *An Outline of Old Testament Theology* (Newton: Charles T. Branford Co., 1960), p. 34.

5. Bentzen compares this reference to Isaiah 10:31 ff. Aage Bentzen, *Daniel* (Tübingen: J.C.B. Mohr, 1952), p. 83.

6. Thus Nebuchadrezzar represents Babylon in Daniel 2:37–39. Actually in the vision itself the kings and the kingdoms are interchanged (7:17).

7. Aage Bentzen, *King and Messiah* (London: Lutterworth Press, 1955), *passim.*

8. Emond Jacob, *Theology of the Old Testament* (New York: Harper & Bros., 1958).

9. W. J. Phythian-Adams, *The Fulness of Israel* (London: Oxford University Press, 1942), p. 188.

Epilogue

The Prophetic Testimony As Christian Revelation

In bringing to a close this discussion of the divine revelation through the prophets, we need to remember that their testimony comes to us in the setting of the Christian Scriptures. Hence it is fitting that we should consider the permanent contribution of this testimony to the movement of Christian thought. It has been said that the Old Testament without the New is like a torso without a head. Our discussion so far has been concerned with the movement of the revelation in the setting of the old covenant. If in Jesus of Nazareth the Old Testament promises have been fulfilled, we may measure such a permanent contribution of the prophetic testimony by the standard of that final and saving revelation. If the message of the prophets is relevant to our time, it is so because the Word which became incarnate in Jesus Christ spoke also through the oracles of these messengers. Their authority rested upon their participation in the heavenly council and their conviction that they bore the divine Word to men. That Word finds its full revelation in the prophet of Galilee who is also Son of God. Here the promise through the prophets becomes actuality. Their disclosure of the divine nature is brought to a focus, and their understanding of the divine purpose in history is confirmed in the Cross and Resurrection of the Christ.

The Disclosure of the Divine Nature

Implicit in the faith of Moses and coming to its full expression in Deutero-Isaiah is the conviction that God is unique and that beside him there is no other. Yahweh their God is one, and beside him all other deities are either his servants or nonentities. This explicit monotheism brought with it the conviction that all nations are his creation and under his control. He is the God of the whole earth, its creator and sustainer. He is the Lord of history, and all peoples are subservient to his purpose. He has elected Israel to be his special concern. Yet such election was seen by the prophets, in their moments of high vision, to have as its objective the redemption of all peoples. Eschatologically, God had no favorites. The promise to Abraham was that through him and his seed all the nations of the earth should evoke blessing.

The prophets understood God as dynamic and personal, a God who acts within human history. They grasped the deep truth that his bond with Israel was not naturalistic and that his relation to his world was not to be understood pantheistically. He neither was a part of the process of nature and the movement of history nor was he to be identified with them in their totality. He was related to Israel by a moral bond which set him over against them in a personal dimension of relationship. He had created them in his absolute freedom, which Deutero-Isaiah grasped in its fullness. He sustained his world in that freedom and could creatively control its natural forces in the interest of his redemptive purpose.

Neither nature nor man was created of the divine substance. Man was flesh and God was spirit. The image of God was never understood by the prophets as signifying a community of nature between man and God. Although the phrase itself was not used by them, they clearly held its implication that man is a creature made with a capacity to have fellowship with God but not a being with a divine status.

Man was related to God as creature to creator, but the relationship was a personal one. Through the media of nature and history, God showed himself to man as moral claim and absolute demand. The universe was moral through and through, and it was so because God was himself a moral God. He had created the world and men in accord with his own nature.

The divine righteousness is consonant with this moral nature. Righteousness means conformance to a standard. God is subject to no norm beyond himself. He is absolutely free, the unique One who alone inhabits eternity. Hence his righteousness means that he cannot belie himself. His actions are always in conformance to his moral nature, and thus in his activity in his creation he is morally righteous. In his demands on men he sets a standard by which his creatures must live. Man's righteousness is thus measured by the divine righteousness.

Yet the prophets were also sure that God is grace. He who demands obedience of his creatures is also gracious. The divine claim is matched by final succor. As the realization of man's stubborn will and sin-corrupted nature was brought home to the prophets, more and more they faced the problem of how God could be gracious to disobedient and impenitent creatures. Convinced that God would find a way to save his rebellious people, they looked for the Day when God would draw near in judgment and in mercy. In some way the divine grace would effect a redemption which would not belie God's righteous demands. His ways are higher than man's. In the mystery of his transcendent being God would show himself both a judge and savior.

The prophetic testimony is very conscious of this transcendent mystery. God is the holy One whose thoughts are higher than man's thoughts and whose ways are past finding out. Yet this transcendent God was also immanent in his world, disclosing his secrets to his servants the prophets. They might be enveloped only in the skirts of his garments, yet even at the foot of his exalted throne they might share enough in his councils to know that, in the end, his grace and not his wrath would prevail. His Day would dawn, and although the end time would be ushered in with judgment, it would yet issue in salvation.

The Divine Lordship over History

Meantime history went on, and within that history God was acting in judgment and in mercy. It is to the prophets that we owe the first vision of world history. For them all history was unified around the divine purpose. God was a God who acted within the movement of man's common life and directed it to the fulfillment of his intention.

For the prophets, as for us today, history is a scene of sin and rebellion. In consequence it is also the realm of divine judgment. God has made his demands on his people. Their failure to obey, their overt rebellion, can have only one consequence. Their sin will turn upon them in judgment. The movements of history will bring them to ruin and destruction. Historical forces bent upon man-made goals will yet serve the divine intention. The divine wrath is operative in history so that rebellious Israel shall not escape disaster.

We notice how the judgment of God is portrayed as employing both the forces of nature and the movements of history. Natural catastrophies like plague and famine may yet manifest the divine wrath. Nature and man are so closely bound together in the moral and covenant structure of God's world that a break in the moral relationship between man and his creator has its repercussions upon the whole created order. This is a truth that modern man still needs to learn despite all his scientific and technical skill. Nature hits back at man bent on the arrogant pursuit of his own ends. Rebellious man will find that his own environment is arraigned against him. Is there a better symbol for this than the mushroom cloud of a nuclear explosion which towers fearfully above our civilization?

Not only nature but also the great political and social forces of history are involved here. Man's rebellion sets in train movements of history which bring about his own undoing. God gives man over to the sin of his heart. Arrogant nations like Israel and Judah, by their own internal dissension, open up avenues for the inroads of aggressors like Egypt, Assyria, and Babylon. World conquerors become the agents of the divine wrath upon a sinful world, only in their own turn to suffer a like doom when they have served the divine purpose.

Yet the judgment is, for the prophets, ever a call to repentance. Although the divine retribution is sure, there is ever the opportunity to turn to God and be saved. That historical man should be so hard of heart and ever refuse to learn is a sore burden on the prophet's soul. He never ceases, however, to believe in the divine graciousness. And so he looks to the final consummation when the judgment of history will be completed in a cataclysm of wrath and yet when, beyond the purging of judgment, God will accomplish his gracious intention and create for himself a true, penitent, and righteous people.

THE ESCHATOLOGICAL PROMISE AND ITS FULFILLMENT

The prophets found the meaning of history in its consummation. For them this end was both chronological and teleological. They looked forward to the Day of Yahweh when God's sovereignty over history would be fully unveiled and his purpose in history be completely actualized. With their insight into the divine counsels they saw this Day as both darkness and light, judgment and grace. Individually they grasped various aspects of the end time. Of none of them can it be said that he sees a total picture. All agree that the end will be won when God will truly have created a people for himself and that this blessed community will live a life of obedience to God with accompanying joy and bliss at every level.

The End is both continuous and discontinuous with the historical process that has preceded it. For the early preexilic and exilic prophets, it will be ushered in by the mediation of historical forces. Assyria and Babylon are to usher in the dawn of judgment. Cyrus is to usher in the dawn of redemption. Their emphasis on the outstanding feature of the final consummation thus moves from judgment to grace, from doom to redemption, as Israel goes into the Babylonian exile. Yet the early message of doom is now eradicated with the promise of a redeemed remnant, and the note of judgment is not missing from the later message of comfort.

Furthermore, there is a note of transcendence in their understanding of the End. They recognize that it will be a miraculous event, a mighty act of God, a wonder which he and he alone will perform. He will set his Messiah on his throne, a scion of the house of David. He will endow his anointed one with charismatic gifts. He will cut a new and inner covenant with the house of

Israel, working miraculously the inner transformation whereby
his law shall be written on their inward parts and they shall
be re-created in individual heart and spirit. Thus the remnant of
the new order shall be his creation, and it is he who will make a
people for himself out of the purging fires of judgment. The
cataclysm of the End and its accompanying redemption will be
a work that he will perform and it will be cosmic in its sweep.
Even nature will participate in it.

With the Exile, the transcendence of the End receives more
emphasis and its discontinuity from the preceding movement of
history becomes more marked. God will intervene directly. The
present orders of nature and history will be dissolved in terrible
cataclysm and warfare. God will war for his people and save them
out of the overwhelming flood of evil. The messianic hope is now
accompanied by variations like the image of the Son of man. The
Davidic Messiah as a figure of the End is an earthly king whom
God has raised and set upon his throne. Now this figure is set
side by side with a transcendent figure of heavenly origin who
is yet also representative of the redeemed saints. He comes, a
heavenly man, on the clouds that hide the divine glory and
establishes God's Kingdom.

From the Exile onward, the emphasis on the individual
rather than on the corporate whole to which he belonged led
to a concern with individual resurrection. God's people would be
resurrected in the last day, but the constitution of this remnant
would result from the individual resurrection of those loyal to
Yahweh. Only after the end of our Old Testament canon was
the scene of this resurrection transferred to a new world. Through
the Book of Daniel some direct continuity is retained between
the present world order and that which will replace it when God's
sovereignty is fully unveiled.

In the center of the final consummation stands the figure of
the Servant of Yahweh, by whom the redemption of Israel and
of all peoples is to be accomplished. Apart from slight traces
elsewhere, the image of the Servant is confined to the oracles of
Deutero-Isaiah. Here he is both a corporate and individual
figure. He is both Messiah and the people of God. In his sufferings
the Servant is individual and messianic, yet his death is redemptive and representative. In his own sacrificial offering of obedience unto death, he represents not only Israel but all nations.
As the people of God are reconstituted by his redeeming act and
participate in his representative sacrifice, their testimony reaches
out to the nations. So in the midst of the prophetic revelation
we have the missionary hope which first found expression in the
promise of Abraham. That Israel failed to catch this vision in
any fullness after the Exile but remained nationalistic and ex-
clusive is a sign that the Day of fulfillment had not yet dawned.
In this image of the Servant the prophetic revelation reaches its

high water mark. Here the veil which hides the mystery of evil and sin in history is partially drawn aside, and we are shown how the innocent may, by his suffering, redeem the many. Undeserved suffering borne redemptively by God's Servant becomes the ground for Good News to all peoples.

It remained for our Lord himself to draw together the fragmentary elements in the eschatological hope of the prophets and to actualize them in history. In him the Day dawned and the Kingdom of God came upon men in judgment and in mercy. In his death and resurrection the End broke into history, and in his Church the remnant of the people of God was reconstituted. We live today under the End in a way that the Old Testament prophets did not. We are still in history, still subject to sin and judgment, yet the life of the Age to Come has been released in our midst. The Servant has suffered, and all nations may share in his redemption. Through his sacrifice the new covenant has been made with the individual believer. The Spirit has been poured out on the faithful, and in the Spirit they have an earnest of their future inheritance. So they wait for a final consummation, the *parousia* of the Lord, which will unveil the hidden presence of the End in the contemporary eschatological scene.

If old Israel and its prophets hoped for the tabernacling presence of God in the midst of his people, that hope has been realized as the Church is incorporated in Christ and permeated by his Spirit. The living risen Lord dwells in the midst of his people. He who became incarnate and tabernacled in our midst in the days of his flesh is still pleased to dwell in the humble and contrite heart. No longer in the Temple on Zion's hill but in the living temple which is his Church, he lives and works in history. The Church is his body, the ongoing of his incarnation, and through it the Gospel goes to all men *until He come*.

Index